INSIGHT GUIDES

Created and Directed by Hans Höfer

BaLI

Update Editors: Garrett Kam and Debe Campbell
Executive Editor: Scott Rutherford

Editorial Director: Brian Bell

Houghton Mifflin

APA PUBLICATIONS

Höfer

In the late 1960s, there were no Insight Guides. There was only a young German photographer who, having spent time rambling through the Indian subcontinent and Southeast Asia, found Bali a pleasant place to rest before continuing his travels.

Hans Höfer hadn't counted on the seductive power of Bali and its people. To say that he fell in love with the island would be an understatement. He was enchanted by the island, passionate about its contours and textures. Rather than moving on as planned, he stayed for a year, painting and photographing and learning about the island's culture and people.

By 1969, Bali's newly-expanded airport and a concerted effort by Indonesia to make itself the next big travel destination in the Pacific marked the beginnings of a new industry for the world's largest archipelago. It was a time of great expectation and some uncertainty, of course, especially for Bali's fledgling hotel and tourist industries. Other places had entertained the same dream. Some failed miserably, others succeeded, but with irreversible alterations in the local cultural and social fabric.

When Höfer heard of a project – sponsored by both the government and local hotels – to create a pilot publication for visitors to Bali, he lost little time in proposing a guidebook that had been sifting through his mind for quite some time. Höfer wanted to produce a book that would not only promote Bali as an important tourist destination, but as importantly, give visitors a better understanding of the island's great cultural vitality, its gracious people, and its exquisite geography. He wanted to convey his own enthusiasm for the island, sharing with others what the real Bali was like. Yet, at the same time, he was acutely aware of the social and economic dilemmas that mass tourism would bring to the island and its people.

Höfer and two friends, photographer **Werner Hahn** and writer **Star Black**, spent months exploring the island when work on the book was approved. The goal: to find the answers to all the questions that any inquisitive reader would ever have about Bali. Given the depth of Balinese culture and society, this was no small undertaking.

Hahn

Villages in the remotest valleys were visited, and every imaginable path and byway investigated. Every possible form of dance-drama and music was encountered, as was Bali's evolving arts scene.

In 1970, *Guide to Bali* was published. That year was one of Bali emerging from a difficult period of economic hardship and civil strife. The 1960s had been bloody and stressful. Bali was ready for a shift in its fortunes, and it was believed that tourism would offer salvation.

Guide to Bali revealed the island to the world as never before, weaving strong color photography and copious informative text into a solid journalistic package. Encouraged by the book's success, Höfer decided to become a publisher, and he registered his new company in Singapore as Apa Publications. The word *apa* was an appropri-

guide to bali

ate choice – doubtful Singaporean registrars notwithstanding – for an endeavor that sought to answer the insightful traveler's questions of who, what, where, why or how. Indeed, *apa* is a Malay interrogative reflecting all of those important queries.

In the nearly three decades since *Guide to Bali* came off the presses, Apa Publications' Insight Guide series has blossomed into over 190 titles. Moreover, two other imprints, Insight Pocket Guides and Insight Compact Guides, have expanded the effort of answering those not-so-simple questions. *Apa.* (Of course, Bali also appears as a Pocket Guide and a Compact Guide.) In 1996, Höfer retired from publishing Insight Guides, choosing to continue his creative journey to new endeavors and horizons.

O ver the decades, the guide book on Bali has gone through numerous reprintings, updates and revamps. Designs have changed, photographs replaced, text updated and overhauled to reflect a changing Bali. As the 1990s approached the end of the millennium, it was time for yet another overhaul of the title.

Apa's executive editor in Singapore, **Scott Rutherford**, went on a search to find contributors who could help in the effort. Rutherford first came to Asia nearly a decade and a half ago, journeying through Japan for three months on a photographic assignment for National Geographic. Years later, he returned to Japan to live for four years in Tokyo, working on publishing and television projects. From Tokyo, he landed in Singapore to take on Apa's Asian and Pacific titles.

Rutherford

On board for this revamp of *Insight Guide: Bali* was **Debe Campbell**, who has lived in Indonesia for over a decade, first in Jakarta and now in Bali. Campbell, who is nearly fluent in Bahasa Indonesian, finds the idyllic air of Bali somewhat preferable to the dusty air of Jakarta. Campbell, who works as a correspondent for several magazines, has been a frequent contributor to Insight Guides, including a new edition of *Insight Guide: Indonesia*. For this book, Campbell updated the Places chapters and rewrote the Travel Tips, no small task.

Garrett Kam, a curator at the Neka Museum and specializing in Indonesian studies, undertook a review and updating of the assorted Features essays. Kam, who comes from Hawaii, has lived on Bali for several years.

Over the years and decades, numerous people have contributed to the many editions of *Insight Guide: Bali*. Much of their work and essays are the core and foundation of this new edition of the guide. The list is a who's-who of Asian expertise: **Rucina Ballinger, John Darling, Fred Eiseman, Willard A. Hanna, David Harnish, Eric Oey, David Stuart-Fox, Made Wijaya, Paul Zach, Mary Zurbuchen**. There are many others, of course.

The difficult work on this book – putting up with editors and putting all the pieces together into the final layout – was handled by **Caroline Low**, of Apa's Singapore office.

Campbell

CONTENTS

Preceding pages: a tourist snaps away in a Balinese painting; a legong dancer from the past.

Places

Maps

TRAVEL TIPS

INTRODUCTION

A great Javanese priest was forced to banish his dissolute son to Bali, which was joined with the larger island Java at the time. The priest then drew a line with his cane across the sands, and Bali became an island.

The legend points to a truth, for Bali was indeed once connected to Java. Less than three kilometers (2 mi) wide, the strait that now separates the two islands reaches a depth of only 60 meters (200 ft). Yet to the east of Bali, on the opposite side, surge through the Lombok Strait some of the deepest waters in the Indonesian archipelago, which is over 5,000 kilometers (3,000 mi) long.

Before the sea rose during the last glacial period, Sumatra, Borneo, Java and Bali were all linked to mainland Asia. In the east, Irian and New Guinea was joined to Australia. The treacherous strait that separates Bali from Lombok is the divide between Asia and Australia.

The earliest rumors of Indonesia to reach the West arose from the distant realities of a huge archipelago, surrounded by eight seas and two oceans. An immense region of six million square kilometers (two million sq mi) encompassing land and sea, Indonesia continues to grow in size. One fourth of its 200 volcanoes, including two in Bali, are still considered active.

Flanked by the Java Sea to the north and the Indian Ocean to the south, Bali has an area of 5,620 square kilometers (2,170 sq mi). Just eight degrees south of the equator, Bali retains the delightfully warm climate of the tropics. The only noticeable changes in weather are between the rainy season, which lasts from October through March, and the dry, balmy season during the remainder of the year.

Bali's volcanoes, stretching from east to west, divide the island in half. The northern region of Buleleng, a narrow coastal strip that quickly merges into foothills, produces Bali's main exports of cattle, coffee and copra. In the highlands are peanuts, cabbage, and onions. Lofty tree-ferns, elephant grass, and wild flowers hang from the cliffs, which in turn hug the roadside. Tall pines and cypress trees soar above the lower embankments. The fertility of the north extends down the mountain slopes to the densely-populated plains of central Bali.

Despite the island's growing population, a lack of water has kept the west uninhabited. Another arid region is the limestone peninsula of Bukit Badung, which rises in sheer cliffs from the deep waters of the south coast. Southeast of Bali lies the barren island of Nusa Penida, the dwelling place of Ratu Gede Mecaling, the fanged giant. The island was once a penal colony used by the kings of Bali. The people of Nusa grow corn and coconut; the dry terrain does not permit irrigation. The smaller island of Serangan is aptly named Turtle Island. Large sea turtles are caught and kept there in the shallow water, to be sold as a special dish for feasts.

Preceding pages: mists clinging to Gunung Batur; carrying deities to the sea during Eka Dasa Rudra; baris dancer; planting rice, Lombok; Kuta youth. **Left**, mask of the topeng dance.

Like the majority of Indonesians, the Balinese are distant descendants of Malays and Polynesians. More recently, Balinese heritage extends to central and eastern Javanese ancestors, perhaps with traces of Indian and Chinese blood. While some people have sleek hair, high nose bridges and cream-yellow skin, others are dark and curly haired, like Melanesians. Over the centuries, numerous groups of foreigners came to Bali, adding to the people's mix. The majority were Chinese, followed by Indian and Arabs. Along with the Indians came Hinduism, which became the dominant belief on Bali, the only remaining stronghold of Hinduism in Indonesia. In fact, over 95 percent of the population practices the Agama Hindu Dharma religion. In the interior, however, especially at the higher elevations, several villages are inhabited by descendants of the animistic people known as Bali Aga.

It is the mountain, not the ocean and distant horizons, that the Balinese see as the source of life and wisdom. Mountains produce lakes and rivers, the source of the land's fertility. The lofty volcano Gunung Agung is the central abode of the deities.

Centuries of rule by a caste of aristocracy ended violently with the Dutch conquest of Bali at the turn of this century. For half a century afterwards, Bali was a colonial island, yet it retained a considerable amount of its identity and culture. It is this culture, plus the exquisite landscape, that brings tourists to its shores. In 1970, less than 15,000 visitors came to Bali. In the 1990s, there were over half a million tourists annually. Over 30,000 hotel rooms were available to them, and more are under construction, including some of the finest resorts in the world.

Tourism is always slammed by purists, who fear the denigration of local culture. Worry not. The cohesive bonds of religion, family and community life have given the Balinese a sound base from which to face problems and outside influences. Moreover, it is probable that, in large part, tourism was responsible for a cultural renaissance. Tourism gave many communities the resources to restore temples and historic sites, and the impetus to create new dance groups and centers of art.

To understand the character of Bali, one must see the island in its true perspective – as an oasis of ceremony and beauty, yet only one of over 13,000 islands in the Indonesian archipelago, itself the fourth-largest nation in the world.

Notes: In most cases, we use Bahasa Indonesian for geographical locations and points of interest in this guide, rather than English. Thus, Mount Agung is Gunung Agung. Similarly, Luhur Uluwatu Temple is Pura Luhur Uluwatu, and Kanginan Palace is Puri Kanginan.

There are two ways to spell President Soeharto's name: Suharto, and Soeharto. The latter is more traditional, and it is how he himself has chosen to spell it, as have most Indonesian media. We do the same. Likewise with the former president, Soekarno.

Right, rice terraces in central Bali.

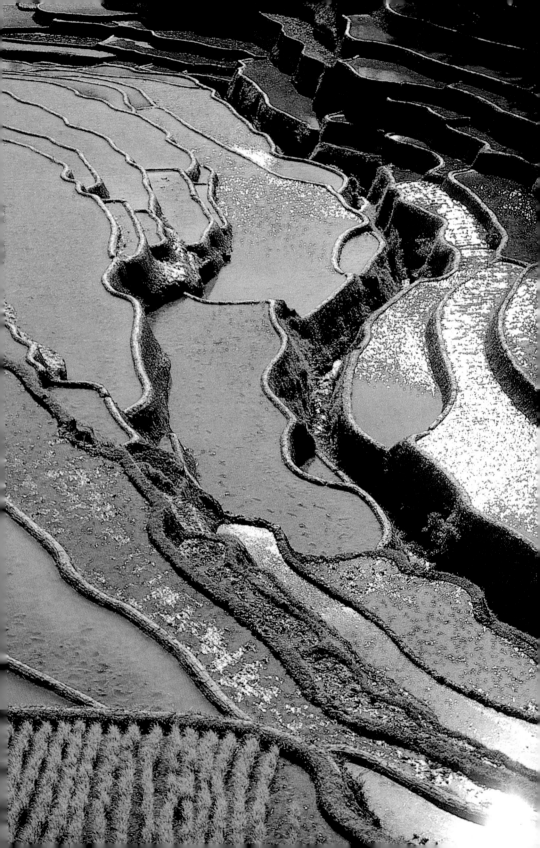

When the world was ready for human habitation, the Great Teacher Batara Guru debated with Brahma regarding the need for people on the world.

The divine duality fashioned figures of clay. When they baked them in an oven, the figures came out in an underdone white finish; the next came out an over-baked black. The last came out just right, a golden brown – the Balinese. Batara Guru and Brahma infused the creatures with life. They created dogs to keep men company and obey his orders. Female counterparts were provided. The first four couples produced numerous children, eventually totaling 117 boys and 118 girls.

This Balinese account of creation has curious echoes of other sacred scriptures and the folklore of both East and West. The evolution of the universe out of the void is not far removed from contemporary speculation. The play between Batara Guru and Brahma is indicative of the spirit of inventiveness and earthiness with which the Balinese endow their drama.

Key elements of the Balinese genesis are several: the imported and indigenous deities, great and small; the invocation of magical names and mythical creatures; the celebration of ancestors and of nature; and both sacred and profane deeds and thoughts.

Hinduism arrives: While the mythical evolution of Bali is preserved in the island's legends, its actual beginnings have faded from memory. Prehistoric Bali remains virtually a blank – few remains of early humans and stone tools have been found.

For tens of thousands of years, small bands hunted the jungles and gathered plants and edible creatures of tidal pools. Bali was heavily populated when the Bronze Age began, in about 300 BC. People lived in villages and buried the dead in pottery jars or stone sarcophagi, along with bronze and iron implements, ornaments and other tools. The early history of Bali is of a theoretical reconstruction of the origins of the population and the evolution of the society. The Balinese are a blend of the various Mongoloid peoples who moved through mainland Southeast Asia into the insular areas long before historic times. Their animistic and agricultural society was inspired by priests and princes.

The first great outside influence upon the early Balinese was of Indian or Indianized traders and travelers, who brought their Hindu-Buddhist learning to Bali. In the latter half of the first millennium, Bali shared in

the waves of Indian influences that spread throughout most of Southeast Asia. The Indians introduced the key concept of the god-king, whose palace reflects the splendors and perfections of Heaven, and whose people prosper as long as the ruler conducts himself with divine law.

Every Balinese ruler had a *puri*, a palace from which he exercised spiritual and temporal power through a hierarchy of courtiers and priests, who nevertheless, and frequently, deposed an evil ruler and replaced him with a better one.

The conversion of Bali into an Indianized society was the result of the rulers who

Preceding pages: temple carving from Bima Swarga depicting hell. **Left**, royal meditation niche, near Gunung Kawi. Dates from 11th century. **Right**, ancient baths, Goa Gajah.

found, in Indian culture, the religious and administrative practices that served their purposes. India provided the literary, artistic, and social model, as well as one of theology and politics.

The Balinese, of course, modified some of the imported beliefs, while still retaining much of the Indian original. By 990, Bali was extensively Indianized.

The Indianization of Bali was a process of many centuries. The most pervasive influence came from nearby Java, which had been subject even earlier to a more extensive process. Documented history of Bali during this period is mainly a catalogue of names of royal personages and references to events.

Rise of empires: Modern archaeologists have reconstructed the approximate historical sequence from fragmentary inscriptions, in Sanskrit or classical Balinese, on objects of stone and metal. Archaeological studies show that Indianized rulers invoked certain deities in commemorating the succession to the throne, building a temple, contracting a marriage, or winning a battle.

In 991, Airlangga, son of Balinese king Dharmodayanawarmadewa (also known as Udayana) was born. Airlangga was sent to the court of Java at an early age to be educated. When the king was overthrown, the victors invited Airlangga to take the throne.

Airlangga devoted himself to rebuilding the empire, adding his home island of Bali to the Javanese domain and ruling it through a regent, his younger brother. Airlangga thus inaugurated a period of close Javanese-Balinese political and cultural contacts, which continued for more than three centuries. The relationship was not without its conflicts, however. The Balinese occasionally asserted their autonomy, and the Javanese Singasari emperors and their Majapahit successors often reasserted their control.

Balinese rulers were implicated in dynastic rivalries, which the Majapahit empire was called upon to settle. For instance, a Javanese ruler, Kretanagara, found it necessary to pacify and reunify Bali in 1284, as did the great general Gajah Mada, in 1343. Thus, the Majapahit empire imposed more of its own institutions upon the Balinese. But when the Majapahit empire finally collapsed in 1515, refugees to Bali from Java resulted in more cultural transfusions.

With the Majapahit period, Balinese history acquires clearer content and pattern. Still, much remains legendary. The visit of Gajah Mada, for instance, is associated with events that might seem to be excessively dramatic even by Balinese standards.

Bali's paramount ruler of the time, King Beda Ulu, was noted for his supernatural powers. He could decapitate himself, hold the head in his hands, then restore his head. This offended the god Siwa (Shiva), who once caused the king to lose his grip on the severed head. It fell into a swift flowing stream and was washed away. The king's quick-witted minister amputated the head of a passing pig as a substitute. Beda Ulu, in fact, means "different head". The king decreed that any one entering his presence must never gaze up into his face. But Gajah Mada raised his head to swallow his food and drink in order to confirm for himself the rumor about the king's features. So enraged was the king by this conduct that he was consumed on the spot by the fires kindled within him.

Gajah Mada then incorporated Bali as a dependent of the Majapahit empire and appointed Javanese nobleman Kapakisan as puppet ruler. Legend identifies him as the offspring of a stone priest and a heavenly nymph. Kapakisan founded a line of princes who ruled Bali, building his palace near present-day Gianyar and ruling justly.

28

Rise of Golden Age: The Majapahit empire fell in 1515, replaced by the new Javanese sultanate of Mataram, built out of small kingdoms inspired and invigorated by Islam. The Majapahit empire's remaining Hindu priests, nobles, soldiers, and artisans moved on to Bali, where they provided more impetus for the predominantly Hindu culture.

For Bali, the sixteenth century marked the beginning of a golden age. Batu Renggong inherited the throne in 1550, and, too, the legacy of the Majapahit empire. From the court at Gelgel, Batu Renggong reigned in undreamed of splendor and authority. He welded the island into a strongly-centralized kingdom, conquering Blambangan in East culture preserved its freshness and animation, while the younger Javanese Mataram society grew both somber and solemn. It is the riddle and the miracle of Bali that, from the embers of Majapahit Java, the fires still burn bright on the neighboring isle.

The Europeans: The sixteenth century also marked Bali's first encounter with Europe. The early Portuguese explorers, adventurers, merchants, missionaries and conquerors, who reached Malacca in 1509 and Maluku (Moluccas) in 1511, all but bypassed Bali in the eager rush to acquire riches, souls and empire. The Spaniards on the Magellan expedition of 1519–22 sighted an island, probably Bali, which they identified as Java

Java, where he installed a vassal ruler and colonized neighboring Lombok island.

The political and military achievements of Batu Renggong were more than matched by a cultural renaissance. Balinese molded the Majapahit influences to their own needs, and in the process, shaped the nucleus of contemporary Balinese culture with that special element of Balinese genius. Balinese still share with the Javanese many common traditions of language, music, dance, sculpture and literature. The older Balinese Majapahit

<u>Left</u>, Airlangga, as Wisnu (Vishnu) on a garuda.
<u>Above</u>, etching on prehistoric gong, Pejeng.

Minor, but apparently no one went ashore. Fernando Mendez Pinto, the great Portuguese navigator, may have visited Bali briefly around 1546, but the evidence is not certain. Various other Portuguese and Spanish sighted Bali, if they did not actually explore it, and they made due notations of the island under various names like *Boly*, *Bale*, and *Bally*. Sir Francis Drake called briefly in 1580, and Thomas Cavendish may have visited in 1585, but they left no written records.

The first Europeans to entertain any designs upon Balinese trade and territory were the Portuguese. In 1588, they dispatched a ship from Malacca with soldiers and merchants, and building materials and trade goods, in an attempt to build a fort and open a trading post on the island. But the ship crashed on the reef off Bukit, and most of the company drowned. The five survivors were put into the service of the king, who gave them homes and wives, but refused to permit them to return to Malacca.

Twelve years later came the earliest Dutch explorer and trader in the East Indies, Cornelis de Houtman. He provided the first substantial body of information about Bali, and his crew conducted themselves in Bali in a reasonably respectable manner. In fact, Houtman was so moved by the beauty and wealth of the island that he indulged in a

Gelgel, surrounded by a harem of 200 wives, a troupe of 50 dwarfs, whose deformed bodies resembled the figures of *kris* hilts, and by many noblemen, who ruled in his name over a population of about 300,000. Lintgens said the state kris was particularly splendid: a two-pound dagger with jewels set in its intricately-wrought golden hilt. Equally showy were the dozens of parasols, lances, vessels of gold and silver and other treasures that would be the envy of any king in Europe.

The king was accompanied by scores of lance and banner bearers whenever he ventured outside his palace. He rode in a procession, either in a palanquin or in a cart drawn by two white oxen, which he himself drove.

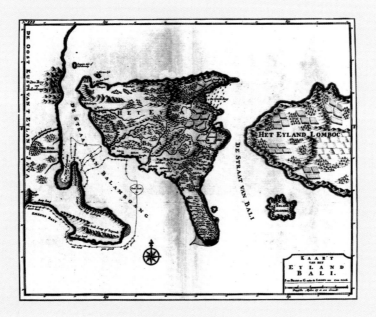

flight of poetic fantasy and christened Bali *Jonck Hollandt*, or Young Holland. It was a description so evocative that it helped persuade later Dutchmen that, by introducing Dutch civilization to Asia, they were guiding the islanders toward their manifest destiny.

Royal court: The four members of the expedition's shore party were treated as honored guests by the Balinese and Raja Bekung, the son of Batu Renggong. The leader of the shore group, Arnouldt Lintgens, described the king as a tall, dark, stout, vigorous man of about 40, who possessed astounding wealth, power and magnificence. Lintgens said he lived in a huge palace in the walled town of

The king commanded the love and respect of his people and his courtiers, and was famous for the clemency of his rule.

Lintgens found the island fascinating: "The Island of Baly lying at the East end of Iaua, is a verie fruitfull Island of Ryce, Hennes, Hogges, that are verie good and great store of cattle: but they are very drie and leane beastes. They haue many horses: the inhabitants are heatens, and haue no religion, for some pray to Kine, other to the Sunne, and euerie man as hee thinketh good. When a man dyeth his wife burneth her selfe with him: there were some of their men aborde our shippes, that told vs, that when some man dyeth in that

Countrey, that sometimes there are at the least fifty women that will burneth themselves with him, and she that doth not so is accounted for a dishonest woman: so that it is a common thing with them."

The king and his people were as curious about the Dutch as the Dutch were about the Balinese. The king managed to extract detailed information about Holland from Lintgens' group, as well as a number of gifts, including a rifle and a chart of the world. However, the Dutch declined an offer from the king to purchase their ship's cannon. Later, the king proposed to write a letter of appreciation to the Dutch king and to send him a kris and a dwarf as gifts, but there is no

Both men settled in Gelgel, took Balinese wives, learned the language, and served the king. Roodenburg returned to Holland, but Claaszoon lived out his life in Bali.

Decline of the court: The next Dutch expedition to Bali, in 1601, was led by Jacob van Heemskerck, with a request from the king of Holland to open trade with the island. The king of Bali granted permission, and also presented van Heemskerck with a token of royal favor – a beautiful Balinese slave. Van Heemskerck was advised that it would be impolite to decline the gift. However, van Heemskerck and his successors proved reluctant to accept the king's consent to reciprocal trading conditions as a charter for one-

evidence that he actually did so. Houtman himself made but one trip ashore, only a few days before setting sail for Holland. Lintgens was safely on board, but two other members of the shore party, Emanuel Roodenburg and Jacob Claaszoon, were mysteriously absent. They had jumped ship to enter the service of the king. Most probably, they had chosen to forego the voyage back to cold, gloomy Holland for the pleasures of tropical Bali.

Left, first Western map of Bali, believed to be from the Houtman expedition. **Above**, *The Crowned Lion*, a famous ship used during the early years of the Dutch East Indies Company.

way trade, or his endorsement of Dutch hopes for unity as acknowledgment of an alliance. Nothing much came of the contact for two centuries, but on the basis of the Heemskerck agreements, the Dutch assured themselves that they had special rights in the island.

The skimpy existing records of Dutch contacts with Bali during the seventeenth and eighteenth centuries refer mainly to opium runners, acts of mutiny, piracy, and treachery, and the ineffectual efforts of the Dutch East India Company (VOC) to either ban or to control and restrict trade.

Meanwhile, the golden age of Gelgel flickered during the latter part of Raja Bekung's reign. His ill-advised adventures in Blambangan provoked a full-scale invasion of Bali by Mataram, in 1639. Bekung lost the respect of the other Balinese princes. His grandson Di Made not only lost Blambangan, but Lombok and the allegiance of the other princes. His prime minister rebelled and ousted Di Made from the throne. After a long war, his successor abandoned Gelgel, clearly under a curse. He built a new palace in nearby Klungkung and sought to rule as the Dewa Agung, like his predecessors, but Bali's golden age set with Klungkung's founding, never matching Gelgel in glory.

The Dewa Agung and his court in Klungkung continued to symbolize Hindu

quent outbreaks of hostilities between the Dewa Agung and the Susuhunan of Java, and both Bali and Mataram applied for Dutch assistance. The Dutch never obliged – at least not openly. But in the years 1717–18, when Balinese troops caused great destruction in East Java and Madura, the Dutch chased the intruders back home.

If the Dutch refrained from intervening in the Balinese-Javanese wars, the English did not. The Dutch believed that the English provided the rajas with arms, and also sold opium and bought slaves; the northern Balinese port of Buleleng was rumored to be a hotbed of British-Balinese intrigue against the Dutch.

grandeur – but never again power. He became less prominent than some of his presumed vassals. The other princes became the Dewa Agung's rivals and even his enemies: their own *punggawa* (chiefs) at times presumed to virtual autonomy; the *pedanda* (high priests) sometimes assumed almost independent power over villages that fell within the domain of the rajas. The ruling families were polygamously intermarried and easily provoked to bloody feuds. Divination, prophecy, and superstition were of comparable significance to jealousy, intrigue and military conflict in personal and state affairs.

In the eighteenth century, there were fre-

The persistent intrusions of the English into Balinese waters caused the Dutch some political and financial agony. They were convinced the English were seeking a new colony and would seize any opportunity to establish a British monopoly in competition with the VOC.

The Dutch suspected that the English would claim one of the many islands that the Dutch regarded as theirs. Dutch and English rivalry over Bali eventually played a minor part in the worldwide English-Dutch conflict. But from the seventeenth to the early nineteenth century, except for a few episodes, Bali enjoyed European neglect.

Birth of Gianyar: As the domain and the authority of the Dewa Agung diminished, there emerged several more or less clearly-defined little independent rajadoms. (Eight still survive as geographical and political entities, now called administrative districts: Gianyar, Badung, Bangli, Tabanan and Klungkung in the south-central region, and Buleleng, Karangasem and Negara, now Jembrana, in the north, the east and west respectively. The history of these eight rajadoms in modern times is closely linked to that of Dutch colonial penetration.)

Klungkung survived but did not flourish, for the Dewa Agung had little power and his kingdom was small. Gianyar came to rival spiracies which characterized the relationships between the rajas themselves.

The founder of the Gianyar line was Dewa Manggis Kuning, now commonly referred to as Dewa Manggis I. The *Dewa* (or divinity, a favorite given name) and *Manggis* (the name of the town where he was born, and the word for mangosteen, a fruit that became the family emblem) became the state title. *Kuning*, the word for yellow, referred to the deep golden glow of the child's skin. His father was Baginda Raja Sri Dalem-Seganing, the fourth king of Gelgel.

This handsome youth so pleased the king that he was sent to Badung to assist the raja there in administering that kingdom. In Puri

Klungkung as a center of traditional culture, and even presumed military might.

The story of the decline of Klungkung merges with the rise, fall and revival of Gianyar, with frequent episodes involving neighbors. It also involves the villages which composed the other rajadoms. The *punggawa* who ruled these villages on behalf of the rajas frequently assumed the airs and even the titles of rajas, built themselves fortified homes, and entered into alliances and con-

Left, 17th-century European drawing of the Dewa Agung. **Above**, royal widow leaping into king's funeral pyre in the rite of suttee.

Badung, he had an affair with the raja's most beautiful wife. Upon being discovered and threatened with arrest and torture, he was wrapped in a woven mat like a bundle of charcoal and carried on the head of an old female servant. He made his way northward and set up shelter in a forest of *bengkel* trees, near present-day Gianyar.

Dewa Manggis Kuning emerged as a major figure upon the death of his father in 1667. He utilized a spear named *Ki Baru Alis* and a kris called *Ki Baru Kama* – the Gianyar-venerated *pusaka*, heirlooms endowed with magical properties. He used the spear to rebuke an attack from Buleleng.

One of the greatest of Kuning's descendants, Dewa Manggis IV, built Puri Gianyar in 1771 and thus became the first actual Raja of Gianyar. It became the most prosperous and powerful of the southern states under Dewa Manggis Disasteria (VII) the following century. But until the latter part of the nineteenth century, Gianyar was never at the focus of Balinese events.

The Dewa Agung's military and political power passed first to Buleleng, which was the focus of foreign commerce and international competition. It passed next to Karangasem, which came to dominate Lombok as well as Bali. Eventually, the power ended up with the Dutch. Buleleng

and Karangasem, long under the rule of members of the same royal family, were to become the two power factors in early contemporary Bali.

Buleleng and Karangasem: Gusti Pandji Sakti, who came to the throne at the end of the seventeenth century, was responsible for Buleleng's rise to power. By skillful political and military maneuvers, he extended his authority throughout most of Karangasem and Jembrana, exacted deferential treatment from the southern states, and put an ally on the throne in Blambangan.

The ruler of Mengwi, Gusti Agung Sakti, usurped the throne of his father-in-law Gusti

Pandji Sakti in 1711, and then consolidated Buleleng's power. The joint rajadom of Buleleng-Mengwi flourished for the better part of the eighteenth century, but then separated again and forfeited power to Karangasem.

Karangasem began its rise to prominence by championing Balinese interests in Lombok, when Buleleng was preoccupied with Java. Karangasem engineered control of Lombok by the middle of the seventeenth century and parceled it out among four weak rajadoms, each ruled by a Balinese prince with allegiance to Karangasem.

At that time, the raja of Karangasem was an ascetic sage so engrossed in meditation that he let his excrement drop where it might. During a visit to Klungkung, this raja shocked and outraged the Dewa Agung, who had the man assassinated. Seeking vengeance, the raja's three sons raised an army and marched into Klungkung. Respect for tradition deterred them from killing or deposing the Dewa Agung, but they made a declaration of independence without much further regard for the authority for the Dewa Agung.

The eldest son succeeded his father as raja of Karangasem and soon conquered Buleleng. Gusti Gde Karangasem became the kingpin of a new coalition. He appointed his brothers as rajas of Buleleng and Lombok, then seized Negara against the protests of Badung. He put pressures upon other states and stirred up wide-spread resentment and resistance.

Balinese power and politics were becoming incomprehensible, as further indicated by the emergence of Gianyar as a rival to Klungkung, and as a military threat to Mengwi and Bangli.

Buleleng rebelled against Karangasem in 1823. Raja Gusti Gde Nugurah Lanang fled to Lombok. He built a new puri and tried to impose his authority over the Lombok rajadoms, which welcomed his defeat in Bali as an invitation to defiance of Karangasem. He also sought to force his one-time vassals in Bali to recognize him as ruler again. Gusti Gde Ngurah Lanang thus did much to create the turbulence that the Dutch found conducive to the imposition of Western – especially Dutch – colonial rule.

Left, the Dutch conquered Java before moving on to Bali and points east. **Right,** painting depicting Balinese mythology.

At the beginning of the nineteenth century, Bali remained relatively unaffected by the Western influences that were already transforming much of the Indonesian archipelago. Dutch traders, agents and colonial officials failed to gain a strong foothold in Bali at first. By 1830, Dutch officials had already engaged in a prolonged exchange of government and company policy alternatives with regard to Bali, eventually deciding to infiltrate traders and then assert sovereignty. The NHM, successor to the trading interests of the bankrupt and defunct VOC, was intimately involved in these intrigues.

A Balinese concept of ship-salvage eventually provided the catalyst for Dutch military intervention. In accordance with their principle of reef rights, *tawan karang*, from the sea deity Baruna, the rajas accepted as a gift of the god whatever ship came to grief on the treacherous reefs. They took the ship, cargo, crew and passengers as their personal property, sharing with those who performed the act of salvage or rescue.

From the Dutch point of view, it was bad enough if the Balinese exercised their reef rights upon a Chinese, Arab, Bugis or Javanese craft, many of which sailed under the Dutch flag and expected Dutch protection. It was even more intolerable if the ship was Dutch-owned.

By the end of the 1830s, circumstances prompted the Dutch to discuss with the Balinese rajas the delicate subjects of trade, politics, slavery and plunder. They tried to blanket these various topics with treaties of friendship and commerce, in fact, recognition of Dutch sovereignty and monopoly.

A Dutch colonial contract-maker, H.J. van Huskus Koopman, was dispatched to the island to coax the rajas into giving Holland sovereignty over the island. His efforts met with little success, and the Dutch finally decided to resort to force. As a pretext for invasion, they used the wreck of the Dutch frigate *Overijssel* on the Kuta reef – and the

plunder of its cargo by Balinese exercising their reef rights.

The sorry saga of the *Overijssel* began in 1841, when the vessel, on its maiden voyage from Plymouth to Surabaya with a valuable cargo of machinery, hit the Kuta reef and was plundered. Dutch outrage served to cloak humiliation that a large and heavily-armed frigate was wrecked by reason of a navigational error – the captain had mistaken the coast of Bali for Java. The Dutch were equally embarrassed that the ship was looted, despite

the presumed vigilance of the ship's company against such possibilities.

As the furor over the incident increased in Holland, a Dutch mission was sent to Bali to demand reconfirmation of earlier promises that the Balinese would give up the practice of reef rights. A new Dutch commissioner arrived with another set of agreements, to be ratified by the rajas and enforced by the Dutch. He landed at Buleleng to meet with its raja and council of state. Gusti Ktut Jelantik, a young prince and brother of the Buleleng and Karangasem rajas, defied the Dutch:

"Never while I live shall the state recognize the sovereignty of the Netherlands in the

Preceding pages: contemporary painting of Balinese-Dutch conflict over the *Sri Kumala*. **Left,** Balinese warriors in battle dress, 1880s. **Right,** Gusti Jelantik with Dutch expedition staff.

sense in which you interpret it. After my death, the raja may do as he chooses. Not by a mere scrap of paper shall any man become the master of another's lands. Rather, let the kris decide."

Preparations for war: The Dutch began preparations for an expeditionary force, which set sail for Bali in 1846. Jelantik began building fortifications, raising troops, and acquiring arms, relying, as the Dutch correctly surmised, upon enterprising merchants in the British colony of Singapore for weapons. Balinese-Dutch relations were rapidly moving into a tragic phase.

Balinese military preparations centered upon Buleleng, ruled by Gusti Madya

tive to Badung. They were not disposed to become involved.

Once the Dutch set themselves to subdue Bali, the outcome was never in doubt. But it took three campaigns to shatter the Balinese defenses and morale, during which the Dutch did not always achieve glory or victory.

Punitive expeditions: The first Dutch military expedition against Bali, in 1846, seemed formidable enough. The fleet consisted of 58 vessels and nearly 3,000 troops. They anchored off Buleleng on 22 June, and dispatched an ultimatum. The rajas ignored them; the Dutch attack began six days later.

The Balinese put up a strong defense, but the Dutch won a swift victory, losing only 18

Karangasem, the elder brother of the raja of Karangasem. Buleleng and Karangasem, the two most powerful rajadoms but longtime rivals, were now closely allied in opposing the political and military aims of the Dutch. They had the blessing of the Dewa Agung of Klungkung, who could not provide much more than that.

The raja of Badung, in the south, who wished to preserve trade and who was no friend of the northerners, remained detached from the conflict and exercised his influence upon his neighbor, the raja of Tabanan, to do likewise. The other states were allied rather tenuously with Klungkung, but were atten-

soldiers, while the Balinese suffered severe losses of life and property. The Dutch victory was empty, however, unless they could enforce their will upon the rajas now firmly entrenched in the nearly hills.

A second military expedition against Bali was mounted in 1848. This time, the Dutch sent even more men and ships. But the Balinese, boldly and brilliantly led by Jelantik, had installed 25 cannons and mustered 16,000 men, 1,500 equipped with firearms. They fought off three attacks with severe Dutch casualties.

The third expedition arrived off Buleleng in March 1849 with over 100 vessels – heavily-armed frigates, steamships, schooners, and scores of auxiliary crafts manned by 3,000 sailors and 5,000 landing troops. They marched into Singaraja, where the Dutch general set up his headquarters in the palace.

The final showdown occurred on 4 April. The Dutch deployed their troops in full dress uniform. The Balinese troops were dressed as if prepared, not for battle, but for the *baris* warrior dance. They carried themselves haughtily, struck theatrical stances, and fingered their weapons suggestively.

The raja and Jelantik were magnificent in brilliant red sarongs gathered up to display short tight trousers, below and above which gleamed bare, bronze skin. Their waists were

Among the victims were the wife of Jelantik and a group of high-born ladies whom she had led in the rite of the *puputan*, advancing in a state of near trance directly into the line of Dutch fire, in a deliberate act of self-destruction. Battles continued into the following year, with the Dutch gaining allies and troops from Lombok. The raja of Karangasem, despairing at the news, killed his family and himself. The Dutch battled their way to Klungkung, but were repelled.

The fluctuating fortunes of war were signaled by the commander of the Lombok forces, who visited a Dutch colonel on shipboard and displayed to him three significant kris. The first was that of the raja of Karan-

nipped in by golden girdles. At the back, each displayed a huge, jeweled kris, the ornate handles extending above shoulder height for quick draw. Their thick, flowing black hair were bound by white headclothes.

What started as a triumph of Dutch and Balinese showmanship deteriorated into a failure of statesmanship, ending without a fight or an agreement. Several weeks later, the Dutch attacked the Balinese fortifications at Jagaraga. They suffered 33 dead and 148 wounded; the Balinese lost thousands.

Left, Buleleng's royal court, c. 1880. <u>Above left</u>, nephew of raja of Buleleng. <u>Right</u>, Dutch ship.

gasem, signifying his death and the fall of that kingdom; the second was the kris of the raja of Buleleng; the third that of Gusti Ktut Jelantik. The raja of Buleleng and Jelantik had been ambushed by the troops from Lombok. The raja was killed on the spot, and Jelantik took poison.

With Jelantik and the two rajas dead, and with the Dewa Agung and his surviving protectors grieved and dismayed, the Balinese resistance was in disarray. The Dutch, decimated by tropical diseases, could scarcely have blundered into defeat.

A Dane, Mads Lange, stepped in. He negotiated a new agreement between the Dutch and the Dewa Agung. It was a difficult task that involved installation of new rulers, and redefining overlord-vassal relationships.

Dutch conquests: As a result of the military expeditions, the Dutch began to exercise increasing control over northern Bali, and to interfere more frequently and more vigorously in Balinese affairs.

Buleleng was the first principality to fall under Dutch administration. In 1855, the Dutch also assumed control over Jembrana. In each case, the Dutch adopted the administrative device found to be effective in Java. They appointed a member of the royal family as regent and assigned him a Dutch *controleur*, who controlled both the regent and

and improvements of economic conditions. By 1875, northern Bali was a profitable colonial enterprise.

The increasing contact between Buleleng and the outside world resulted in an attempt to introduce Christian missions, which met with little success. The colonial successes and failures produced a policy of benevolent paternalism that resulted in a relatively enlightened administration. Still, the darkest days of the Dutch penetration lay ahead.

Ambush in Lombok: Gianyar enjoyed its turn at the top during the middle of the nineteenth century. Under Dewa Manggis Disasteria (VII), Gianyar became the most prosperous and powerful of the states of the

the kingdom. Thus, as of the mid 1850s, the Dutch actually began to acquire the sovereign power that they had long claimed, at least in northern and western Bali. Half a century later, they ruled the entire island. The colonial administration in Bali remained centered in the royal capital of Singaraja.

The latter part of the nineteenth century was reasonably peaceful and saw satisfactory development for the northern states. But continuing strife between the warring factions in the south resulted in several more Dutch military campaigns. The Dutch, under van Bloemen Waanders and his successor, announced new regulations against slavery

south. He earned fame as a shrewd ruler, who made a host of enemies among other rajas by swallowing up villages in their areas.

The Dewa Agung even created a military coalition against Gianyar and found a ready ally in the raja of Bangli, whose sister was a favorite in the Klungkung harem. But Disasteria enlisted the aid of Karangasem and Lombok and shattered the Klungkung army in 1868. After its victory, Gianyar enjoyed well more than a decade of peace and prosperity.

The island of Lombok also played an integral part in the tragedies that marked Bali's total takeover by the Dutch, after the turn of the century. The trouble began when the Dutch sent a military expedition in 1894 to punish the Balinese rulers of Lombok for complaints of cruelty and discrimination toward Lombok's Sasak Muslims.

The Dutch, led by generals J.A. Vetter and P.P.H. van Ham, marched into the heart of the island without resistance. Just as it seemed they would win a bloodless victory, thousands of Balinese warriors staged a surprise attack on the Dutch camp in the town of Cakranegara. They fired their rifles with deadly aim and massacred Dutch soldiers, who had no place to take cover. General van Ham himself was fatally wounded. Dutch casualties totaled 98 dead and 272 injured.

nobles of that kingdom perished. The Dutch got their victory – by default. The events in Lombok in 1894 left deep scars upon the Balinese soul and the Dutch conscience.

The events in Lombok also disturbed the Dewa Agung and other leaders in Bali. They grew uneasy about the Dutch presence. It was assumed that some incident would launch yet another Dutch expeditionary force, which in fact happened, in 1904. Again, it involved a shipwreck and the Balinese right of salvage. The vessel was a Chinese-owned schooner, the *Sri Kumala*, which struck the reef near Sanur, not far from the Badung-Gianyar border. The area's people plundered the ship with the complicity, it was alleged, of the

The Dutch government was outraged at the "Lombok Treachery".

The Dutch sent in reinforcements to revenge their defeat in Lombok. They laid waste to the island. In Mataram, the Balinese defenders chose the rite of puputan over defeat or surrender. The island's raja chose the same fate in another village. As the Dutch advanced, men, women and children emerged from the village as if in a trance. If they did not die by the kris, they rushed into the rifle fire of the troops. Ten of the highest-ranking

Left, raja of Karangasem and grandson, circa 1900. **Above**, Dutch guns on Sanur Beach.

rajas. The owner of the craft gave an implausible account of his misfortune and demanded compensation for the cargo. To the original claim, he added large quantities of gold and silver. The Dutch scaled down his claims and presented the bill to the raja of Badung, who refused to pay.

The Dewa Agung backed him in his defiance. So did the raja of Tabanan, who was also involved in a crisis over a recent ceremony of *suttee*, which he had permitted despite Dutch protest. So in June of 1904, the Dutch blockaded the coasts of Badung and Tabanan, while at the same time drawing up ultimatums and assembling a military expedition. The sixth military expedition to Bali, consisting of infantry, cavalry, artillery and naval support, arrived off the southern coast in September 1906. The Dutch sent the raja of Badung a final ultimatum. He rejected it. On 14 September, the Dutch landed their troops on Sanur Beach.

Blood of the puputan: Without meeting any significant resistance, the Dutch troops marched through Kesiman toward Denpasar, expecting more of a dress parade than a pitched battle. Marching in orderly ranks along a roadway, walled on either side, that led to the royal palace, they found the town deserted and smoke rising over the puri, or palace. Most disquieting was the wild beat-

his dagger into the raja's breast. Others of the company also turned their daggers upon themselves or one another. The Dutch troops, startled into action, directed rifle and artillery fire into the surging crowd. Some of the women mockingly threw jewels and gold coins to the soldiers. More people emerged from the palace gate. The mounds of corpses rose higher and higher.

The soldiers stripped the valuables from the corpses and then sacked the palace ruins. It was a slaughter of the innocents made more appalling by its recurrence that same afternoon in nearby Pemecutan, a minor court of Badung. There, the old raja and his court, having heard what happened in Denpasar,

ing of drums within the palace walls. As the Dutch drew closer, they observed a silent procession emerging from the main gate of the puri. It was led by the raja, seated in his state palanquin carried by four bearers, dressed in white garments but splendidly bejeweled and armed with a magnificent kris. The raja was followed by officials of his court, armed guards, priests, wives, children and retainers, likewise dressed in white, and many of them as richly ornamented and as splendidly armed as their ruler.

One hundred paces from the Dutch, the raja halted his bearers, stepped from his palanquin, and gave a signal. A priest plunged

elected the same fate. When the Dutch troops marched from Denpasar to Pemecutan, the raja and his retainers chose the puputan. This time, however, the Dutch refrained from participation, if not from profit.

The Dutch expeditionary force marched to Tabanan, where the wives of its venerable old raja had earlier followed their husband faithfully in death – jumping into his cremation fire in the rite of suttee.

The new raja and crown prince fled from the puri as the Dutch advanced. When they gave themselves up, the Dutch informed them that they would be exiled to Madura or Lombok. In the Denpasar prison, the raja plunged a betel-cutting knife into his throat, and the crown prince took poison – and so Tabanan followed into the Dutch sphere.

The Dutch made a show of force in Klungkung, hoping that they would provoke a show of resistance by the Dewa Agung. However, the Dewa Agung did not oblige and the Dutch withheld.

Later, the Dutch presented the Dewa Agung with new agreements almost indistinguishable from ultimatums. He accepted them at sight. All knew that the Dutch would impose an administrative system upon Klungkung.

By 1908, disorders broke out in the area. In Gelgel, men of the *punggawa* intimidated and attacked agents of the opium monopoly.

200 meters (660 ft) from the main gate. The Dewa Agung led a procession of some 200 people, which emerged from the puri to confront the Dutch soldiers. Clad in white, he carried in one hand a lance with a golden tip and in the other, his ancestral kris.

Pausing about 100 meters (330 ft) from the momentarily-silent cannon, he bent over and thrust the kris blade into the ground. Thus, if the prophecy came true, his magical kris would create a great chasm that would swallow up all of his enemies.

As the Dewa Agung straightened up, he received a bullet and was killed outright by another. Six of his wives knelt around him and drove kris blades into their own hearts.

The Dutch landed a small party of troops to punish the punggawa, who mounted a counterattack. So many Dutch soldiers were injured that the detachment withdrew to the seacoast. The punggawa sought shelter in Klungkung, where the Dewa Agung had authorized measures of defense.

Bombardment swiftly followed, which demolished Gelgel and destroyed parts of Klungkung. Then came the troops with their field pieces, which they fired at a distance of

The whole company – men, women and children – engaged in ritual suicide or sacrificed one another, while murderous cannon and gunfire contributed to the mayhem.

There were very few royal or other survivors of the Klungkung puputan. The puri was razed, except for one gateway and a few pavilions. What little remained of Klungkung's ancient glory had vanished, but the last bright blaze of martyrdom had burnt away many stains.

On 18 April 1908, after 600 years of rule in Bali, the lineal descendants of the vast Majapahit empire were decimated, the victims of Western occupation.

Left, the aftermath of the 1906 *puputan* in Badung outside the Pemecutan palace. **Above**, the body of the raja of Badung wrapped in a woven mat.

Although the punitive expeditions against Bali in the 1840s passed almost unnoticed in the outside world, the reports of the *puputan* of 1906 in Badung, and of 1908 in Klungkung, shocked people and governments worldwide. Protests poured into the colonial office condemning Dutch reprisals as disproportionate to Balinese offenses. Under pressure with regard to their policies in Java, Sumatra and the eastern islands, the Dutch made amends.

In 1914, the Dutch replaced their army with a police force and reorganized the government. The raja continued to reign as regent. He ruled by consent of the Dutch resident and *controleur*. The latter prompted his important decisions and relieved him of much routine by controlling the *punggawa* as well. Visitors to Bali reported that the island was the prettiest exhibit in the Indies of Dutch enlightenment.

From the beginning, the Residency opposed all efforts to open up rubber or tea plantations, or sugar or tobacco estates, as had successfully been done in Java. Only a very few Dutch business interests opened offices in Bali, mostly in Buleleng and Denpasar. The most conspicuous was the giant steamship line that linked Bali to Java and the eastern islands. The important foreign enterprises in Bali were those of the Chinese, who acquired urban property, coffee gardens and coconut groves. The Chinese generally held them in the name of a Balinese wife, but were excluded from acquiring other agricultural land. Protection of the Balinese farmers against the exploitation of foreigners, and the protection of Balinese culture against disruptive outside influences, constituted the two most significant achievements of the Dutch colonial administration.

Early tourism: The Dutch policy of cultural conservationism resulted in colonial officials who became distinguished scholars regarding many aspects of Balinese life. Diligent research even refreshed Balinese traditions and customs that might otherwise have

lapsed. Whether or not Dutch policy and practice had anything to do with it, Balinese culture in the early part of the twentieth century had numerous distinguished achievements in art and architecture, and many aspects of Balinese culture and life were sustained through the rajas' increased wealth.

The residency that sheltered Bali from missionaries and merchants also sheltered the island from world travelers. But foreign anthropologists, archaeologists, ethnologists, artists, musicians, dancers and actors – and,

eventually, sociologists, economists and political scientists – inevitably and eagerly sought out Bali on missions often indistinguishable from tourism.

Tourism began in Bali in the 1920s. By 1930, as many as 100 visitors a month were experiencing the delights of the island. They came for a few days of romantic escapism; artists and writers often came to stay.

One of the most famous was a German musician and painter, Walter Spies. He moved to Bali in 1927, after spending a few years as bandmaster in the court of the sultan of Yogyakarta. In Bali, Spies built himself a house on the edge of a scenic ravine, just

Preceding pages: temple relief in Kubutambahan. **Left**, a gold garuda radiator cap – a Balinese icon gone modern. **Right**, German artist Walter Spies, 1930s.

outside Ubud. He produced two or three paintings annually of such radiant and revealing beauty, in a new aesthetics that the Balinese have since made their own.

Spies was joined in the early 1930s by the German novelist Vicki Baum, who wrote *A Tale of Bali*, a classic of Balinese studies. The Mexican artist-ethnologist Miguel Covarrubias, and his wife, Rose, produced the great study *Island of Bali*, which remains unrivaled in English as an exposition of Balinese culture. Even the sociologist Margaret Mead carried out important anthropological inquiries in Bali.

The painters, however, usually outnumbered the writers. In addition to Spies, they

the Japanese landed about 500 troops on Sanur Beach, marching unopposed into Denpasar. In the next few days, they assumed control of the entire island and installed administrative offices in Denpasar and Singaraja.

The Japanese immediately acquired the reputation of being arrogant and obtuse. The Japanese Kempeitai police soon began making arrests, especially among persons associated with the Dutch civil or military establishment. As elsewhere, Japanese occupation was brutal, harsh and unforgiving.

In 1945, the Japanese military capitulated. On 17 August 1945, Soekarno and Mohammed Hatta declared Indonesia's national in-

included Dutch painters Rudolf Bonnet and Willem Geraid Hofker, and a Belgian, Adrien Le Mayeur de Merpres.

Japanese occupation: The only real cause for concern in Bali during the 1930s was the prospect of war in the Pacific, a threat that suddenly became a reality in December 1941. Japanese troops marched down the Malay Peninsula and captured Singapore, key to the entire region, including the weakly-defended Indonesian archipelago.

Japanese forces made Bali an early target of their campaign, sending in a small expeditionary force several weeks before invading Java. On the morning of 19 February 1942,

dependence. New Balinese officials soon occupied the provincial offices and residences. In December 1945, the Dutch returned and attempted to re-establish a Dutch civil administration based on the pattern of prewar days.

One prominent Balinese leader was a young military officer, Gusti Ngurai Rai. He proved to be a charismatic hero and martyr, a military leader who relied, not upon tactics and logistics, but rather upon intuition and mystical guidance. His slogan was *merdeka atau mati* – freedom or death – which he put to the ultimate test. Ngurah Rai created the Tentara Keamanan Rakyat, or the People's Security

Force. In time, he merged it with most other paramilitary movements and thus commanded what was regarded as a Balinese people's army.

Ngurah Rai undertook the Long March to Gunung Agung. He rallied all available men in western and southern Bali, concentrating them in eastern Bali with safe sanctuary on the slopes of the sacred mountain, hoping to lure Dutch forces, who had returned after the Japanese left, into areas vulnerable to guerrilla attacks. The Dutch forces surrounded the encampment, but Ngurah Rai and his men escaped annihilation by climbing over the volcanic peak and across formidable mountain terrain to Tabanan. There, on 16

the Dutch and pressure from Holland's own allies, along with a United Nations resolution, finally led the Dutch to concede Indonesian independence. Bali became part of the Republic of Indonesia in 1949.

Era of Soekarno: Under the leadership of its first president, Soekarno, the Indonesian archipelago underwent the growing pains that accompanied transition to nationhood.

In Bali, this proved difficult, in part due to historic Balinese-Javanese antagonisms. Even though Soekarno was half Balinese, he ruled the vast new nation from Jakarta, an old city on Java dating back to Dutch colonial times, when it was called Batavia. Soekarno always claimed empathy with the Balinese

November 1946, the Dutch again surrounded them. Called upon to surrender and negotiate, Ngurah Rai asked his men to join in a suicide attack upon the heavily-armed Dutch, another puputan. Ngurah Rai and 95 of his men were killed. The site of the Margarana Incident, as it is now known, is a national heroes' cemetery.

With Ngurah's defeat, the Balinese military resistance was effectively broken. But in the ensuing years, continued attacks against

Left, the Dutch *controleur* arrives at his residence in a 1930s photograph. **Above**, Soekarno reads a statement handing over power to Soeharto, right.

soul. He saw himself as the age-old raja, but he did not discharge the raja's responsibilities for enhancing the spiritual and material welfare of his people. He left on Bali a collection of monuments, such as the Tampaksiring palace and the Bali Beach Hotel – symbolic of ill-chosen priorities if not ill-advised objectives. On the other hand, Soekarno established Udayana University.

By the early 1960s, there prevailed throughout Bali the premonition of disaster. It was feared that the supernatural powers were being provoked. People would be compelled by the gods to revert to the standards and the values of the past, thought some, and to

Despite its size, Bali offers an astonishing variety of landscapes. The southern part of the island, the most fertile region, is characterized by luxuriant tropical vegetation. In the center lie the misty, cloud-covered highlands. The emerald-green rice terraces found in the southcentral region are irrigated by the waters from mountain lakes and rivers. The Bukit Badung peninsula in the extreme south, on the other hand, is very arid. The northern beaches are formed out of black lava, while the west is largely covered with impenetrable jungle. The east coast, by contrast, is largely dry and inhospitable.

Bali is the westernmost island in the chain that makes up the Lesser Sundas group. It covers 5,600 square kilometers (2,021 sq mi), which makes it one of the smallest provinces of the Indonesian archipelago, itself the largest in the world. Indonesia's 13,677 islands stretch from the Pacific to the Indian Ocean, lying on both sides of the equator between the Malay Peninsula and New Guinea. Lying eight degrees south of the equator and 115 degrees east longitude, Bali is separated to the west from neighboring Java by a narrow strip of sea. The Strait of Lombok, which divides Bali from the island of Lombok to the east, is not only considerably wider (30 km/19 mi), but also considerably much deeper.

In the nineteenth century, the geographer-scientist Alfred Wallace established that there were marked differences of both vegetation and animal life between Bali and Lombok. The large mammals of western Indonesia, from tiger and rhinoceros to elephants, gave way at the strait between the two islands to marsupials and a number of bird species, which were otherwise found only in Australia. From this, Wallace concluded that, 100 million years ago, the Strait of Lombok represented the dividing line between the Asian and Australian continents. The division is known to this day as the Wallace Line.

A chain of volcanoes runs through the islands of Sumatra and Java, and continues into Bali, forming Gunung Agung (3,142 m/

Preceding pages: terraces of rice. **Left**, Tanah Lot, West Bali. **Right**, village of Iseh.

10,308 ft), the island's highest mountain (*gunung*), and Gunung Batur (1,717 m/5,633 ft). The islanders believe these volcanoes to be the abode of the gods, who in their taciturn manner bless the island with mineral-rich volcanic ash for bountiful harvests, yet remain a permanent threat when the people anger the gods. (The last major eruptions occurred as recently as the 1960s.) Also of volcanic origin are the mountain lakes (*danau*), of which the largest are Danau Batur and Danau Bratan. These lakes feed

the rivers that flow through central and southern Bali, providing the water for the irrigation of the rice fields.

Climate: Bali's climate is determined by the monsoon winds and consists of two seasons. During the wet season, between November and March, the northwest monsoon brings rain and humidity that can be as high as 95 percent. The dry season, from May until October, is the most pleasant time to visit. Since the island lies virtually on the equator, daytime temperatures climb to about 30°C (86°F) almost every day, although the mountains tend to be about 10°C (18°F) cooler, and may even seem chilly at night.

The summer months of the northern hemisphere are definitely the best time to visit Bali, which explains why July and August are high season on the island. Fewer tourists arrive during the northern winter, except for Christmas, which is the summer holiday season for Australians. During these months, take an umbrella, although there is seldom a day of continuous rain, and several wet days at a stretch are a rare occurrence.

Nature and environment: Bali's countryside is largely determined by its year-round rice-farming culture. Rice farming is an important activity, and the countryside is characterised by a series of artistically laid-out rice terraces (*sawah*). When ripe, the golden yel-

during the entire period of growth, until the rice is ready for harvesting. The water from streams and rivers is diverted to the fields via channels cut into the soft volcanic rock. Thanks to its fertile soil and an irrigation system perfected over centuries, a Balinese farmer can harvest two to three crops a year.

A cooperative (*subak*) ensures that the water is fairly distributed to the fields and that the dams are properly maintained. Shortly before harvest time, the fields are drained and the women of the neighborhood congregate to cut the rice, ear by ear, using a small knife called the *ani-ani*, hiding the blade in their hands in order not to frighten Dewi Sri. Today, this traditional method of harvesting

low stalks sway in the breeze, caressed by Dewi Sri, the Balinese goddess of fertility – her shrine, laden with offerings, is found in a corner of every field.

Side by side with the dry fields ready for harvest are freshly-flooded green paddies containing young seedlings, and just around the next corner may be a farmer plowing the land with the help of oxen.

Depending on the variety of rice grown, a period of three to six months will elapse between sowing and harvesting. The seedlings initially take root in seed beds before being transplanted into the irrigated fields, where they must be kept immersed in water

the grain is used only for Balinese rice, and not for other Indonesian varieties.

Progress ignores religious sentiments, and since the 1970s, President Soeharto's "Green Revolution" has propagated new types of high-yield rice, which have largely been responsible for making Indonesia self-sufficient in rice production. Recently, however, it has been discovered that these new varieties rapidly exhaust the soil. As a result, Balinese farmers are returning increasingly to the traditional Balinese rice varieties. Not only are they ecologically-more friendly, but they also taste better, as the Balinese point out with a smile.

Other important crops include coconuts, coffee, peanuts, spices such as cloves, cinnamon and vanilla, and tropical fruits such as bananas, pineapples, papayas and mangoes, as well as vegetables. The local wine (*anggur*) production in the north of the island is declining because of poor-quality grapes.

Flora and fauna: Bali has been compared to a tropical garden because of the wide variety of plants flourishing on the island. There are various species of palm trees, bamboo groves, and flowering shrubs – frangipani, poinsettia, bougainvillea and a profusion of orchids. The focal point of most villages is the banyan tree (*ficus bengalensis*), with its typical aerial roots. The dry Bukit Badung peninsula is

kilometers (253 sq mi) and is a paradise for ornithologists. It is one of the last habitats of the Bali starling, also known as the Rothschild mynah bird, a species threatened with extinction. With luck and patience, visitors to the park will be able to see several species of deer and monkey, as well as the endangered wild Javan buffalo.

Of the large mammal species once found on Bali, only the wild boar and deer remain. Monkeys are common, and some forests, such as Alas Kedaton, are inhabited by colonies of macaques.

Lizards are also found everywhere, including the insect-eating geckos that serve a useful pest-control function in many hotel

also home to the pandanus (screw-pine) and even cacti. Mangrove swamps fringe the coast between Sanur and Nusa Dua, and throughout the northwest.

Tropical rain forests, which once covered the entire island, are still found in the west. Many of them lie within Taman Nasional Bali Barat, the West Bali National Park. This is Bali's wild west, where, until a few decades ago, one could still find the island's last remaining tigers, rhinoceroses and crocodiles. The park covers an area of 700 square

Left, Bali's volcanoes are always nearby. **Above**, crater lake on Gunung Rinjani, Lombok.

rooms. Snakes, too, are also commonplace. The most important domestic animals are the sway-back pig and the pretty doe-faced Balinese cow, as well as chickens and ducks.

Population: Bali's present population of some three million people can trace their ancestry to various ethnic groups, which migrated to the island from southern China between 2500 and 1500 BC. The population density of 500 people per square kilometer (1,400/sq mi) is one of the world's highest. More than 85 percent of the population still lives in the rural areas. Bali's annual population growth rate is 3.4 percent, and the average life expectancy is 64 years.

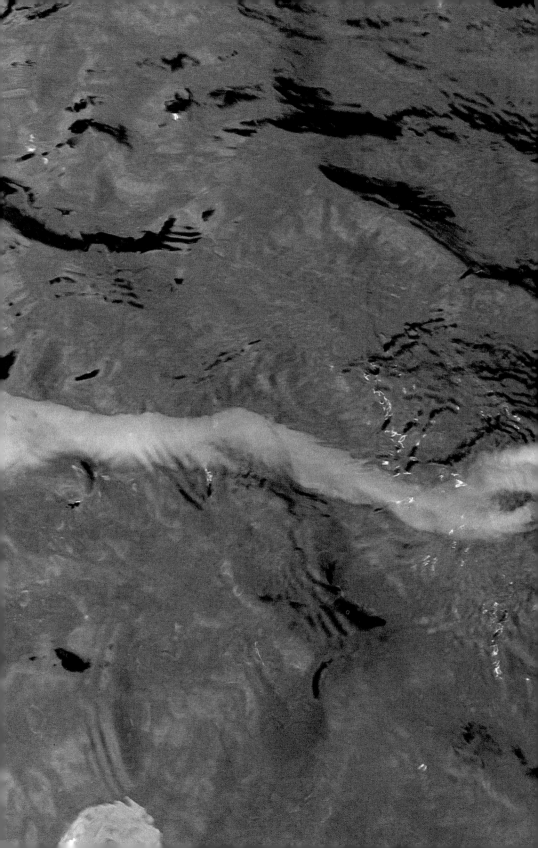

THE BALINESE

The Balinese world is one of sharing. Everyday life merges with social duties and religious obligations, in the same way that personal fears are projected onto the mysteries of nature. The arts reflect an integration of environment, religion and community, in which every individual is a part.

This feeling of continuity is the cornerstone of local society. Every form of work or creativity is given group expression. The organization of villages, the cultivation of farmlands, and even the creative arts are a communal effort.

Within a village, a person belongs to family, clan, caste, community, and to the total of the Balinese people. Religion is as essential as livelihood. Every new occasion, whether it be the first birthday of a child or the completion of a house, receives the priest's blessing. Every personal calamity is treated as a shared problem among family, friends and divine guardians. Only in rare moments throughout life would a Balinese feel solitude. Nor is death a separation, but rather a journey of the soul to a resting place in heaven, where life is just as in Bali, but devoid of all trouble and illness – until the soul is reborn on earth, possibly in the person of a great-grandchild. A father has long centered his hopes on having children, preferably male, who will care for him in his old age and, after his death, perform the rites to liberate his soul for reincarnation.

Children are privileged Balinese. The younger the child, the closer is the soul to heaven, and the purer is the spirit. A child born in Bali awakens to a wondrous world. A newborn baby emerges into this life from a spiritual realm, and is thus holy.

An infant is not permitted to touch the impure earth, and so is carried everywhere. Ceremonies are held at prescribed intervals, culminating in the first birthday according to the Balinese calendar, at 210 days of age. Offerings are made, and the baby is allowed to touch the ground for the first time.

Preceding pages: raja of Gianyar with his wife and attendants; wet smile. **Left**, priest reads from lontar palm-leaf book. **Right**, children assume responsibilities at an early age.

As soon as the child can walk, she or he wanders all over the village with other children. In this society, children grow to be self-reliant at a very early age. At home, the child is treated cordially, taken by his parents wherever they go, and coaxed into obedience as an equal. A child is never beaten, for it may harm the tender spirit. Raising children with independence and respect accounts for the maturity and sense of responsibility in Balinese children. In the most crowded villages, seldom do children cry or fight.

Adulthood: During adolescence, a child is formally initiated into the adult community. When a young girl of a high-caste family reaches puberty, a ceremony announces her status as a mature woman. First, she goes into seclusion and cleanses her body. After three days, she emerges in gold brocades and a crown of flowers to receive a purification blessing from the priest. Frequently, a tooth-filing ceremony follows, for both boys and girls. A specialist, usually a priest, files a small portion of the six upper teeth to form a straight line, so as to diminish the six evil qualities of human nature: passion, greed, anger, intoxication, stupidity, and jealousy.

After this ceremony, a Balinese is less prone to human frailty and error. Long canines are reserved for animals, witches and demons.

The average marriage age for a woman is 20 to 25, and for a man, between 25 and 30. A young Balinese feels it is one's most important duty to marry, and to raise a family to perpetuate family line. Only a settled married man can become a member of the village association.

Marriage customs vary from village to village, and from caste to caste. The most popular forms of marriage are the *mapedik* – by request – and *ngrorod* – by elopement. Mapedik is the respectable form in which the boy's family, bearing offerings and presents,

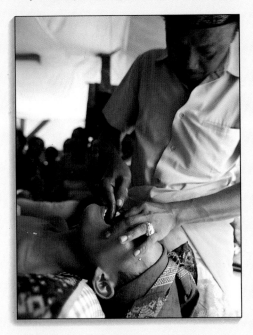

visits the girl's family and openly proposes the marriage. Ngrorod is more exciting and clandestine, in which the honeymoon precedes the wedding, and the man is considered to be more heroic.

In ngrorod, the couple decides to run away, usually to a friend's house a good distance from the girl's village. On the appointed day, the girl is suddenly carried off by her suitor. (Nowadays, it's fashionable to kidnap one's bride in a car.) The girl's family pretends to be very worried (and sometimes is). The enraged father searches the surroundings, asking everyone in the village who took his daughter. Even a close friend, who may have

helped the daughter pack her clothes, innocently denies any knowledge of the affair. Sometimes a search party is organized.

Usually an envoy is sent to inform the girl's parents, who generally know the suitor and then realize that their daughter has willingly eloped.

Most Balinese agree that the advantage of ngrorod is that it is economical. (In the formal courtship that precedes a mapedik marriage, the suitor must visit the girl's home several times – the cost of small gifts mounts up.) On the first night of elopement, a small ceremony is held to make the marriage official by customary law. Offerings are presented to Ibu Pertiwi, goddess of the earth, who witnesses the union. Later, villagers are invited to a formal ceremony, when the couple is blessed by the priest and their union is announced through offerings and prayer to their ancestors and deities of the house temple. The woman formally joins the man's family, thus becoming a member of his caste, family and clan.

Divorce is not difficult. A man reports to village authorities that his marriage is finished; or, if a woman, she simply returns to her home and the children are cared for by the man's family. However, divorce does not occur often. It is more likely that a man takes a second wife, but the first remains as head of the household.

Caste system: The Hindu caste system was introduced by the Javanese Majapahit kingdom, which invaded Bali in the fifteenth century. The spread of the Hindu religion at the beginning of the sixteenth century was resisted by the Bali Aga, the original pre-Hindu inhabitants of the island, who still live in a handful of remote villages.

There are four castes, each associated with a title that indicates the caste to which the individual belongs.

Brahmana, or priests, form the top caste in Balinese society. Members of this caste are known as Ida Bagu (male) and Ida Ayu (female). The next caste, *Ksatria*, comprises the high nobility who once ruled the island, and are distinguished by titles like Anak Agung, Dewa and Cokorde. *Wesi*, who form the lower nobility, go by the title of Gusti. Only three percent of all Balinese belong to one of these castes, which together are known as *Triwangsa*. Most Balinese are *Sudra* or *Jaba*, literally the outsiders of the court.

Unlike India, there are no lower-caste untouchables on Bali.

Community life: The community revolves around family and religion. A man raises a family that worships common ancestors in the family shrine. The various families composing a village all worship at three major village temples: *pura puseh,* dedicated to Brahma and where the village founders are honored; *pura desa,* honoring Vishnu for official ceremonies involving the living village community; and *pura dalem* of the dead, for revering the deities of death and the afterlife Siwa (Shiva) and his consort Durga. Together, these temples form the core of the community.

for the signal drums *(kulkul)* to call meetings, announce events or give warnings – and usually a giant banyan, the sacred tree of the Hindus and Buddhists.

On the outskirts of the village are the public baths, often a riverine laundry, and the cemetery near the temple of the dead.

Although every male citizen with a family generally owns the land he lives upon and labors, theoretically the island is divine property and borrowed from deities by the people who cultivate it and live from it. The *krama desa* authority, a governing council of married villagers, oversees all that is built upon village land. Formerly, desa control was very strict. If a man moved to another town,

For thousands of people, the community is in the crowded neighborhoods of district capitals. But for the majority of Balinese, whose livelihood is agriculture, the community is near the rice fields of rural villages. A village *(desa)* is made up of family compounds that line several streets and lanes. Where the two main streets cross at right angles in the center of the village are temples, a market, a cockfight arena, the home of the local royal descendants *(puri)*, a tower

Left, tooth-filing. **Above left**, only men plant rice, but everyone joins in the harvest. **Right**, portrait of Balinese man.

he was released from the desa association and took the value of his share in village property, but his house and land remained with the desa. Nowadays, the desa authority is more lenient. Decisions concerning land ultimately rest with the individual landowner.

Within the village are smaller communities, the *banjar,* which are cooperative groups of neighbors bound to assist each other in marriages, festivals and especially during cremations. Every adult belongs both to desa and banjar, where he carries out most of his responsibilities to the village. The banjar owns the community's orchestras and dance properties, and has a kitchen for preparing banquets, a signal-drum tower to call meetings, and a communal temple. The banjar's meeting hall, an open pavilion, is a familiar sight to every traveler. The *bale banjar* serves as a local clubhouse, where villagers can gather in their leisure hours to practice with their gamelan troupe, watch a rehearsal of a play, hold council, or just sit and chat.

Working the rice: After the looming volcanoes, the cascading terraces of rice fields are the most striking feature of the Balinese landscape. Each individual plot of rice, *sawah*, is irrigated and contained by dikes of earth, one flowing into the next. Every farmer owning a sawah must join a *subak*, an agricultural society that controls the distribution

neighboring farmers, the Balinese are famed as the most efficient rice growers in the Indonesian archipelago.

Before the fields are planted, offerings are made to gain the goodwill of deities, who provide water and favorable conditions for a successful harvest. A little shrine stands near every sawah as an altar for the offerings that are placed there at specific times during the growing season.

Farmers begin work soon after daybreak, and are also at work at dusk – working is most comfortable during these cooler parts of the day. Noontime is spent at home or at the bale banjar. Some seasons demand more labor than others.

of irrigation water to its members. Like other Balinese associations, the spirit of the subak is communal. All members abide by the same rules. The subak helps the small farmers by assuring them of water, guarding irrigation channels against strangers diverting the water for their own use, repairing any damage in the dikes, and organizing festivals. At least once a month, a general meeting is held in the temple of the subak dedicated to the agricultural deities. Subak associations are important to the prosperity of the Balinese, as the mountainous nature of the land makes irrigation extremely difficult. Through this full cooperation among

During a harvest, the village streets are almost deserted, the banjar empty. Everyone joins in the harvest, and often it is also an opportunity to meet future mates. At other times, after the rice has just been planted, few hands are needed.

In the home: The household is run by the women. They are up at dawn preparing snacks for the men, fetching water and laying out morsels of rice and bouquets of flowers as small offerings to protect the homestead from evil spirits.

The Balinese house is a living organism. Like a human being, it has a head, the ancestral shrine; arms, the sleeping quarters and living room; legs and feet, the kitchen and rice granaries; and an anus, the garbage pit in the back yard. For affluent families, the sleeping and living rooms are combined in a modern building with a tiled roof.

Usually, however, all the bale are constructed of brick and wood, with thick roofs of thatch. The bale are distributed within a courtyard surrounded by a high wall for privacy during the day and security at night. Directly behind the entrance gate stands a small wall, *aling-aling*, which not only screens the interior of the compound, but also guards against dangerous influences, for evil spirits have trouble turning corners.

Outside the compound lies a fruit garden, with soups and food wrapped in banana leaves, local medicines, fruits and betel nuts. The grounds are so filled with determined saleswomen that one wonders who is doing all the buying.

Yet, there is always a constant coming and going of people and the voices of excited bargainers. Prices vary with the buyer. They are lowest to fellow villagers, higher to strangers, and considerably higher to foreigners – a customary procedure that is logical in a society so strongly oriented to the village community. After a jaunt to the market, the women return to prepare the morning meal: steamed rice with spicy side dishes and hot sauce. During a harvest, they deliver food to

with a corner reserved for a pigsty. The Balinese pig, a tamed descendant of the wild hog, is the dweller of most households; raising pigs and chickens is one of the main sources of income for the women.

With the exception of cattle sales, the market is the woman's dominion. There, she may spend the entire morning gossiping with friends. The market has a mood about it – smells of the island's delicacies and the colors of the seeds, beans, ferns, pastes of all hues and textures, portable one-pot kitchens

the fields, but ordinarily the meal is set out for the family, who may eat when they wish. Meals are eaten silently, leaving the time after dining for conversation.

In the early evening, after a refreshing bath, the men return home for dinner, usually the same food as lunch, served cold. Night is the time to put on clean clothes and stroll in the night markets, or meet at the lamp-lit food stands in the villages. The roads after dark provide lively scenes of gamelan recitals, banjar activities, or gatherings of friends.

If a temple festival or a cremation is approaching, the village is mobilized into making preparations. Women fashion high offer-

Left, rice farmer's art. <u>Above</u>, cremation of a Balinese raja.

ings and palm-leaf decorations, musicians and dancers rehearse, and men construct ornamental gateways of bamboo and long slender poles, *penjor*.

Death rites: Death is a passage from this life to the next in the soul's journey to heaven. A death is the time for sharing one's feelings, when friends of the deceased gather in the home to visit. During the period when the body remains in the house, visitors and relatives stay up until late hours to keep the family company.

On the appropriate date, the body is purified for burial in the village graveyard. The body is buried underground, until it is cremated. Many villagers, who may not be able to hold a cremation on the first auspicious day indicated by the religious calendar, may wait several years until a collective cremation is held, for which everyone shares the expenses. On the other hand, the body of a priest cannot be buried and must be cremated as soon as possible. A cremation is the most important and most costly of ceremonies, so a fund to aid the family may be set aside.

The cremation returns the material body to its five constituent elements – water, fire, air, earth and metal – and weakens the attachment of the soul towards worldly desires. Only when the body is destroyed and the soul freed from all worldly attractions can the soul be reunited with the Supreme Being. Thus, a cremation represents the accomplishment of the most sacred duty of every Balinese: liberating a relation's soul.

The soul of the dead has been brought from the graveyard to the home in an effigy, and placed upon a special pavilion. Throughout the morning, the guests are entertained with refreshments, and at midday are treated to a banquet. What seems a casual reception later explodes with activity. Urged by the thunderous beat of the gamelan, dozens of village men rush into the household and carry the effigy from its resting place. All try to participate, for by doing so one shows loyalty to the deceased. The carriers hoist the effigy to the awaiting tower, a high structure of wood or bamboo glittering with paper ornaments, mirrors and bright fabrics.

The tower represents the cosmos. Its wide base is in the shape of a turtle entwined by two *naga* (crowned snakes) – symbol of the foundation of the world. Above is an open platform where the effigy is placed, repre-senting the space between heaven and earth; the platform itself supports roofs symbolizing the heavens, with the number of roofs varying according to the caste of the deceased. Brahmans have eleven roofs, the lower aristocracy seven or nine roofs, and the common people, from one to five. The cremation tower of a priest has no roofs at all.

A large wooden animal sarcophagus also varies with each caste. The Brahmans burn their dead in a bull, or a cow if it is a woman. Other nobility use different representations, but since customs are changing, nowadays most of the nobility uses the bull.

The procession to the cremation ground provides an astonishing spectacle. Larger ceremonies need as many as a hundred men to carry the tower and sarcophagus in a tumultuous parade through town to the burning site. Led by a single line of women, who carry the offerings and holy water, the bearers lift the towering constructions above a sea of followers. The tower is led by a long white cloth held by the relatives. In the cremations for high aristocracy, the cloth takes the form of a serpent.

As the procession crowds into the cremation ground, the effigy is passed from tower to sarcophagus, and the exhumed remains also put inside. The priest mounts the bull's platform to recite the final prayers and pour holy water upon the remains, breaking the pots of water as is the custom. The *adegan*, an effigy used in the ceremony as a symbolic container of the soul, is placed upon the remains, and old Chinese coins *(kepeng)* or Indonesian currency notes are spread all over it, as a ransom to Yama, the god of the underworld. When proper offerings and prayers have been made to ensure the soul a safe journey, the sarcophagus is set ablaze.

A procession marches to the sea to deposit the ashes, or to the river if the sea is too far away. This custom is a purification, the washing away of all uncleanliness.

Twelve or 42 days after cremation, but sometimes even decades, the Balinese hold a second funeral ceremony – *nyekah* or *mukur* or *ngasti* – which releases the soul of any thought and feeling still clinging to it. Finally, the deified soul is enshrined in the family temple, but a distinction remains between it and the gods.

<u>Right</u>, final send off in Hindu-style cremation.

It is natural for the Balinese who live so close to the earth to bestow nature with a magic and spiritual significance. On top of the lofty mountains dwell divine spirits, who bring prosperity and good fortune to the people. Beneath the unfamiliar sea lurk fanged giants and demons – forces dangerous to humanity. So all nature is eternally divided into pairs – high and low, right and left, day and night, east and west, strong and weak, healthy and sick, clean and unclean – in general, good and evil, life and death.

Each illuminates the other within the scope of creation, and Balinese rituals strive always to maintain a middle ground, a harmony between the two poles.

From earliest times, the people of Bali have conceived of an ordered universe stretching from the heavens above the mountains down to the depths of the sea. Everything within nature has direction, rank and place. All that is holy is associated with height, the mountains and the direction upstream toward the volcano Gunung Agung. All that is threatening or harmful belongs to the forces of the underworld, the ocean and the direction downstream toward the sea. The people dwell in the intermediary sphere of fertile plains, wedged between the mountains and the sea.

Religious rites and festivals guide a Balinese from birth to death, and into the world thereafter. They provide the cohesive forces within the family and a village community. Religion regulates the plan of a town, the order of a home and the ethical code of the people. Holidays, entertainment and social gatherings are based upon the calendar and occur within the milieu of religious ceremonies. In the innumerable shrines that mark the landscapes, in the *pendet* offering dance, even in the gracious personality of the people, religion is essential to the identity of the Balinese and to their life.

Agama Hindu Dharma, the religion of Bali, upholds the peaceful life of a people.

Preceding pages: gebogan – pyramids of fruits, flowers and rice cookies on way to a temple. **Left,** odalan ritual at Pura Meru, Lombok. **Right,** female pemangku entering a trance.

The divine spirits (the deities and ancestors) are honored through worship and devotion. The evil spirits (demons, witches and ghosts) are placated through purification and exorcism. Both must be provided for, since happiness and contentment come only to those who take both forces into consideration.

Yet beyond good and evil, life and death, there exists a single unity – the source and totality of creation. This is Sanghyang Widi Wasa, god omnipotent to the Balinese. In this universal god, all the deities and ances-

tral spirits achieve a higher unity. It is Sanghyang Widi Wasa who lies behind the offerings, rituals and temples. But though Agama Hindu Dharma is a monotheistic religion, the supreme god – Sanghyang Widi Wasa – is not often directly worshipped. A few temples and shrines are dedicated to the supreme god directly, but most are for the many manifestations.

The Balinese are a deeply religious people. The common folk – villagers and farmers – dutifully perform the devotions they have been taught since infancy. During a temple festival, nobody is excluded, however young. Even the smallest child, hands closed in prayer between those of a parent, participates in a faith that grows and remains throughout life. The educated and the priests, who have studied the complicated theology of Agama Hindu Dharma, guide the villagers in their reverences. One Brahmana explained, "The Balinese know but one god, yet they honor many deities and ancestors. The multiplicity of divine spirits involves function. As we are one person but use our eyes to see, our hands to work and our feet to walk, so Sanghyang Widi Wasa is one god. Yet in his power as creator he is Brahma, in his power as preserver he is Wisnu, and in his power to destroy he is Siwa."

The high priest was speaking of the Hindu

(female) – each closely linked to nature. Again, the Brahman has an example. "If one could imagine an indivisible whole seen from many different angles, so the dewa and dewi are different angles, so the dewa and dewi are different manifestations of Sanghyang Widi Wasa, each having its own associations." God in the manifestation of rice, Dewi Sri (goddess of fertility), and of the ocean, Dewa Baruna (deity of the sea). Thus, the Balinese venerate many personifications of the universal god. But, whatever deity the people honor, their reverence is also paid to Sanghyang Widi Wasa, but indirectly through tangible things such as the sea, the rice, or even a remembered ancestor.

Trinity – Brahma, Wisnu (Vishnu) and Siwa (Shiva) – which in Bali is called the *Trimurti*. In many of the large state temples there stands a three-seated pedestal enshrining the Trimurti. Before a ceremony, the temple guardians decorate the pedestal with bright wraps of colored cloth: red for Brahma, white for Siwa and black for Wisnu.

Most Balinese worship according to the Siwaistic sect of Agama Hindu Dharma, since Siwa – destroyer and reincarnator – is most seen and felt by the people.

In the hierarchy of the divine, below Sanghyang Widi Wasa and the Trinity are many other deities – *dewa* (male) and *dewi*

The dark side: Were Bali to be under the care of only the deities and guardian ancestors, it would be heavenly. But there is a darker, mysterious side to the island. The graveyards and crossroads are inhabited by nocturnal goblins and witches who assume the forms of weird animals and monsters to waylay innocent passers-by. Reports range from monkeys with golden teeth to bald-headed giants sighted walking along the roads at midnight.

Of course, everyone knows who is responsible for the ghostly visions: *leyak* – the spirits of living persons practicing the art of black magic.

Almost every Balinese has a tale to tell about leyaks, whether by hearing a spooky story, watching a play about Rangda (queen of the leyak and a manifestation of Siwa's consort), or possibly even a personal encounter. Like vampires, they are fond of sucking the blood from sleeping people and like to eat little children. They also grow indignant if one neglects to bring them offerings, and may vent their anger by plaguing the community with sickness or death.

Yet, somehow, leyaks seldom reveal themselves to outsiders. Those who are curious content themselves with hearsay, dramas of magic, stone statues at the *pura dalem* (temple of the dead), and of course, the gruesome,

rate rites of purification are necessary to cleanse it back to health again. The deities and demons are as much a part of Bali's population as the people themselves.

Yet, as noted before, it would be misleading to think the Balinese believe in many gods. Their religion grew from a long succession of Hindu and Buddhist influences upon deeply-rooted beliefs in animism and ancestor worship. From the teachings brought by priests from India and Java, the people adopted practices to suit their needs.

The strength of Agama Hindu Dharma has long been its flexibility in adapting to the changing times. In its pertinence to customary law *(adat)*, civil ceremonies, science,

saber-toothed masks with flaming tongues and long tendrils of goat's hair. Witches are the most vivid characters in the spirit world of the Balinese. And they are not alone.

The wicked *buta* and *kala* – invisible spirits that haunt the desolate seashores and dark woods – also pollute villages with uncleanliness and disease. Should these evil spirits predominate even in one household, the entire village is thrown into jeopardy, and elabo-

Far left, symbolic male figure representing Sanghyang Widi Wasa. **Left**, Bali's world depicted as a turtle and coiled serpents as world's foundation. **Above**, trance dancers and Rangda.

superstition, labor and leisure – to the whole of Balinese society – Agama Hindu Dharma guides a community.

Holiest people: The serene figure of the priest, clad in white and seated upon a high pavilion, is a familiar sight. Villagers make their devotions with the guidance of a priest so that their prayers are properly directed and received. Ceremonies connected with civil law, such as marriage or the blessing of a newborn child, are conducted by a priest to bestow official authority. Even for completing a house, the priest is called upon to give god's blessing before the family moves into their new home.

The community turns to its holy men and women, who are divided into two levels: the *pedanda* or high priest, and the *pemangku*, or temple priest.

No momentous ceremony would be complete without the services of a pedanda. As spiritual leader and carrier of the Agama Hindu Dharma theology, the high priest serves as a medium for the people during ceremonies. Through an intricate ritual of hymns, mantras, bell-ringing and hand gestures, the priest temporarily achieves unity with god. By absorbing divine power into the self, he or she is able to prepare the purifying holy water essential to worship. This ritual may take several hours.

meditation, theology, and ritual. The assistants of priests are their wives, who through marriage become priestesses and take on the same responsibilities as their husbands.

Places of worship: Temples – large or small, plain or elaborate – are found everywhere on the island. Besides the house temple in every compound, most villages have three major temples – the *pura desa*, *pura puseh* and *pura dalem*. There are countless others: the *subak* irrigation temples, the clan temples, the *banjar* hamlet temples, and those shrines near public bathing places dedicated to the spirits of rivers and springs. As sites for making contact with the spiritual world through offerings and prayer, temples are

The divine spirit of god is embodied in the water prepared by the high priest. When the ritual has been completed, the priest passes the holy water to the pemangku (the temple priest), who sprinkles it upon the people as a blessing and purification.

The hard-working pemangku are the supervisors of temple feasts. Whether distributing holy water to their congregation, receiving offerings or directing a large procession, it is they who officiate at the temple and take an active part in the ceremonies. The high priest does not participate in worldly things, but rather is respected as a holy person set above the people. Life is dedicated to

essential to the Balinese. If not, the harmony with nature would be disrupted, leaving people susceptible to accidents and danger.

Most of the time, the temples are unoccupied. It is only during holy days, when the deities and ancestral spirits descend from heaven to visit their devotees, that temples flourish with festivity. Everyone arrives beautifully dressed, presenting the deities with food, music, prayer, devotions and the best entertainment to amuse them during their sojourn on earth. Usually after one or three days, the deities return to heaven and the temple empties until the next holiday. As places for contacting the divine, temples are the true centers of the arts and the focus of Balinese culture.

Rather than a somber and massive structure, the temple is a spacious enclosure surrounded by walls and partitioned into courtyards. Entrance is through the *candi bentar*, or split gate. Resembling a tower cut into two halves, it probably took its form from the old *candi* monuments of ancient Java.

Inside seems far away from the hurried traffic and commerce of the street-side. In the absence of all the ceremonial decorations, the crowds, dances and food stands, a temple is quiet and withdrawn. Stone carvings of demonic faces, overgrown with weeds and moss, peer out from the walls onto the

temple proper. Here, lined in rows on the sides closest to the mountains and the east, are the shrines that serve as "sitting places" for the visiting deities. Perhaps the pemangku is there placing some small offerings before the shrines and brushing the fallen leaves aside to keep the place tidy. The multi-roofed towers of the *meru* shrines taper upwards to the sky. The receding roofs are always in odd numbers, the highest meru having eleven roofs.

In the inner courtyard are shrines that house the temple's heirlooms. Stone statues of Hindu deities, jewels, ancient manuscripts and shapeless stones are sacred relics. Either because of their antiquity or because they

wide courtyard. Around the courtyard stand thatched pavilions: an assembly hall where the village authority holds meetings (*bale agung*), a pavilion for the temple gamelan (*bale gong*), a kitchen for preparing offerings, and sometimes a cockfight arena.

Shaded by frangipani trees and a tall *kulkul* (signal drum) tower, the outer courtyard functions as an antechamber for social affairs and preparations. A second covered gateway, *paduraksa*, guarded by statues of two fierce giants, leads to the inner courtyard – the

Left, a pedanda, or high priest, in meditation. **Above**, Pura Besakih.

were found under extraordinary circumstances, these objects are divine gifts to the people. Yet a statue is never venerated for its own sake. There are no idols in Bali. Both a thing and a person may be respected as holy if a spiritual presence that dwells within.

Festivals and rituals: Certain days are designated for special prayers, some for purification rites, and others for making offerings to the lower spirits. If a village is threatened by disease or an unexpected mishap, a ritual exorcism is necessary. A ceremony may also be prompted by divine inspiration through a trance medium, or by the fear of black magic. In addition, there are also holiday seasons with festivals in all of Bali's temples, and the nights of the full moon and new moon are favorable for religious observances and rites.

When the Balinese first settle upon new land and wish to build a village, they erect a temple of origin, *pura puseh,* where they may pray to Sanghyang Widi Wasa. Later, when the village temples and all the altars have been constructed, the people pay homage to the deities of the village.

Generations afterwards, when the souls of the village founders have been purified to attain a divine state, the people revere their ancestors in the pura puseh. (The title of *leluhur* is used to address the deified soul of a deceased person.)

A government law from 1981 forbades cockfighting outside of religious festivals. Although cockfighting still retains its traditional place, the ban was aimed primarily at limiting gambling. It is unlikely that cockfighting will disappear from the Balinese way of life, however.

For months, the cocks have been groomed, tested and coaxed for the special event. Before the fight, two men exchange their roosters to see if in strength and size the birds are matched, and if they have a mean eye for each other. When the contest is agreed upon, the cocks' left legs are armed with vicious blades of polished steel. The thread bindings must be tight and bound properly. An expert

Among the most frequent ceremonies is the *odalan.* Held on the anniversary of the temple's initial consecration, an odalan festival is long anticipated by the entire village as a day of prayer, feasting and entertainment lasting late into the night.

On the morning of an odalan, all the men gather around the *wantilan* – an open pavilion for cockfights. Originally, cockfighting served as an essential preliminary to temple feasts. The spilt blood of the cocks was a sacrifice to evil spirits so they would not interfere with the religious proceedings to follow. Later, ritual became secularized into a favorite sport.

stands by to see they are fixed by regulation. Amid all this excitement, the cocks are put down in a small square.

The arena falls silent as the cocks are provoked and released. In attacks too swift for the eye to follow, the cocks entwine in aerial combat, each striving to gain leverage for the lethal descent of its spur. A round may last a few seconds, and for all the commotion that precedes them, the fights are quick and to the point – a bloodstained cock unable to rise marks a defeat. The birds are swiftly retrieved and, if they are not too badly injured, nursed back to health to fight another day. The less fortunate reappear as dinner.

Cockfighting is a man's sport. Women rarely watch, but usually they are either selling snacks at the surrounding food stands (*warung*) or arranging the high offerings. All during the odalan, lofty pyramids – *gebogan* – of fruit, cakes and flowers arrive at the temple, sometimes in colorful processions.

Offerings: Offerings are given in the same spirit as presenting gifts – a sort of token to strengthen the people's request that the divine bring prosperity to the community, and that the evil spirits bring the least possible trouble. Thus, offerings are always sharply divided into two kinds: those to the evil spirits, which are left upon the ground, and those to the deities, exquisitely made and appropriately placed upon high altars. Near the high offerings burn fragrant wood and incense, to carry their essence (*sari*) upward toward the divine. The material part is later brought home and eaten by the family, so both the divine recipients and the donors enjoy the banquet.

While the offerings continue to arrive, the pemangku recites prayers of invitation that request the deities to descend to the temple, their earthly residence. Often, the deities are represented by little figurines of gold, bronze or gilded wood called *pratima*. The deities are asked to occupy the pratima as a more tangible form to which the ceremony may be directed. These figures in themselves have no power. Like the temple shrines that support them, they are merely receptacles for a divine presence.

All the shrines are smothered with splendid offerings and hung with traditional paintings and glittering brocades. The pratima stand with flowers upon the shrines and high altars. Nearby, the pemangku sits before a brazier of incense and a water vessel, and blesses the people who have come with offerings. Everyone performs their duties seriously, yet there is no solemnity about a temple festival.

At times, the temple's gamelan sounds a rhythmic march and a procession is formed to take the deities to the ocean or nearest river for a ceremonial bath. When the procession reaches the sea, the deities are entertained with music, dancing and hymns of praise, and receive many offerings before they are carried back to the temple.

Left, cockfighting.

At night, the outer temple grounds are a fair. Outside the towering gate is a carnival of sideshows, with rows of food and candy stands, toys, balloons, clothing sales, animated card games, lively displays of wonder medicines, and invariably a drama performance, which begins around midnight and lasts late into the morning hours. Everybody looks their best, especially the shy young women who sell food at the warung. (It's a custom in Bali for a girl who reaches the age of marriage to set up a food stand. In the public eye, she attracts many suitors. The young man who wins her fancy pays less. Needless to say, girl-watching is the number one attraction for the bachelors present.)

Once inside the temple, the proceedings take on a more formal, mystic tone. Pemangku continue to chant songs of praise before shrines clouded with smoking incense. They are joined by a group of women who rise to dance a *pendet*, honoring the deities of each shrine with incense and offerings and prayers. The women may go unnoticed among other villagers, but come alive with exuberant individuality and grace. They do not use costume or make-up. The dance is an offering to the deities, and true to the Balinese spirit to pay homage to god through the beauty of motion, song and music.

Trance is a religious experience, a form of communication with the spiritual world. Certain men and women in every village serve the deities as established trance mediums in the temple ceremonies. Each temple has its own trance mediums, who attend all the ceremonies there. Moreover, every medium has a special deity with which to communicate during a trance.

Through a trance medium, a divine request may be made or advice given. If a person goes into trance and speaks during a ceremony, it is taken as a good sign to the people that their prayers have been heard and their offerings accepted. When the message is passed on to the priest, he revives the person with prayers and libations of holy water. The medium awakes fatigued and dazed, rarely recalling what was spoken.

An odalan ends as the long tragic tale of the drama reaches its climax, and the pemangku recite prayers politely requesting the deities to depart in hopes that they have been well provided for during their visit and will return to heaven pleased.

RAMAYANA AND MAHABHARATA

Two great and ancient Hindu epics, *Ramayana* (Story of Prince Rama) and *Mahabharata* (War of the Bharatas), originated in India, spreading throughout Southeast Asia – including Cambodia, Thailand and Indonesia – over a thousand years ago. In Bali, in addition to dance-drama and shadow plays, artists have shared the epics in stone reliefs, woodcarvings and paintings.

In both Hindu epics is woven a thread of high moral purpose – the ultimate triumph of virtue and the subjugation of vice. Every episode that is performed on stage or portrayed in art is a parable of great relevance to Indonesians.

Whereas the *Ramayana* illuminates the ethics of human relationships, the *Mahabharata* sings of the glorious battle exploits and deeds in the war of the Bharatas, an ancient and warlike race of northern India. The verses ring of dazzling feats of warriors, daring escapes and merciless revenge in a feud between two rival royal houses.

The oldest version of the *Ramayana* was written around the third or fourth century BC. The *Ramayana* in India consists of 24,000 verses divided into 500 songs. The *Mahabharata* probably reached its present form in the fourth century AD. The *Mahabharata* is nearly 90,000 stanzas in its final form. The Indonesian versions, written during the tenth to thirteenth centuries in Java, are among the most beautiful poems in Old Javanese literature.

Ramayana: In the kingdom of Kosala, near the Himalayas, reigned King Dasarata and his four sons: Rama, Barata, Laksmana and Satrugna. Raised in wisdom and righteousness, the princes lived in harmony and were an endless source of happiness to the king and his people. At a great age, Dasarata realized he must give up his throne to his eldest son, Rama.

Kekayi, Darasata's second wife and mother of Barata, fosters secret ambitions for her own son. Urged by her wicked servant Muntara, she reminds the king that he owes her two unfulfilled vows. Now she makes her demands: that Barata be king, and that Rama be banished.

Rama, obeying his father, prepares to go. Sita, Rama's wife, begs permission to accompany him. Laksmana also insists on following, and the three start for the forest.

The king, overcome by sadness, soon dies. Much to Kekayi's dismay, Barata refuses the crown and rules the kingdom as Rama's deputy, with his elder brother's sandals on the throne.

Rama, Sita and Laksmana live peacefully in the forest for 13 years. Their peace is shattered by horrible Rawana, the many-headed ogre king with a retinue of giants. Rawana is captivated by Sita's beauty and is determined to kidnap her. His minister, the giant Marica, is ordered to lure Rama away. Marica goes to Sita as a golden deer; Sita begs Rama to catch it. He sets off in pursuit. Far from the cottage, he shoots an arrow at the golden deer. Before Marica dies, the giant cries out for help in Rama's voice. Hearing the cry, Sita urges Laksamana to go to the rescue. Laksamana hurries off.

Meanwhile, Rawana arrives in the disguise of a begging Brahmana. With much flattery, he persuades Sita to give him some water. Rawana seizes her in his arms, and flies to his home in Langka (Sri Lanka). On the way, he is attacked by the brave bird Jatayu, who tries to rescue Sita. Mortally wounded, Jatayu manages to tell Rama of Sita's abduction before dying.

Rama and Laksmana set out in search of Sita. Rama meets the monkey, Hanuman, servant of the monkey king, Sugriwa, who was deprived of his rightful throne by his wicked brother Subali. Rama regains the kingdom for Sugriwa by killing Subali with an arrow. In gratitude, Sugriwa orders his armies, under the command of Hanuman, to search for Sita.

They reach the shore opposite Langka, and Hanuman leaps across the sea to find Sita in the garden of Rawana's palace. He tells her that Rama will rescue her and, in token, gives her Rama's ring. Sita gives him her ring to take to Rama. The army of monkeys forms a causeway of boulders across the sea.

Rama and his allies invade Langka and a violent battle ensues, ending with Rawana's death by an arrow from Rama's magic bow.

Reunited, Rama, Sita and Laksmana return to Kosala. Barata gladly cedes his regency and Kosala attains new heights of glory and prosperity under King Rama.

Mahabharata: Once there lived two families of the Kuru clan, descended from Bharata. The Pandawa family has five brothers, sons of the king's brother, Pandu, who ruled the kingdom in his brother's name. The Korawa family are the one hundred sons of the blind king Dretarastra.

The Pandawa sons are of semi-divine origin - the eldest son, Yudistira, a man of truth and piety, is descended from Dharma, god of virtue; the dauntless warrior Bima from Bayu, god of the wind; Arjuna, the peerless archer, from Indra, god of elements; and the twins Nakula and Sahadewa, from the celestial Aswin twins.

Years before, Pandu's wife had given birth to yet another son, Karna. He later joined the Korawa family, becoming their warlord and the chief opponent of his half-brother Arjuna.

As cousins, the boys of the two families grow up together. In every contest between the rival families, the Pandawas are victorious. The Korawas grow more jealous and revengeful with each passing year. When Pandu dies, Yudistira becomes heir to the throne. The ruthless Duryodana contrives a plot to destroy the sons of Pandu.

One day, the Pandawa boys and their mother are persuaded to pay a visit to the Korawa family. A special abode has been built for them, but the house is mysteriously torched. The brothers and their mother barely escape through an underground tunnel and flee to the forest. The Pandawa brothers hear of a contest for the hand of a princess, so they journey to the kingdom, ruled by King Drupada. Arjuna easily defeats all his rivals and wins the daughter of King Drupada. The sons return and tell their mother they received a great gift. Not knowing what it is, their mother replies, "Share the gift in common." Thus, the princess becomes the wife of all the brothers. Soon afterwards, Arjuna also marries the sister of King Krishna.

Meanwhile, the devious Duryodana learns of the failure of his plot to kill the Pandawa brothers. Moreover, he now knows that his cousins have powerful allies, Drupada and Krishna.

The Pandawas clear the forest and build a new capital called Ngamerta (supposedly the present-day region of Delhi). Yudistira, as eldest brother the king of Ngamerta, has a sacrifice to declare his sovereignty over all the kings of India, and his brothers subsequently set out in all directions to proclaim his rule. The hundred Korawa brothers and their aging father also attend, but in great humiliation and envy.

Left, modern carving of Hanuman protecting Sita. Above, temple relief of the Hindu epics.

Still determined to secure the ruin of the Pandawas, Duryodana gains the assistance of his minister, Sakuni, an expert at loading dice and who shares in his hatred. Yudistira has one incurable weakness: gambling. Sakuni challenges Yudistira, who loses game after game. Yudistira forfeits everything – wealth, horses, elephants, slaves and possessions. Lastly, his kingdom. In a final gamble, he stakes himself, his brothers, and even the princess Drupadi, against Sakuni - and loses! Duryodana, eager to claim the Pandawa brothers as slaves, is persuaded by his father to soften the claim: the Pandawas must go into twelve years of exile.

The Pandawas pass the next twelve years in the wilderness. Duryodana, now king, is still not satisfied with his revenge and pursues them. Along the way, he is taken captive in a skirmish

with sprites. The Pandawa brothers, hearing of his plight, go to his rescue and allow him to return to his kingdom safely; however, this act of generosity only deepens Duryodana's hatred and jealousy.

In council with Krishna, the Pandawas decide to recapture their kingdom by force, and so the Bharatayudha, the great war of the Bharatas, begins. For 18 days, the skies are dark with clouds of arrows and the dust of charioteers and cavalry. The venerated teachers of both families are killed, as are Arjuna's and Bima's sons. Then the undefeated rivals, Arjuna and Karna, meet in mortal combat.

Arjuna avenges the death of his son with that of his arch enemy. Both Bima and Duryodana fight on until Duryodana falls dead. ∎

Ceremonial dances and dramas directly relate to religious ceremonies by serving as offerings, prayers, or exorcisms. With the active participation of the *pemangku* (the people's priest and caretaker of the village temple), they are a dramatic form of contact with the spiritual world.

Religious dances are usually held within or near a temple. The presentation of an offering in the form of a ritual dance is known as *pendet*. Unlike the exhibition dances that demand arduous training, pendet may be danced by anyone: male and female pemangku, or women and girls of the village.

Pendet is taught simply by imitation. Younger girls follow the movements of the elder women, who recognize their responsibility in setting a good example. Proficiency comes with age, and the grandmothers are the best.

As a religious dance, pendet is performed during temple ceremonies. All dancers carry in their right hand a small offering of incense, cakes, water vessels, or flower formations set in palm leaf. With these they dance from shrine to shrine within the temple. Pendet may continue intermittently throughout the day and late into the night during temple feasts.

In the *sanghyang*, in which the dancers enter a trance prior to dancing, the ceremony begins in the temple and moves to a clearing nearby. Because of their association with evil spirits, the Calon Arang and Barong plays are generally held near the temple of the dead and the graveyard, favorite meeting places of witches and the like.

Trance: An elevated state of consciousness, trance is part of Balinese life and is viewed as quite natural. An entranced person communicating with a divine presence is respected as holy, guided by a directive influence, usually a priest. The Balinese are careful never to let someone in a trance get out of hand. There are always guardians who stand by to exercise control, if needed.

Although there were once more variations

of the sanghyang than will be found today in Bali, trance continues to be influential. Kecak and janger, for example, are direct offshoots of the sanghyang, and a dancer becoming possessed by a role is manifest in a *topeng* actor "entered" by the characters of the masks.

Sanghyang: In the temple, two girls kneel before a brazier of smoking incense. The pemangku makes offerings to the deity, requesting protection for the village during the trance ceremony. Behind the girls kneels a group of women who chant the *sanghyang*

song, asking celestial nymphs to descend from heaven and dance through the bodies of the young girls.

With eyes closed, the girls sway back and forth above the incense until they fall over in trance. The attending women put flowered crowns upon their heads and lift them to the shoulders of male retainers, who carry them to the dance area.

Set upon the ground between the female choir and male chorus, the little dancers perform a dreamy version of the *legong*. Their eyes remain shut during the entire performance. When the chanting ceases, the girls are brought out of trance by the

Preceding pages: open-air performance; trance procession. **Left,** kris dancers under the spell of Rangda. **Right,** sanghyang jaran.

pemangku, who prays and blesses them with holy water. This is *sanghyang dedari* – divine angel – a ritual dance in which a spirit temporarily descends and reveals itself through the entranced dancers. The girls dancing as "divine angels" are always underage, for a virgin child is holy. And as with legong, the girls retire from the dance as no longer pure when menstruation begins.

There are other forms of the sanghyang trance dance as well. In *sanghyang jaran,* an entranced boy (or priest) dances on a horse, *jaran,* represented by a hobbyhorse. He dances around a bonfire, sometimes stepping on the glowing embers. Mountain villages near Kintamani perform the *sanghyang*

sanghyang dedari dancers have little or no formal dance training, nor can a sanghyang jaran dancer normally walk on fire.

Barong and Rangda: The natural world to the Balinese is held in balance by two opposing forces, benign and malign. The destructive power of sickness and death is associated with the latter force and the evil influence of black magic.

If black magic prevails, a village falls into danger, and extensive purification ceremonies are necessary to restore a proper equilibrium. Dramatic art is a means of cleansing the village, by strengthening its resistance to harmful forces, including natural disasters.

Barong – a mystical creature with a long,

deling, where puppets dance suspended on a string, between poles manipulated by two girls, who will fall into trances.

Sanghyang dances developed from the essential religious function of maintaining the health and well-being of the village. They are performed to exorcise evil spirits, which infest the community as sickness, calamity or death.

Boys and girls selected as sanghyang dancers are highly regarded by the community and exempted from certain village responsibilities. The feats they perform while dancing are a medium of spiritual expression, since the dancer is possessed by a deity –

sway back and curved tail – represents the favorable spirits, the protectors of humanity. The widow-witch Rangda – a manifestation of Siwa's consort – is the opposite. She rules the evil spirits and witches who haunt the graveyards. Her world is darkness, and her specialities lie with the practice of black magic, the negative and destructive force of the left.

Often, the struggle between Barong and Rangda occurs within the framework of a popular story, an episode from the *Mahabharata*, for example. Yet the essence of the play remains the eternal conflict of two cosmic forces, symbolized by the two figures. Because the play is charged with sorcery and magic, extensive offerings are made to the deities to protect the players during the dance performance.

Usually Barong enters first, cleverly danced by two men who form the forelegs and hind legs, the front man manipulating the mask. Barong's appearance varies with the kind of mask it wears, which may be a stylized wild boar, tiger, lion, or occasionally an elephant.

The most holy mask, and the type used in the play, is that of the *barong keket,* the Lord of the Forest, a beast representing no known animal. The fantastic creature mischievously sidesteps, snapping its jaws at the gamelan,

vation of the community, represented by the *kris* dancers, men armed with daggers. At one point in the fight, when the victory of the barong is threatened, the kris dancers rush to the barong's assistance and violently attack Rangda. The witch's spell reverses their fury back onto themselves, and they plunge the blades of their daggers against their own bodies. But the barong protects the crazed men from inflicting self-harm.

This phenomenal self-stabbing is enacted when the kris dancers are in trance. No matter how forcefully they plunge the daggers against their chest, the tips of the blades do not puncture the skin. Occasional wounds do occur, a sign of divine displeasure with

swishing its tail, seeming to threaten but actually there to protect the village.

After Barong's dance, everyone falls silent. Splintery fingernails foreshadow the dreadful vision of Rangda. From her mouth hangs a flaming tongue signifying her consuming fire, and around her neck, a necklace of human entrails falls over her pendulous breasts. Howling a low, gurgling curse, she stalks Barong while waving a white cloth, issuing her overwhelming magic.

In the protection of Barong lies the preser-

Left and above, scenes from Barong and Rangda, a story of good and evil.

the individual or even with the community. Injuries are "cured" with petals of the red hibiscus flowers that decorate the holy masks. At the end of the play, the kris dancers are revived by the pemangku, who sprinkles them with holy water, into which has been dipped in the beard of the barong. (The beard, made of human hair, is one of the most sacred parts of the barong.)

A final offering is made to the evil spirits by spilling the blood of a live chicken and pairing alcoholic liquids.

Barong landung: On the island of Nusa Penida lives a demon, Jero Gede Mecaling, the Tusked Giant. Once he came to Bali,

The exuberance of Balinese dances gives them an air of spontaneity, yet beneath lies a learned set of motions presented in a highly-stylized technique. Each gesture has a name that describes its action, usually in terms of nature, especially animals. A flurry of turns, for example, may bear the name of a tiger defending itself, or a sidestep may be named after the way a raven jumps. A tilt of the head may be a duck looking up at the sky, and the shimmering of the fingers are two birds moving on a coconut leaf. The names are descriptive, in fact, and have no meaning except in identifying, metaphorically, the character and feeling of an action.

Balinese dances and drama cover a wide array of theatrical forms. Most performances are a combination of dance, music, song and acting. No play is complete without music of some kind, and no dance, even the most abstract, is without story or meaning.

In classical Balinese dances, space is usually partitioned in measured steps, with the weight close to the ground. Rarely do dancers merge in a single form. Although the motion of the dancers may be highly-synchronized, the dancers remain separate and relate to each other through the choreography, usually in lines and rows. The movements of wrist and fingers vary tremendously, making them an important criterion as to the quality of the dancer.

The accent in Balinese drama is upon the unraveling of a story more than the heightened counterpoint between music and dance. The gamelan orchestra is always essential, but it is not as commanding as the development of plot and the colorful spectrum of personalities.

Tales of passion, historical romances, love adventures and military chivalry are popular themes in dance-drama. Most of the stories are drawn from the eleventh to thirteenth century courts of eastern Java, from where the costumes, language and gestures are of-

ten derived. Characters speak in the classical language of royal families, and dance in the refined manner of the aristocracy.

Comic interludes are provided by lower members of the court, the retainers and ladies-in-waiting. There are always two male clowns, usually servants of the king's prime minister, who function within the drama as interpreters of the narrative, translating the poetic language spoken by their masters into common Balinese.

Indeed, the clowns are exempt from re-

fined styles of dancing. The Balinese are so accustomed to the stylized postures, dress and movements of dance that, when a clown appears, who obviously has no style at all, he or she is intrinsically funny. Witches, animals and demons, also exempt from the behavior of humans, have license to adopt styles of their own and often constitute a large part of the comedy.

Costume is inseparable from the dance itself. Make-up is a stylized facade of the character, and by putting on a mask, the dancer totally adopts the character's personality. The immobile face seems to transform the dancer into a new being. The imperson-

Left, tightly bound in gold brocade and crowned with frangipani blossoms, this young dancer is poised in classical legong dance. **Above**, a dance teacher with her young student, refining the delicate body movements and positions.

ality of Balinese dancers, with their intense stares and closed lips, is striking. It is in movement of body and hands through which dancers define their personality.

Dance is taught by imitation, and a pupil always studies just a single dance. A young pupil follows every movement of the teacher. After the basic motions, the teacher comes behind and forces the arms and fingers into the correct postures, tilts the head to the proper accents of the drum, and adjusts the position of the body.

This body-to-body lesson is repeated as often as necessary for the pupil to "feel" the dance. The dancer follows the beat of the drum, which dictates the rhythm of the dance.

The drummer is the conductor of the *gamelan* orchestra and leads the changing tempo, which serves to guide the movements of the dancer. An exceptional dancer, by adding personal modifications of style to the traditional choreography, elevates the dance to new heights.

One of the oldest of Balinese dances is the *gambuh*, which may be 1,000 years old. Many of Bali's most popular dances were derived or influenced by it, including the *topeng, cupak, calon arang, legong* and *arja*. Most of these dances were created between 1850 and 1900, a period of exceptional vitality for dance under the patronage of nobles.

The *sanghyang* trance dance influenced such dances as the *kecak* and *janger*. Other dances, such as *kebyar,* which dates from this century, were created by such great dancers as I Ketut Mario and I Nyoman Kaler.

Gambuh: This rare courtly dance-drama of gambuh uses the repertoire of eastern Javanese romances, known as *panji* or *malat*. Believed to originally date from the tenth century, gambuh is courtly refinement at its best, and has influenced other forms of Balinese dance. During the eighteenth and nineteenth centuries, the nobles of Bali sponsored dozens of groups in elaborate performances, some of them even on floating barges in moats.

Elaborately-costumed dancers perform extended choreographies to the soft wailing sounds of meter-long bamboo flutes, lutes, drums, and metal percussion instruments, including bells. In the stylized speech of Old Javanese and High Balinese, the memorized dialogues in gambuh are not translated into common language by comic figures, as in other types of performances. The story is not important, in fact. Rather, the elegance and skills of the dancers are the focus in gambuh. Humor is virtually absent.

Gambuh recreates the splendor of ancient kingdoms. The repertoire is extensive but revolves around rival princes, contested maidens, abductions, rescues, and magical weapons. The scenes are formal, with precise arrangements and movements of characters on stage. Ladies-in-waiting, princesses, ministers, lords, kings, and clowns appear in a pageant of courtly love, intrigue, and warfare. Battles tend to be short sequences using drawn daggers.

Once exclusively entertainment for the court, gambuh is now performed at some temple ceremonies, large weddings, and even death rites. Only a few groups are active, mostly in Batuan, Denpasar, and Budakeling.

Arja: A folk opera, arja is a social event for the entire village, when everyone gathers to watch this long love story unfold. Like gambuh, arja uses the same catalogue of east Javanese romance stories.

Arja developed around 1880 as an all-male dance-drama from the traditional gambuh. Stories are mostly drawn from court romances of the Javanese kingdoms, of the eleventh to thirteenth centuries. Leading characters are members of the court, who move in the stylized dance of the nobility, while singing in poetic Balinese.

Arja plays are packed with sentimentality and melodrama. Like most great love stories, there is invariably some tragic issue causing the lovers' union to be near impossible – their families prohibit the marriage, a jealous rival makes war on the hero, the princess is abducted, the hero falls in love with another woman while under a magic spell. Fallen from grace, the prince may be misunderstood, beaten, kicked and thrown out of his house. His tragic song reaches the peak of suffering, while angry jeers of enemies continue their abuse. But, by this time, reconciliation takes place and arja quickly ends.

Cupak makes a belated attempt to rescue the princess, but fear gets the better of his valor, and so he shimmies up a tree in order to shout directions to his younger brother. In the skirmish, Grantang, the princess and the ogress all fall into a well. Grantang defeats the ogress, but just as he is about to emerge victorious, Cupak yanks the rope, saving the princess but letting his brave brother fall back into the well.

The unscrupulous glutton then goes to the king and tells of how he himself killed the ogress and rescued the princess. The joyous king offers Cupak whatever he wants, which, of course, is food – two mounds of rice and one suckling pig.

Cupak: A boisterous man with a huge belly, Cupak is Bali's notorious glutton. Cupak's story is more like an epic drama, as it has a kingdom and a mysterious forest; a villain, princess, witch and hero; disaster, resolution, and great joy. The focus of the story is the hand of a princess, held captive by an ogress who likes to eat flesh. Cupak and his brave and handsome younger brother, Grantang, journey deep into the dark forest to find the princess.

They meet the witch and violence follows.

Left, a young dancer makes preparations. **Above**, a janger performance earlier this century.

Meanwhile, Grantang manages to climb out of the well on a ladder made from the ogress's bones. Cupak refuses to recognize him and has him thrown into the sea, but Grantang is saved by a humble fisherman. Before Cupak is about to be crowned king, Grantang challenges him to a fight. He easily defeats the glutton, much to the relief and joy of the princess, who then marries the more preferable Grantang.

Legong: Of all classical Balinese dances, legong is the quintessence of femininity and grace, and girls from the age of five aspire to be legong dancers. Formerly, the dance was patronized by local princes and held in the *puri*, residence of the royal family. Dancers were recruited from the ablest and prettiest children. Today, the dance is frequently seen at village temple ceremonies throughout Bali. The dancers are usually still quite young.

The highly-stylized legong enacts an abstract drama by three dancers: the *condong*, a female attendant, and two identically-dressed legong, or dancers, who perform the main roles. Originally, a storyteller sat with the gamelan orchestra and chanted the narrative, but this has been stopped in most legong dance performances. Only the suggestive themes of the magnificent *gamelan semar pegulingan* – and the minds of the audience – conjure up imaginary changes of scene in

and his ominous encounter with the bird. It opens with an introductory solo by the condong. She moves with suppleness, dipping to the ground and rising, her torso poised in an arch with elbows and head held high, fingers trembling from flexed wrists. Her eyes focus on two fans laid before her, takes them, and meets the legong.

The legong glitter and dazzle. Bound from head to foot in gold brocade, it is a wonder the legong can move with such fervent agitation. The tight composure of the body, the flash of an eye, the tremble of fingers – all blend in precision. After a short dance, the condong retires, leaving the two legong to enact the story within the dance.

the underlying play. The most popular version performed today is *lasem,* also called *legong kraton.*

The story is derived from the history of eastern Java in the twelfth and thirteenth centuries. The king of Lasem finds the maiden Rangkesari lost in the forest and abducts her. Her brother, the prince of Daha, threatens war unless she is set free. Rangkesari asks to be released, but the king prefers to fight. On his way to the battlefield, he is met by a bird of ill omen that predicts his death. In the fight that ensues, he is killed.

The dance dramatizes the departure of the king of Lasem as he goes to the battlefield

The dancers flow from one identity into the next without disrupting the harmony of the choreography. They may enter as the double image of one character, their movements marked by tight synchronization and rhythmic verve. Then they may split, each enacting a separate role, and then come together in complementary halves to form a unified pattern, as in the playful love scene in which they kiss by rubbing noses.

Rangkesari repels Lasem's advances by hitting him with her fan and departs in anger. It is then that the condong reappears as a bird with wild eyes fixed upon the king. Beating its golden wings, it attacks the king. The ancient narrative relates that a black bird came flying out of the sky and swooped down upon the king, who saw it and said, "Raven, why do you swoop down on me? In spite of all, I shall go out and fight. This I shall do, oh raven!" With the king's decision understood, the dance may end, or else the other legong may return on stage as his prime minister, and in shimmering unison, they whirl the final steps to war.

Baris: A traditional war dance, baris glorifies the manhood of the Balinese warrior. (The word *baris* means a line or file, and refers to the formation of soldiers.)

There are numerous kinds of baris, distinguished by the weapons held by the dancers

A good baris dancer must undergo rigorous training to obtain the necessary skill and flexibility, and he must be supple, able to keep his knees spread wide apart in line with his body. His face must be mobile to convey fierceness, disdain, pride, acute alertness, and, equally important, compassion and regret – the characteristics of a warlike noble.

A good baris performance is a test of wits for both dancer and musicians; the relation between the dancer and orchestra is an intimate one, since the gamelan must be entirely attuned to the warrior's changing moods.

At first, the warrior's movements are studied and careful, as if seeking out foes in an unfamiliar place. Hesitation gives way to

– spear, lance, *kris*, bow and arrow, sword, or shield. Originally, the dance was a religious ritual of warriors expelling evil forces during a temple feast. The ancient *baris gede* is performed by groups of men with lances ready for the enemy's advance. From the ritualistic baris gede grew the dramatic baris, a story with a series of exhibition solo dances depicting a warrior's prowess in battle, a performance that is never done any more. It is from these that the popular baris solo, which uses no weapons, takes its form.

Left, a village *gamelan* orchestra. **Above**, *baris* dancers prepare for battle.

self-assurance as he rises on his toes to full stature, his body motionless with quivering limbs. In a flash, he whirls on one leg, and his face expresses the storm of passions of a quick-tempered warrior.

Such a spectacular show of style, mental control and physical dexterity would intimidate any enemy.

Jauk: A solo performance expressing the movements of a demon, jauk is derived from a traditional play in which the dancers, wearing frightening demon masks, enacted the exorcistic *calon arang* drama. The harsh stare of the eyes, the thick, black moustache, and a frozen smile give the masked jauk dancer an uncanny appearance of being from a distinctly evil world. He wears a high crown covering a thick mass of tangled hair, and gloves with long fingernails that flitter incessantly to the music.

Jauk is considered difficult to execute well. The dancer's aim is to express the character revealed in the appearance of the mask – that of a strong, forceful personality. The round, protruding eyes and tentacle-like fingernails are the identification marks of a demon. A jauk performer cannot rely on powerful facial expressions to convey feeling. He can dart his hidden eyes here and there, but he is obliged to express his demoniac exuberance through gestures.

electrifies. No other dance is so amazing as the kecak: 100 men who, by a regimented counterplay of sounds, simulate the interlocking rhythms of the gamelan. Kecak, a name indicating the *chak-a-chak* sounds, evolved from the male chorus of the ritual sanghyang trance ceremony.

By ingenious choreography, the chorus is transfigured into ecstasy. The annihilation of the individual, the cries, the pulse of sound and sublimated drama of the kecak are contained in the precise use of head, arms and torso motions. Various parts of the dance merge in a startling continuum of collective motion and voice. The words and gestures have no meaning, other than as derivatives of

The jauk dancer's movements are exaggerated and violent. He peers out like a crouching tiger ready to leap upon its prey. Suddenly he lunges, the music becomes frenetic with loud, clashing sounds, and he spins then stops, precise and controlled. Only the shimmering of the crown and fingernails mirror his intensity. Slowly, he retreats, as if preoccupied by dark, treacherous thoughts.

Kecak: In the uneven light, a serpentine stream of bodies coils itself, circle within circle, around a large, branching torch. The half-seen multitude waits in silence. A priest enters to gave a blessing of holy water. One piercing voice cracks the suspense; the circle

incantations to drive out evil, as was the original purpose of the sanghyang ritual.

Kecak includes a drama in which the circle of light around the torch becomes a stage, and its periphery of men, a living theater with all dramatic effects. Accompanied by the music of human voices, a storyteller narrates an episode usually drawn from the *Ramayana*. When demon-king Rawana leaps to the center, the chorus simulates his flight with a long hissing sound. When Hanuman enters the mystic circle, the men become an army of chattering monkeys.

Janger: The flute begins a simple tune, and faraway voices chant a song. Two girls appear, wearing splendid floral crowns with multicolored spikes. They advance, allowing the next pair of dancers to enter, until twelve girls have filed on stage. Slowly, they kneel opposite each other, tilting their heads and darting their eyes to accent the rhythm of the orchestra.

As the chanting continues, twelve youths repeat the girls' entrance. In contrast to the girls, the boys' movements are deliberate and strong. All wear painted moustaches and bear the self-assured look of slick courtiers.

Suddenly, the male formation breaks into frenzied activity of twists, jerks and lunges – all in the tight syncopation with brisk shouts. Instantly, the youths freeze in their positions,

first appeared, it spread like fire to nearly every village.

Kebyar: A solo dance of a more individualistic kind, kebyar places the accent upon the dancer, who interprets every nuance of the music in facial expressions and movement. Kebyar (literally, a flash of lightning or a burst of fire) is based upon a later form of gamelan music of the same name that appeared in northern Bali around 1920.

The man most often credited with its creation is the late I Ketut Mario, a dancer whose superb performances of kebyar remain unparalleled. The most popular dance is *kebyar duduk*, the "seated" kebyar, where the dancer sits cross-legged throughout most of the

and once again, the flute carries the dance back to the soft sways and melodious chanting of the girls.

The juxtaposition of harmonious feminine song against the jagged yells of male voices makes janger an artful composition of dance, music and chorus. A folk dance that developed in the 1930s, janger also has its origin in the sanghyang trance ceremony, in which the women chant the lyrical sanghyang songs and the men alternate with the rhythmic sounds of the kecak. When the new dance

dance. By not emphasizing the legs and decreasing the space to a small sphere, the relation between dancer and gamelan is intensified. The dance is concentrated in the flexibility of the wrists and elbows, the magnetic power of the face, and the suppleness of the dancer's torso.

The music seems infused in the dancer's body. The fingers bend with a singular beauty to catch the light melodies of the metallophones, while the body sways back and forth to the resounding beat of the gong. The dancer crosses the floor on the outer edges of his feet and woos the the lead drummer with side glances and smiles.

Left, kecak, Pura Tanah Lot. **Above**, I Ketut Mario, originator of kebyar, 1930s.

The kebyar is the most strenuous and subtle of Balinese dances. It is said that a great kebyar dancer can play every instrument of the orchestra. To attain perfection, all the moods of the music – lyrical and idyllic, dark and ominous – must be reflected in the disposition and skill of the dancer. In *kebyar trompong*, the dancer actually joins the orchestra by playing a long instrument of circular, knobbed kettles called the *trompong*, while continuing to dance and twirling the trompong sticks between the fingers.

Oleg tambulilingan: A modern dance choreographed by the late I Ketut Mario in 1952, *oleg tambulilingan* is a popular addition to the repertoire of dances included in a per-

formance. Originally, it was a female solo called *oleg*, a general term meaning the swaying of a dancer. Later, a male part was added to make it a duet, and the dance gained a new theme of two bumblebees (*tambulilingan*) flirting in a garden.

The female enters first. In light, quick steps she circles about, fluttering the long scarfs hanging from her sides. If the dancer is good, she conveys all the beguiling qualities of a young coquette. At one moment, she is moody and temperamental, eyes narrow and lips spread slightly into a seductive smile. The next, she is scornful, only to return as most feminine with an air of innocence.

The female's role is strenuous. Her movements must flow from subdued and delicate to tense gestures of haughtiness and disdain. At one point, she dances in the kneeling position. The sensuous sweeps of her hands, the tremble of her fingers and the fluctuating moods that pass and change epitomize an idea of femininity.

The male enters unnoticed, eyes her, and tilts his head with a half-smile of affirmation. He moves forward to make a conquest. At first, they shy away, yet woo with a display of grace while pretending to be unaware of the other's presence.

As the circle of flight grows smaller, the flirting increases. The female teases him, he moves forward, she draws back in feigned surprise, yet is secretly pleased with her success. They bring their faces close in an affectionate caress, then swirl away again. In the end, they fall in love and leave together.

Wayang wong: The *Ramayana* epic has long been rendered on the Balinese stage through the *wayang wong,* a classical dance-drama enacting scenes from the Hindu epic, in sequel performances that take place over several days. In the 1960s, a new dance interpretation of the *Ramayana* was introduced by KOKAR, the Conservatory of Musical Arts and Dance. It was called *sendratari,* from *seni* (art), drama, and *tari* (dance).

The *sendratari Ramayana* is a mixture of traditional dance technique and storytelling through gesture and narrator. Because of their refined movements, the royal brothers are usually danced by women.

Rama wears a golden crown, and Laksmana a black headdress. Their manner is stately and heroic – the refined style of dance for regal personages. In contrast, the ogre king Rawana takes large and dynamic steps – a fiery mode of dance which shows the arrogance of a tyrant.

And then there are the inevitable monkeys, wheeling about in the most comical situations. Hanuman, the monkey general, outwits two giants by cleverly maneuvering out of their way, so that they end up knocking each other out. A charging monkey, by mistake, trips on his tail. Stories from the epic *Mahabhrata* also are sometimes performed as sendratari.

Left, after a strenuous performance of oleg tambulilingan. **Right**, topeng masks.

TOPENG

Both the stoic and the clown were enacted by one man – the principal *topeng* actor, who, by changing masks, impersonates a series of different characters.

Topeng, or *tapel,* means something pressed against the face – a mask. Some masks survive from the sixteenth century. Today's mask play, commemorating historical exploits of local kings and heroes, was influenced by the traditional *gambuh* dance. Often called the chronicle play, topeng stories are drawn from the genealogical histories of important noble families.

Behind the curtain, a *topeng* actor places his masks, all neatly covered with white cloth, in their proper order of appearance. After dedicating an offering, he unwraps the first mask, eyeing it for some time as if he were absorbing the personality of the character reflected in the immobile mask. He then quickly puts on the mask. Already his movements are rendered as dance, and a transformation is apparent.

The curtain trembles, the gamelan builds to a fervent pace of expectation. A stoic-looking man with wide eyes and a questionable smile draws apart the curtain. Then, marching forward, he

The medium of topeng alters the telling of history. The borderline between fact, legend, and the miraculous has little importance in topeng, in which many episodes include divine intervention or acts of magic. The intent is not to reconstruct exact personalities of the past, but

gazes inquisitively, puts a finger to his forehead, takes a bit of his clothing, and in one delicate gesture, lets it drop from his hand. He resolves to dance, radiating the sound of the gamelan in the vibration of his fingertips and pattering feet. After a few minutes, he retreats and vanishes.

The curtain shakes again. Suddenly, it is pushed aside with the grand gesture of a movie star stepping into the limelight. There stands an extremely shy and effeminate young man, who draws a limp hand to his mouth and blushes at his abrupt exposure. He coyly moves on stage, swinging to and fro, with his hands dangling. He stands there looking ridiculous, fluttering his eyelashes while the audience rocks in laughter. Such abusiveness is too much for him, and he quickly seeks sanctuary behind the curtain.

to portray their types. Their stature is so lofty, they do not speak and express themselves in pantomime. They are accompanied by two clumsy clowns, who wear half-masks that leave their mouths free to talk as interpreters for their dignified masters. A marvelous parade of crude caricatures appear.

There are many forms of topeng, depending upon the masks used and the performer's style. A popular solo performance is the *topeng tua,* representing the movements of an old man. In a *topeng panca* play, up to five actors, usually all men, impersonate all the characters. A full set of topeng belongs to the principal actor, who is responsible for the series of eccentric personalities that produce the comedy of the play. To watch a good topeng actor is inspirational. ∎

Among all of Bali's lively dramatic arts, *wayang kulit* – shadow-puppet theater – is perhaps the most enduring, the most popular, and the most revealing of Balinese concepts regarding this world, and the next. Wayang kulit (shadow-leather) is a procession of lamp-lit puppet shadows and speaking, shouting, singing, and chanting voices – all performed by one man behind a screen.

The wayang kulit travels to nearly any venue. Performances take place in *banjar* (neighborhood) meeting halls, courtyard or temple pavilions, or household verandas, or else on temporary platforms of bamboo.

At the bottom of the white cotton screen is the *gedebong*, a banana-tree trunk forming the base, into which puppets may be inserted by puncturing the soft trunk with their long stick-like handles. Suspended at center-screen is the *damar*, a coconut-oil lamp that illuminates and casts shadows on the screen.

The audience sits on the other side of the screen and is entertained by the shadows; the *dalang* – storyteller and puppeteer – remains behind the screen with his assistants (right and left) and musicians. On the dalang's left is his puppet chest (*grobag*), while the quartet of musicians, playing intricate and brilliant patterns on the 10-keyed *gender* instruments, sits behind him.

In Bali, the shadow-puppet theater exists in more than half a dozen forms. The best-known is *wayang parwa*, which takes its name, and stories, from the *Mahabharata*, the Indian epic. *Wayang Ramayana*, with the addition of gongs and drums, takes its name from the other major Indian epic.

While these two genres are clearly linked to the ancient period of Indian influences in Bali, *wayang gambuh* takes its material from the Javanese epic romance about the adventures of the heroic Prince Panji. Both wayang gambuh and *wayang arja*, with a repertoire of indigenous legends and romantic tales, have particular types of musical accompaniment, and are infrequently performed.

Another type of shadow theater concerns

the exploits of a bawdy anti-hero, Cupak, and his refined brother, Grantang. A recently-created form, *wayang tantri*, uses animals as the main characters.

Witchcraft, possession and black magic are themes of *wayang Calon Arang*, which tells of an evil witch and her attempt to destroy an ancient kingdom in East Java. This wayang is particularly *tenget* – magically dangerous – and if not correctly performed, may bring disastrous results for both dalang and audience.

In fact, a powerful dalang can call forth the village *leyak,* or people who through black magic transform themselves into malevolent creatures.

Finally, there is shadow theater for particular ritual needs. The *wayang lemah* is performed during ceremonies at the moment a high priest is consecrating holy water. The dalang sits on the ground but with no screen or lamp; instead, the puppets are leaned against raw cotton thread stretched between two branches of the sacred *dapdap* tree. As wayang lemah is intended for a divine, rather than a human, audience, people usually pay scant attention during its performance.

Another ritual-based wayang – *wayang sapu leger* – is performed to free a victim of illness or misfortune. It is most commonly performed for people born under the inauspicious Balinese "week" called *wuku wayang*, ruled by Batara Kala, the time-consuming deity of time. In order to liberate a victim from his curse, a wayang performance of the *sapu leger* story must be commissioned at some point in the individual's life. The story features a play-within-a-play, as gods descend to earth to perform the first shadow play and thus charm ravenous Kala from devouring his human prey.

The dalang who performs it must be spiritually pure, and thus able to create holy may wish to hire a *wayang parwa* troupe when celebrating their child's *otonan*, or birthday, calculated according to the 210-day Balinese calendar. They would prepare a stage for the performance in their own house yard. The dalang might choose a story showing the *Mahabharata* heroes during their childhood, evoking a parallel with the baby whose birthday is being celebrated.

A wayang held in conjunction with a cremation might show when the Pandawa brother Bima travels to the underworld to rescue his parents' souls. Shadow plays commissioned for temple ceremonies might feature the story of a royal sacrifice or the fulfillment of some sacred duty or obligation.

water via the performance, combining the roles of both exorcist and priest.

Another juncture between wayang and religious ritual is illustrated by the way in which wayang kulit is commissioned in Bali. All Balinese ceremony can be classified according to a scheme called *panca yadnya*, or Five Rites. These include rites of passage for humans; ceremonies for the deceased; worship of deities' consecration ceremonies for priests; and, finally, rituals in honor of demonic forces.

The location of the performance and the story being played all vary depending on the ritual. For instance, parents of a new baby

Other occasions call for shadow theater, including a new house or building, or the fulfillment of a person's earlier vow to commission a wayang if he or she recovers from serious illness. Wayang are also performed on secular national holidays and during regional festivals.

Wayang origins: The origins of shadow theater are lost in time. There is no way of knowing when it began, how it was performed, or its social and religious setting in ancient times.

The earliest historical sources are ancient inscriptions, mostly on metal plates, issued by courts in the ninth through eleventh centuries; wayang is mentioned with other kinds of entertainment whose performers moved from community to community, and whose performances were subject to royal tax. Later historical evidence confirms that some Balinese wayang was under royal control, with fees levied on performances.

It is likely that early Balinese shadow theater used the *Mahabharata* and *Ramayana* epics as dramatic material, evolving during the thirteenth to fifteenth centuries, when Java and Bali were united under the Majapahit empire. Today, these epics represent the large majority of wayang performances in Bali, well-known through temple sculpture, painting, literary works and dance-

toire of music and stories, and to the ritual and social context of wayang.

Not all dalang have inherited their art, however. Some individuals take up the study of wayang after being a dancer or other type of performer; others start after an illness or profound spiritual experience. Even those who have grown up within the tradition are not guaranteed performers. Beyond the acquisition of skills, the dalang must know how to weave a story and entertain.

The dalang must be a verbal artist, using language to inspire the story, bring puppet characters to life, and win the attention of the audience. The *Dharma Pawayangan*, an important text that dalang use as a source for the

drama. But it is in the shadow play that epic heroes and events come most vividly alive.

The dalang: The shadow-theater dalang embodies skills and dramatic techniques that have evolved over centuries, the fruit of artistry passed from one generation to another. There is no guidebook to becoming a dalang, nor rules dictating what may or may not be done behind the screen.

Young relatives of dalang become musicians and assistants; joining a troupe in this way exposes junior artists to the full reper-

Left, profile of detailed leather work. **Above**, the dalang moves the kulit and narrates.

legendary and spiritual aspects of their art, states that the dalang is "one who is empowered to command speech", and that "his voice says all that can be spoken".

The dalang must also be an accomplished musician, intimately familiar with the repertoire played by instrumental accompanists. He also must have a pleasing singing voice, so as to embellish his dialogue with songs. He needs outstanding manual dexterity to manipulate the puppet figures, and knowledge of Balinese dance to articulate dance movements through the puppets. In addition to literary and dramatic knowledge, the dalang must command the details of Balinese religious practice and philosophy, be familiar with folk tales and proverbial knowledge, be an adept comedian, and communicate the wisdom of the past as well as comment on current public affairs.

The dalang has no written script, and does not memorize dialogue, but rather composes each play in performance, using knowledge and experience.

A basic part of the dalang's storytelling art is *lampahan*, or plot, which gives a particular story shape and coherence. It is an abstract notion adhered to in a general way by all dalang, combining themes and dramatic episodes in similar patterns. The major parts in each story are marked by the *kayonan*, a

puppet representing the tree of life. Within each division, the dalang puts together scenes of standard types, depending on the particular story being played.

This overall dramatic structure is enlivened by the music of the *gender* metallophones, whose repertoire encompasses every mood and situation, whether sadness or combat. The music is integral to each performance, and gender musicians lay interlocking parts that are astounding in speed, synchronization, and kinesthetic awareness.

Attentive to the dalang's cues, the musicians must anticipate changes in scene, alteration of dramatic mood, and the appearance of puppet characters on screen. The puppeteer signals by means of the *cempala*, a wooden knocker held in the hand or between the toes and rapped on the side of the puppet-box, or else by means of verbal cues concealed in dialogue.

Balinese wayang employs two languages: *Kawi* or Old Javanese, a literary language, and modern Balinese. The dalang uses Kawi for the speech of most puppet characters, including the gods, priests, kings and other nobles, as well as demons and monster-like creatures.

Kawi is also used for the dalang's narrative interludes, his songs and quotations from literary texts, the opening chants and introductions to the play, and for a lengthy series of ritual invocations the puppet master must use in preparation for performance. These invocations, or mantra, are not spoken aloud but rather uttered within his mind. They purify and protect him spiritually, putting him in close touch with the unseen guiding forces that can charm the audience, so that "delight comes to the hearts of everyone listening to the sound of my voice," as one dalang's mantra puts it.

Generally, there are clown-servants in a story, who provide humor, pungent critique, slapstick and a "commoner" Balinese perspective to the play. Their linguistic function is to translate the Kawi speech of their noble masters into the more accessible Balinese vernacular. Dramatically, they provide some levity, plot summaries, linkages, and running commentary.

Part of the dalang's task is to know something about the audience in order to address local tastes and concerns. He may use specific references to familiar places, such as a temple or market, as part of the setting of his play. The dalang might try to mirror a local controversy or important event in the story he chooses to perform, and thus evoke a parallel between the wayang world and everyday experience.

The puppet master is at once an entertainer and an interpreter of the world for the Balinese audience. It is traditional for the dalang to be revered as one of the community's important teachers, using the *Mahabharata* and *Ramayana* tales as the sources of instruction.

Left, wayang performed without a screen. Right, gamelan gong.

110

GAMELAN

In Bali, it is easy to know when something is happening. Just listen for the sounds of the *gamelan* orchestra, with its bronze kettles, gongs and metallophones. Often, in the evenings, the softened tones of the music float outwards from a distant village, sifting through the thick air as if from another world.

Music accompanies every theatrical, religious and social function, and the magic of the gamelan gives the occasion an aura of vibration with its metallic energy.

In Bali, the word *gong* is used to described the many kinds of orchestras. Balinese music has undergone considerable change during its history. In the 1920s and 1930s, for example, the old *gong gede* was replaced by the faster *gong kebyar,* which is now the commonest form of gamelan orchestra.

A basic principle of gamelan music is that instruments with a higher range of notes are struck more frequently than those with lower ranges. At given intervals, gongs of various sizes mark off the structure of the music, the other instruments adding their complicated, shimmering ornamentation.

Most of the musicians play a variety of *gangsa* metallophones, which consist of bronze bars suspended over bamboo resonators. With one hand the player strikes the keys with a wooden mallet; with the other he dampens the key he struck just before.

At the heart of the orchestra are the two drums, *kendang*. The drummers control the tempo of the music. Sometimes using their hands, at other times a knobbed stick, the drummers' rhythmic techniques are mind-boggling. The male drum is slightly smaller than the other, the female. The small hand cymbals (*cengceng*) accent the music. Helping to keep the orchestra together is the steady beat of the *kempli*, a single small gong struck with a stick. The rich tones of the *trompong*, a set of kettles like the *reyong* but played by one man instead of four, occurs in certain pieces and in the *kebyar trompong* dance.

Other instruments that accompany particular dances or drama performances include *tingklik* (bamboo xylophones), *suling* (flutes) and *rebab* (the two-stringed violin). *Wayang kulit,* the shadow play, has its own little ensemble consisting of four *gender* metallophones.

Archaic ensembles still play in a few old villages in eastern Bali, include the *gamelan selonding* of instruments with iron keys, and the wooden-keyed *gambang*. And finally there is *genggong*, a type of jew's-harp and one of the world's oldest instruments.

Gamelan instruments are still made in Bali, the leading craftsmen living in the village of Tihingan, near Klungkung, and Blahbatuh and Sawan in north Bali.

Most villages have their music clubs, *sekaa*, which own and cooperatively maintain the village gamelan. The clubs are communal organizations in which everyone has a share in the responsibilities. Every practicing musician belongs to a music club of some kind. Frequently, these clubs are a prime source of entertainment to villagers, who casually gather around the *bale gong* – pavilion where the village gamelan orchestra is kept – to listen to the gamelan practice. At informal practices, a baby rests on the lap of his father while he plays. The child remains there, awake or asleep, throughout the session. Some clubs practice nightly to perfect

new and difficult compositions, or to rehearse with a dance troupe.

The polyphonic compositions are learned by memory. Musicians do not use musical notation, as their remarkable sense of rhythm is instilled from childhood. Experienced musicians say there is no conscious effort to remember compositions. They have heard and played them so often that their hands work instinctively.

Gamelan music is organic, and changes with time. Some music is no longer performed, replaced by more contemporary interpretations. There are old recordings, however, now on CD, that present gamelan music as it was over half a century ago. The Fahnestock brothers, in a sailing expedition, made these exceptional historical recordings. (*See page 53.*) ∎

The spirit of creativity pervades everything in Balinese life. The very fertility of the land and splendor of its natural forms seem to invoke the worshipping hand of the artist. In ancient times, the people of the Indonesian archipelago followed types of animism and ancestor worship.

By around the first century AD, Buddhism and Hinduism became forces on Sumatra and Java. When Islam gained control of Java in the sixteenth century, Hindu princes and craftsmen went to Bali.

Balinese expertise at rice farming allowed ample leisure time for everyone to develop a highly refined and artistic way of life, one in which art and the artisan were given a place in the system.

A convergence of beauty and ceremony explains why the arts have endured in Bali. Art was never a conscious production for its own sake. Rather, it was an obligation to make things beautiful, and done with a definite purpose: to create beauty in service to society and religion. The artist was a respected member of the community. Works were not signed. The prime aim was to serve the community.

At the end of the nineteenth century, the indigenous arts of Bali mirrored a society governed by feudal lords and sustained by the rituals of religion. The palaces and temples, as political and religious centers, were also centers of the arts. A prince supported actors, artists and musicians as part of his retinue. Most importantly, ordinary people were skilled in the arts of dancing, poetry, music and painting. These arts found their expression when a village honored the deities of their temples, or in the elaborate rituals surrounding death.

Ritual demanded a continuous renewal of communion with the divine through temple celebrations. The people focused artistic talents into these occasions. Offerings had to be made, shrines repaired, dances rehearsed, music practiced and dramas created.

Preceding pages: early 20th-century painting; woodcarving is found throughout Bali. **Left,** fine metalwork on a kris handle. **Right,** detailed painting of egret.

Climate and materials made frequent renovations necessary. Soft volcanic stone quickly eroded in the rain. This kept carvers and masons constantly occupied creating new sculptures or repairing older ones. Artists replaced cloth paintings that had rotted in the humidity, or woodcarvings eaten away by white ants. Earthquakes destroyed temples, causing scores of villages to engage in massive reconstruction. Because artifacts had limited life, the Balinese were continually building and rebuilding.

In the first decades of this century, Bali entered a new era as a Dutch colony. Western education, modern technology, films, magazines, and a steady tourist trade opened up a new world for many Balinese. Craftsmen began to treat their work as art for art's sake, experimenting in new styles, themes and media. Some artists received recognition abroad, and it was during the 1930s that many of Bali's finest works were produced.

Unfortunately, much of the superb execution in the antique carvings and early modern paintings is often absent today. One of the reasons for this lies in the structure of Balinese society. Modern art, created for its own sake, does not have a traditional place and function within the community. The patronage of Balinese nobles virtually ceased in this century, and with it an influential aesthetic guidance. Except for established painters and woodcarvers who have their own studios, working artists have little choice but to display their works in commercial art shops. Many of the most beautiful examples go overseas and are lost to Bali.

What distinguishes Balinese art today is a fusion of the lively, ornamental folk art – beauty in service – and the added element of self-conscious "art". Many paintings, carvings and sculptures are made communally in workshops, where a master craftsman supervises apprentices. A small number of outstanding artists have developed unique styles, with their best work setting the trend for imitations.

Balinese artists and artisans rarely work from nature; they *know* nature, and in their art they distill from it an essence that is uniquely Balinese. They scan their experience, select details from it, and give each element a fresh significance. One would never find here, as in Chinese painting, a quick brush stroke representing a tree. In Bali, a tree is a trunk with branches and leaves drawn or carved with precision and care. A tree is also a house for mysterious birds, snakes, lizards, butterflies and monsters. Such a vision is true to an island community charged with cosmic and magical influences.

Due to the constantly changing acceleration of life and art in Bali, it is not surprising that the search for new forms to express experiences sometimes seems confused. Despite the present diversity of expression, few have achieved the deeper search for perfection personified by the best artists of Pita Maha, especially as they strive to meet the demands of tourists. Hopefully this search for meaning will lead Balinese artists back to their deepest roots, so that they will face the call of change with all the power of the past.

Painting: Balinese painting became codified in the court of Gelgel, near Klungkung in southeast Bali, during the sixteenth century. This style of painting, using natural pigment on hand-woven cotton, was derived from the two-dimensional cutout figures of *wayang kulit* – the shadow-puppet theater of Bali. Variously called *wayang*, classical, traditional or *kamasan,* it is still practiced today in the village of Kamasan, whose craftsmen were supported by the court.

In ancient days, many Balinese artisans were multifaceted. They could sculpt, draw and paint. By the mid nineteenth century, however, armed conflicts between rival kingdoms caused the Dutch to become more involved with island affairs. Between 1908 and 1938, Dutch administrators did their best to preserve Balinese culture by interfering as little as possible in the centuries-old traditions. But while they brought peace, they also brought taxes and tourists.

Among the Westerners who arrived on Bali's shores were established artists, including Walter Spies, Rudolf Bonnet and Miguel Covarrubias. They brought with them not only a background in Western art, both classical and contemporary, but also the tools of their profession: watercolors, oil paints, commercial paper and canvas. Within this context new styles of Balinese painting came into being, to some extent influenced by these artists.

The conventions of the traditional style were no longer binding. Instead of illustrating stories from the great Hindu epics, some Balinese artists began to depict scenes of secular life and nature.

Although both Sanur and Ubud had close contact with Western artists, the theory that Balinese art leaped from medieval to modern because of the intervention of foreigners ignores the distinctly individual achievement of artists who were active before 1930.

The most important of Balinese art's transitional figures was I Gusti Nyoman Lempad (1862–1978), master craftsman and architect of the court of Ubud. Lempad was in his 60s when he got his first art paper from Spies, who moved to Ubud in 1927. In the 50 years after that, the pen-and-ink drawings that flowed from his hand were never a naive imitation of European techniques. While his style originated in tradition, he developed an unusual freedom in exploring the rich legends of his homeland.

Other older painters of the transitional period, using a background in the wayang tradition to embrace the new freedom and energy, were Ida Bagus Gelgel (1900–1937), from Kamasan, and Ida Bagus Kembang (1897–1952), from Ubud. Gusti Made Deblog (1906–1986), who came from a small village north of Denpasar, lived far from Western artists. Trained by a Chinese photographer as a photo retoucher and in the use of charcoal and ink, he painted magical scenes, fascinated by the old myths.

Between 1936 and 1942, Bali's new art was in full bloom under the guidance of Pita Maha (Noble Aspiration), an artists' organization founded by the prince of Ubud, Corkoda Gede Agung Sukawati, with guidance from Lempad, Spies and Bonnet. More than 150 artists from all over Bali joined Pita Maha, which provided both inspiration and a forum of consultation, quality control and promotion. It also provided artists with a sense of creative community.

Pita Maha was dissolved in 1942 with the Japanese occupation. Although Indonesian independence was acknowledged by the Dutch in 1949, the stability so essential to Balinese well-being had been severely shaken by the war. Despite the relative calm of the 1950s, painting never regained the vitality of the prewar years, although Pita Maha artists who kept working became the recognized older generation.

A new school of young artists sprang up in the village of Penestanan, near Ubud, initiated by Dutch artist Arie Smit, who introduced bright oils to Bali in the 1960s. Like the artists of the Ubud, Batuan and Sanur schools, the young artists of Penestanan de-

It is possible to make a broad division of the artists of the 1930s into three schools. The Ubud school was generally more concerned with the tranquil scenes of nature. In Batuan, the paintings were often of a haphazard perspective, as if the artist conceived each section of his mosaic from a different viewpoint. The Sanur painters – including Ida Bagus Nyoman Rai – used their geographical location by the sea for different subject matter, often dealing with marine subjects, many composed of interwoven patterns of the same motif.

Village painting by Walter Spies.

veloped refinements in their naive works. Nyoman Mandra, a painter from Kamasan, founded a school of traditional Balinese painting that has been subsidized by the Indonesian government since 1974. Interesting work has appeared in Batuan, especially in the work of I Wayan Rajin, and in the artistic wit of I Made Budi and I Wayan Bendi, who paint tourists, surfers and motorbikes.

Other contemporary Balinese artists turn to the deeper patterns that unconsciously rule their lives. I Nyoman Gunasara, for example, received academic training in Java and elaborates on the wayang figures. I Gusti Ngurah Gede Pemecutan reinterprets

Balinese myth, dances or cockfights in a pointillist style using his fingertips.

Crafts: The Balinese word for craftsman is *tukang*, practitioner or expert. Before Western influence, the crafts of Bali were directed almost entirely toward utilitarian ends. Bamboo and coconut were the raw materials for most houses and utensils. Metalworking, fabric-making, and carving focused on decorating public buildings, especially temples. The average Balinese farmer had – and has today – a very simple home, devoid of art. Most creations are for religious purposes.

By 1908, the Dutch had systematically destroyed the *puri* and slaughtered the rajas, and with them also perished the decorative

crafts they sponsored. There were two exceptions. The rajas of the districts of Gianyar and Karangasem made treaties with Dutch, under which they were able to retain their titles, wealth, and influence. With Dutch blessings, Gianyar became an area in which craft activities flourished.

The prince of Ubud used his influence to invite European artists to visit his area, study the local crafts, and suggest ways to appeal to the blossoming tourist trade. The Westerners showed the Balinese new techniques and uses for old materials. They directed the focus away from the traditional decorative and utilitarian ends, and towards the making

of commercially-appealing objects. They did not seek to obliterate the old techniques, but rather to redirect them.

It would be unrealistic to claim that the Balinese are more creative and artistic than other cultures. But from an early age, many Balinese learn to make intricate and elaborate offerings for deities, and to develop considerable manual dexterity. Balinese coconut-leaf offerings are ornate, delicate and lovely to behold. All that is required is a knowledge of the rules and the skill to follow them. It is not easy, neither is it creative.

Textiles: Bali's home-produced cloth, *endek*, is not popular with visitors, but the Balinese themselves use it a great deal. Endek is classed as a weft ikat textile. The weft threads that run perpendicular to the length of the cloth are wound on a frame that is of the same width as the finished product. Sections of the weft are bound with plastic ties, then the weft is removed from the frame and dyed, with the ties preventing the dye from reaching portions of the thread. Repeated tyings and dyeings produces colorful, intricate and varied patterns.

Endek is woven by hand on horizontal wooden looms. There are several well-known factories in both the Denpasar and Gianyar areas, and numerous smaller factories as well. Endek is available in long bolts, or ready-made into shirts, dresses, and other articles. It is made with either cotton or rayon, or in a mixture of the two. A few shops offer expensive silk endek. Quality endek is color-fast.

Tenganan Pegeringsingan, in eastern Bali, is one of only three places in the world (the other two are India and Japan) to traditionally produce the fabulously difficult double *ikat* – fabrics decorated by tie-dyeing both warp and weft before weaving. These *geringsing* cloths are dyed with indigo and *mengkudu* red, producing a reddish-purple design on a cream background. Loosely woven, some seem to imitate the Indian patola, also a double ikat.

Others are clearly indigenous in design, such as the *geringsing wayang kebo*, with its symmetrical groupings of wayang figures around a central four-pointed star. The pieces are extremely expensive.

Considered by the Balinese to be the most sacred of all textiles, geringsing cloths are used in many important ceremonies throughout the island, including tooth-filings and cremations. Within the village of Tenganan, wearers of these cloths were once said to be protected from evil influences and illness. (Indeed, geringsing means without sickness.) The fact that Tenganan is one of the few Bali Aga (original, or non-Hindu) villages on the island is intriguing. Either the geringsing cloth is of very ancient, pre-Hindu origin, or else the production of the cloth was surrounded by certain taboos or restrictions that only the Bali Aga disregarded.

A favorite textile with the Balinese for festive and religious occasions is a brocade called *songket,* with threads of a gold or silver. It is widely available and is beautiful

the wax with hot water and scraping, then applying wax to other areas, a series of dyeings produces intricate, characteristic patterns. Both Balinese men and women buy batik in two-meter lengths and wrap it, untailored, around the waist as skirt-like *kamben*. Many of the large batik manufacturers in Java have branch stores in Denpasar.

Woodcarving: Balinese woodcarving consists largely of painted statues using local wood. Some are representations of demons, heroes of the Hindu epics, or manifestations of deities. Others, such as the mythical *garuda*, vehicle of Wisnu (Vishnu), decorate traditional Balinese pavilions called *bale*. Painted masks are also produced and used in

when new. However, the silver or gold threads snag and break quickly – songket cloth rapidly acquires a ragged, worn look.

Visitors to Indonesia expect to find a wide variety of *batik* available. Batik is a product of central Java, and almost none is made in Bali. That does not mean it is not available. On the contrary, large selections in every imaginable style and quality are readily found in stores and markets. Batik is made by applying wax to cloth, which acts as a barrier to the penetration of the dye. By removing

performances of a religious nature. Figures from everyday life, on the other hand, are rare. Realism is not a consideration.

Painted carvings are still widely available. The centers of production are in the Tegalalang and Sebatu areas, north of Peliatan. The industry has spread because of the relative cheapness and popularity of carvings. Traditional garuda are still made. But, increasingly, most painted carvings tend to be on the cute side – cartoon animals, representations of fruits of varying degrees of quality, decoy-like ducks, and tropical fruit trees.

Painted masks in the traditional style are still made by a few carvers for Balinese

<u>Left</u>, Bali-style souvenir. <u>Above left</u>, wooden door carvings. <u>Right</u>, carved mask.

performers. I Wayan Tangguh, of Singapadu, grinds the paint pigments by hand in the traditional manner, and makes masks of the traditional *pule* wood. But most masks are made for tourists as wall decorations.

The European artists of the 1930s influenced some Balinese carvers to change techniques and materials. Instead of painted, highly-stylized statues of heroes and ogres, emphasis was directed toward forms from everyday life. Carvers were encouraged to leave the wood unpainted, using the natural grain to emphasize the curve and flow of carved shapes.

Today, deliberately distorted, elongated, compressed, impressionistic carvings are

sanded to a fine finish and waxed with a thin layer of shoe polish to bring out the luster. Most of Bali's soft woods are not very attractive if unpainted, however, and it is more difficult, sometimes impossible, to hide defects in the wood when it is not covered with a layer of paint. Some more attractive woods are available only in remote parts of Bali; ebony and sandalwood are imported.

About 15 different kinds of wood are used for unpainted statues, ranging from the red-striped black ebony to the almost pure-white *panggal buaya*. Carvers often use the difference in color between the heartwood and sapwood to emphasize the features of their statues. For example, the *waru lot* tree has a dark red interior and a pale tan exterior, and this is used to enhance that which might otherwise be a very ordinary subject. The so-called driftwood carvings are not mass produced, since each root is different.

The centers of unpainted-wood statue carving are Mas and Peliatan, near Ubud, and Buruan and Kemenuh, near Blahbatuh. Mas has dozens of woodcarving specialty shops, as do Buruan and Kemenuh.

Still another style of carving was done by I Nyoman Cokot, who lived near Sebatu in the village of Jati. He was known for large hollow logs carved with hordes of overlapping monsters, spooks and demons peering out from the irregular recesses of the wood. Cokot died in 1971, but his two sons, I Ketut Nongos, in Teges near Mas, and I Made Dini, in Teges Kanginan in Peliatan, carry on the traditions of their father.

Gold and silver: Of the precious metals, gold appeals to Balinese taste. A small amount of goldsmith work is done in Celuk, but the Balinese buy their personal gold jewelry from shops in major towns.

Economics being what they are, silverwork, primarily in jewelry, is most popular. A great variety of rings, bracelets, necklaces, boxes, pins, and utilitarian objects, some set with semiprecious stones, are available in the village of Celuk. Some silver jewelry is also made in Kuta and in Kamasan. Modern Balinese silverwork tends to be rather ornate, full of filigrees and curlicues. Most of the smaller pieces are made with 90 to 95 percent pure silver, but the larger pieces are usually plated to keep the price down.

Stone carvings: A half-ton stone statue is not the sort of Balinese souvenir that would appeal to the average visitor. Batubulan, the home of the daily *barong* dance, is also the center for stonecarving. *Paras*, a soft ashy sandstone that is technically called tuff, is cut from the walls of the deep gorges of Balinese streams, with most of it still going to temples and other public buildings. Stone carvings require frequent replacement because of the rapid weathering. The subjects have broadened to include human and animal figures from everyday life, as well as fanciful shapes that are quite appealing.

Left, portrait of beach vender. **Right**, Bali's geringsingah cloth.

FOOD

Framed with style and filled with flavor, an Indonesian rice table is an introduction to a variety of island specialities. *Nasi goreng* (1) – rice fried with shrimps, meats, and spices – and *bakmi goreng* (2), fried noodles, are the basis of a colorful array of side dishes accompanying the Indonesian meal. *Babi guling* (3), roasted suckling pig, and *betutu bebek* (4), duckling broiled in banana leaf, are favorites at Balinese banquets.

Popular dishes of the archipelago include *ikan assem manis* (5), sweet-sour fish; *kare udang* (6), curried shrimp; *babi kecap* (7), pork cooked in sweet soy sauce; lobster (8), caught just off Kuta Beach in South Bali; *opor ayam* (9), chicken simmered in coconut milk; *semur sapi* (10), beef stew with tomato; and, of course, *sate* (11), roasted chunks of beef, pork, chicken, or turtle meat served with a peanut sauce (12). For new and simple tastes, try *lontong* (13), rice steamed in banana leaf, and *ketupat* (14), boiled rice wrapped in coconut. No Indonesian meal is complete without a dish of *sambal* (15), a hot sauce made from chili peppers. Finish with a tasty rice pudding (16), cooked in palm sugar and coconut milk.

FRUITS

The customary dessert in Indonesia is an ample serving of fruit, of which the archipelago has a countless number. Many of the fruits of Bali come from Karangasem, the easternmost district of the island. Some of the specialities of this region include *salak* (1), a brown fruit with a taste similar to an apple, but with a skin resembling a snake's; dark-seeded grapes (2); mangoes (3); bananas of numerous sizes and flavors (4); tangerines (5); guavas (6); and a local variety of grapefruit, *jeruk bali* (7).

Seen frequently in religious offerings is *sawo* (8), which looks like a small potato but tastes like a ripe pear. Every family compound grows *blimbing* (9), a delicious tiny fruit and a favorite of Balinese women. Village markets have the many-seeded pomegranate (10); *rambutan* (11); *sirsak* (12), an extremely juicy fruit; jackfruit, or *nangka* (13); pineapples (14); papayas (15); and the famous mangosteen – not to mention the infamous durian (17).

134

PLACES

Bali is a magnet for the most consistently overused cliches to be found in any catalogue of travel writing. Exquisite, seductive, mesmerizing, enchanting, magical – the words lose their power and importance after a while. It's a writer's dilemma, this island of Bali, for those words are, in fact, accurate and to the point. In the end, of course, words don't matter. Perceptions and impressions do.

The thinker who first said that great things come in small packages must have been to Bali, if not in this life then in an earlier one. A comparatively small parcel of island in the world's largest archipelago, Bali reveals an astonishing diversity in land and culture. Not only can one retreat to an ideal setting of whatever contour, but one can seek out specific centers of specific arts. One village is noted for banana-tree carvings, another village for silver jewelry. Still another is noted for *topeng* masks.

Bali's social cohesion is derived from deities and history – and rice. The cultivation of rice defines the community, and the collection of communities that make up Bali. More important, perhaps, has been the communal sharing of irrigation water – and the cooperation necessary to do so – for the rice terraces.

Bali's amazing terraces of rice are not the visitor's first impression, however. The international airport is in the extreme south, and southern Bali is urban Bali. This is where serious tanning, playing and partying are to be found, most often in Denpasar, Sanur or Kuta. This is not to suggest that these areas are without redemption, for beneath said tanning, playing and partying, there are ancient undercurrents that give Balinese their grounding.

Inland to the north and east, away from the urban fuss of the south, the contours become softer, the villages smaller, and the culture more seductive. Indeed, Central and East Bali are centers of art and culture, not to mention most of Bali's history. Traditionally, art had a communal and religious function, and thus was intrinsic with daily life. A modern traveler must intentionally go out of the way *not* to encounter dance-drama, gamelan, painting and woodcarving. And the multitudinous temples and palaces that were traditionally served by the arts are equally difficult to avoid.

Anchoring the island and the people are three volcanic peaks to the north: Agung, Batur and Batukau. The mountains are holy, and the source of all water that nurtures life. They help to define Bali, geographically, culturally and spiritually. The west of Bali – sometimes dry, sometimes lush – is typically ignored by travelers, but such is unwarranted. Much of the west is covered by a national park, the last refuge of many endangered species of animals.

Lombok, of course, exists in the shadow of Bali. Although lacking in the spectacular cultural artifacts of Bali, Lombok has a back-roads feel to it, and its people radiate a sense of satisfaction with what the gods have offered to them.

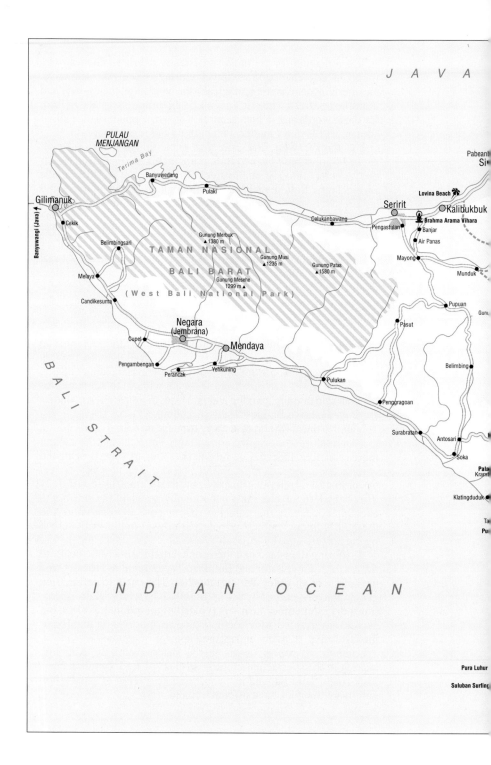

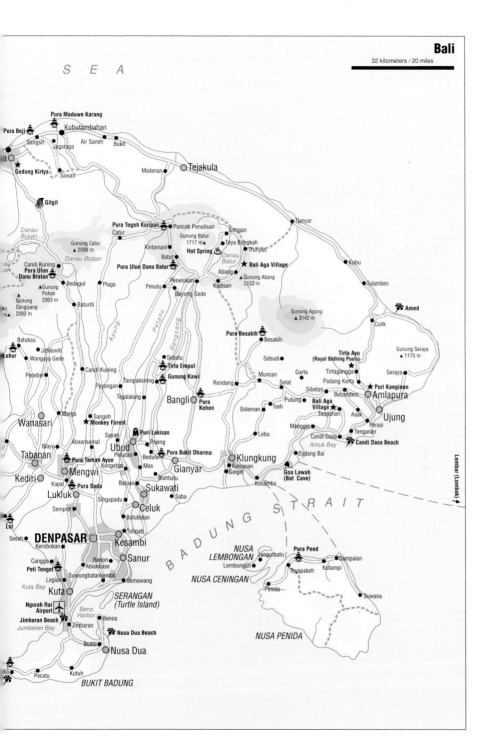

Bali

32 kilometers / 20 miles

S E A

Pura Maduwe Karang
Pura Beji
Kubutambahan
Sangsit
Jagaraga
Air Saneh
Bukit
Gedong Kirtya
Madenan
Tejakula
Sawan
Gitgit
Tianyar
Pura Tegeh Koripan
Puncak Penulisan
Catur
Songan
Gunung Batur
1717 m ▲
Toya Bungkah
Danau
Buyan
Gunung Catur
▲ 2096 m
Danau Bratan
Kintamani
Batur
Hot Spring
Trunyan
Danau
Batur
Kubu
Candi Kuning
Pura Ulun
Danu Bratan
Pura Ulun Danu Batur
Abang
Bali Aga Village
▲Gunung
Pohan
2063 m
Bedugul
Plaga
Peludu
Penelokan
Kadisan
Tulamben
Gunung
Sangiyang
2093 m
Baturiti
Bayung Gede
Gunung Abang
2153 m
Gunung Agung
▲ 3142 m
Amed
Culik
Batukau
Jatiluwih
Wangaya Gede
uhur
Pura Besakih
Besakih
Gunung Seraya
▲ 1175 m
Penebel
Candi Kuning
Sebatu
Tirta Empul
Gunung Kawi
Sebudi
Tirta Ayu
(Royal Bathing Pools)
Tampaksiring
Rendang
Muncan
Garta
Tirtagangga
Seraya
Payangan
Tegalalang
Selat
Padang Kerta
Sibetan
Bebandem
Puri Kanginan
Amlapura
Bangli
Pura
Kehen
Sideman
Iseh
Putung
Bali Aga
Village
Asak
Perasi
Ujung
Marga
Sanggeh
Monkey Forest
Sayan
Pejeng
Tenganan
Tenganan
Wanasari
Abeansemal
Puri Lukisan
Lebu
Manggis
Candi Dasa
Tenganan
Blayu
Pelatan
Pura Bukit Dharma
Klungkung
Kamasan
Padang Bai
Candi Dasa Beach
Ubud
Bedulu
Amuk Bay
Tabanan
Pura Taman Ayun
Kengetan
Mas
Blahbatu
Gelgel
Goa Lawah
(Bat Cave)
Kediri
Mengwi
Batuan
Gianyar
Kusamba
Kapal
Pura Sada
Sukawati
Saba
Lukluk
Singapadu
Celuk
Sempidi
Batubulan
Lot
DENPASAR
Tohpati
Kesambi
B A D U N G   S T R A I T
Seseh
Kerobokan
Sanur
NUSA
LEMBONGAN
Pura Peed
Sampalan
Canggu
Renon
Abianbase
Ujungutbatu
Lembongan
Kintampi
Peti Tenget
Suwungbatankendal
Semawang
Toyapakeh
Kuta Bay
Legian
NUSA CENINGAN
Penida
Kuta
SERANGAN
(Turtle Island)
Suwana
Ngurah Rai
Airport
Beno
Harbor
Jimbaran Beach
Benoa
Jimbaran
NUSA PENIDA
Jumbaran Bay
Nusa Dua Beach
Bualu
Nusa Dua
Pecatu
Kutuh
BUKIT BADUNG

Lembar (Lombok)

Ayung
Petanu
Sangsang
Unda

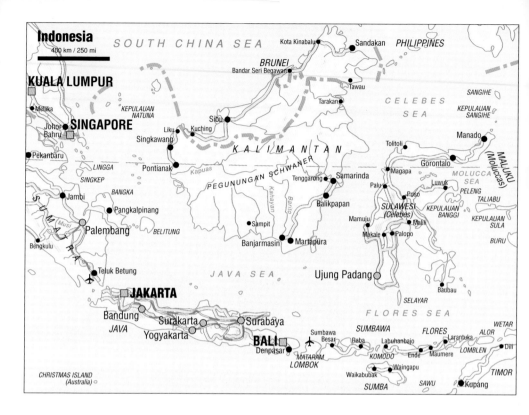

Indemnesia

400 km / 250 mi

SOUTH CHINA SEA

Kota Kinabalu
Sandakan
PHILIPPINES

BRUNEI
Bandar Seri Begawan

KUALA LUMPUR

Tawau

Tarakan

CELEBES
SEA

SANGIHE

KEPULAUAN
NATUNA

Melaka

Sibu

KEPULAUAN
SANGIHE

Johor
Bahru

SINGAPORE

Liku
Kuching

Singkawang

Manado

Tolitoli

Pekanbaru

LINGGA

Pontianak

Kapuas

KALIMANTAN

Gorontalo

MALUKU
(Moluccas)

SINGKEP

PEGUNUNGAN SCHWANER

Magapa

MOLUCCA
SEA

Jambi

BANGKA

Tenggarong
Samarinda

Palu

Luwuk

PELENG

TALIABU

Pangkalpinang

Balikpapan

Poso

KEPULAUAN
BANGGI

Palembang

BELITUNG

Sampit

Mamuju

SULAWESI
(Celebes)

Malili

KEPULAUAN
SULA

Bengkulu

Banjarmasin
Martapura

Makale
Palopo

BURU

Teluk Betung

JAVA SEA

Ujung Padang

Baubau

SELAYAR

FLORES SEA

WETAR

JAKARTA

Bandung

Surakarta
Surabaya

JAVA

Yogyakarta

SUMBAWA

FLORES

ALOR

Sumbawa
Besar
Raba

Labuhanbajo

Larantuka

LOMBLEN

Dili

BALI

Denpasar

MATARAM
LOMBOK

KOMODO

Ende
Maumere

TIMOR

CHRISTMAS ISLAND
(Australia)

Waikabubak

Waingapu

SUMBA

SAWU

Kupang

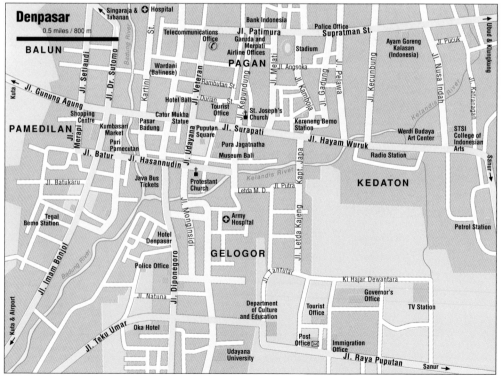

Denpasar

0.5 miles / 800 m

Singaraja &
Tabanan

Hospital

Bank Indonesia

Police Office

BALUN

Telecommunications
Office

Jl. Patimura

Supratman St.

Garuda and
Merpati
Airline Offices

Stadium

Ayam Goreng
Kalasan
(Indonesia)

Jl. Pucuk

Wardani
(Balinese)

PAGAN

Kuta

Jl. Gunung Agung

Hotel Bali

Hambutan St.

Jl. Angsoka

Tourist
Office

Durian
St.

Shopping
Centre

Catur Mukha
Statue

St. Joseph's
Church

PAMEDILAN

Kumbasari
Market

Pasar
Badung

Puputan
Square

Jl. Surapati

Kereneng Bemo
Station

Werdi Budaya
Art Center

STSI
College of
Indonesian
Arts

Puri
Pamecutan

Jl. Batur

Jl. Hasannudin

Pura Jagatnatha

Jl. Hayam Wuruk

Jl. Batukaru

Museum Bali

Radio Station

Kelandis River

Java Bus
Tickets

Protestant
Church

Letda M. D.

Jl. Putra

KEDATON

Tegal
Bemo Station

Army
Hospital

Petrol Station

Hotel
Denpasar

GELOGOR

Ki Hajar Dewantara

Police Office

Jl. Natuna

Governor's
Office

TV Station

Jl. Teku Umar

Department
of Culture
and Education

Tourist
Office

Oka Hotel

Post
Office

Immigration
Office

Udayana
University

Jl. Raya Puputan

Sanur

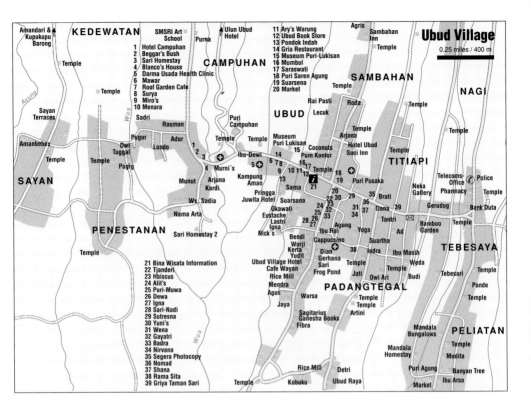

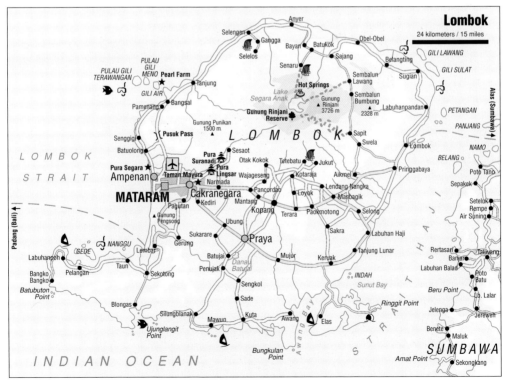

DENPASAR AND THE SOUTH

A growing metropolis of nearly half a million people, Denpasar is a crowded, hot, dusty city full of winding alleys, one-way streets and traffic jams. Yet there are more than a few jewels to be found in this capital city.

The center of town is the **Pasar Badung** (*den pasar* means north of the market), a four-story market building where one can find fruits and vegetables, clothing, spices, baskets, ritual paraphernalia, stainless and bamboo cooking utensils, and more. Surrounding streets are filled with fabrics (Jalan Sulawesi), goldsmiths (Jalan Sulawesi and Jalan Hasanuddin), and electronic shops (Jalan Gajah Mada – the main town boulevard).

At the Kumbasari shopping center, just west of the canal on Jalan Gajah Mada, are movie theaters and kiosks full of handicrafts. Many of the major banks are on Jalan Gajah Mada, but for changing money, use money changers as they're quicker (and many Denpasar banks don't cash travelers checks).

Denpasar does not sport any grand hotels, but there are many small hotels in the city. One hotel of historical note, on Jalan Thamrin, is **Puri Pemecutan**, a renovated palace. At the turn of the century, much of it was destroyed in battles with the Dutch, during which the Balinese royalty here committed *puputan* – a mass suicide. The hotel follows the design of royal residences of the old Badung kingdom.

One of the two centers of culture is **Puputan Square**, a large and open square commemorating the battle between the rajas of the Badung regency and the Dutch militia in 1906.

On the east side stand the Museum Bali, with its striking architecture, and Pura Jagatnatha, a state temple where young people go to worship every full and new moon. Across the square is the national military complex, and on the third side is the former residence of the island's governor.

Museum Bali was built by the Dutch government in 1932, presenting a commendable survey of Balinese art, from prehistoric times to the early twentieth century, although the upkeep leaves something to be desired. Items range from neolithic stone implements, Bronze Age sarcophagi, and Buddhist and Hindu bronzes through a fine variety of modern woodcarvings and paintings, to ceremonial masks and *ukur* – human effigies made from silver and Chinese coins, and used in death rituals.

The architecture of the museum combines the two principal edifices in Bali: the temple and the palace. The split gate, the outer and inner courtyards, and *kulkul* (signal drum) tower are characteristic of temples. Opposite stands an elevated pavilion, once used as a palace lookout for a prince viewing his lands.

The main building, with its wide pillared veranda, resembles the Karangasem palaces of East Bali, where the porch once served ministers and authorities who had an audience with the raja. The windowless building on

the right reflects the Tabanan palace style of West Bali, while the brick building on the left belongs to the northern palace style of Singaraja, making the museum a true monument to Bali.

Every full moon, young people pay homage at **Pura Jagatnatha**, the recently-built temple next to the museum, dedicated to Sanghyang Widi Wasa, the supreme god (in contrast to Bali's numerous local deities, or to ancestral spirits). The tall *padmasana*, constructed of white coral, symbolizes universal order. The turtle Bedawangnala and two *naga* serpents represent the foundation of the world; the towering throne signifies the receding heavens. This design, so prevalent on the island, relates to the Hindu myth of the churning of the sea of milk, when the gods and the demons stirred the cosmic ocean to create the nectar of immortality.

The great statue with four faces and eight arms, at Denpasar's main intersection (at the northwest corner of Puputan Square), represents Siwa (Shiva) manifesting himself as the lords of the four directions. It was erected in 1972 as a secular monument to commemorate the puputan, though its imagery symbolizes Hindu concepts.

A permanent exhibition of modern Balinese painting and woodcarving may be seen at the **Werdi Budaya Art Center**, at Abiankapas (south end of Jalan Nusa Indah and on the east side of town). This grand complex includes an outdoor theater that hosts colossal dance-dramas, two smaller theaters, a sales room and lovely grounds to wander through. Every June and July, the Pesta Seni, or Balinese Arts Festival, is held here. Traditional music and dance are performed almost nightly, and there are exhibitions and sales of local handicrafts, foodstuffs and hand-loomed fabrics.

Just north on Jalan Nusa Indah lies **Sekolah Tinggi Seni Indonesia** (STSI), the College of Indonesian Arts. Formerly known as ASTI, college students here have been studying traditional dance, music and puppetry, and choreographing both classical and contemporary performing arts, since 1967.

Family off to somewhere, Kuta.

For the serious student of Balinese culture, a visit to the **Pusat Dokumentasi** (Documentation Center) is a must. Here is the beginning of a collection of works in all languages on Balinese life and culture. Documents may not be taken out, but one can photocopy them on the premises. Adjacent is the Culture Center, **Pusat Budaya**. The centers is located at Jalan Ir. Juanda.

Nightlife in Denpasar revolves around the three **night markets** at the Kumbasari shopping center, the Kereneng bus station cum market, and the Pasar Malam Pekambinan, just off Jalan Diponegoro in front of the Kertawijaya shopping center. Here one can find all sorts of cooked foods for sale next to hawkers selling snake oil and charms, as well as the standard fare of T-shirts and sandals.

For those craving more modern conveniences, there are a number of modern shopping centers.

South Bali: It is interesting to note that Bali's three major tourism centers – Sanur, Kuta and Nusa Dua – are all in the most southern part of the island. South is considered as the most impure direction, *kelod* or towards the sea, according to Balinese cosmology. And indeed, many Balinese and foreigners alike feel that these areas have been spoiled, and are no longer Balinese.

Kuta, once an isolated fishing village, is now a vigorous commercial area, attracting young budget travelers and the international surfing set. Sanur still manages to retain some flavor as a Brahman-dominated village, where incredible trance performances still occur at local temple festivals. Nusa Dua, on the other hand, is not so much a village as a tourist resort for well-off visitors.

All three areas are fringed with white-sand beaches. Kuta is famous for its great waves and spectacular sunsets. Sanur's waters are calm and shallow. Nusa Dua has a fabulous beach front, which, however, is not particularly suitable for swimming.

Historical context: Throughout the island's history, southern Bali, together with the northern seaports in Buleleng,

Below, nautical kite. Right, beach vendor.

have always been the first to welcome – or repel – outsiders.

At Belanjong, beyond the Hotel Sanur Beach, an inscription engraved on a low pillar commemorates the victories of Sri Kesari Warmadewa, Bali's first king, over his enemies in AD 913.

In later times, famous priests from Java trod these shores. The three best known temples of the area – Pura Sakenan on Turtle Island, Pura Luhur Uluwatu on the Bukit, and Pura Petitenget at Kerobokan – are associated with the itinerant sixteenth-century priest Danghyang Nirartha, also known as Pedanda Sakti Wawu Rauh.

This eminent teacher brought the concept of the Lotus Throne, or Padmasana, for the worship of Sanghyang Widi Wasa, who is Bali's supreme god. Empu Kuturan, another prominent priest, came to Bali in the tenth century and introduced the *meru*, or roofed shrine. The number of meru is dependent upon which *dewa*, or deity, is being worshipped; except for those shrines used for storage of ritual paraphernalia, the number of roofs is always odd, with eleven being the most supreme.

The first European to settle in South Bali was a Danish trader, Mads Lange, who built a copra (coconut-shell husk) factory in Kuta, around 1830. By befriending kings of these regions, he persuaded the squabbling rajas to give up their quarrelling to some degree, and to unite against Dutch pressures.

Partially successful at promoting Bali's independence, Mads Lange was beloved by some rulers and detested by others. He was believed to be poisoned by his enemies in the late nineteenth century. His grave is in Kuta.

In 1906, a Chinese schooner wrecked off the shores of Sanur. Local tradition had it that shipwrecks were bounty from Baruna, the god of the sea, and thus anyone had rights to it. This was, in fact, a breach of a previous treaty between the Balinese and the Dutch, and was the excuse the Dutch needed to wage battle against the raja of Badung.

Rather than continuing the hopeless fight against the better-equipped Dutch

forces, the king and his entire entourage, dressed in white and carrying daggers, walked straight into the gunfire of the Dutch, in a ritual suicide known as *puputan* – literally, end. Only one small child survived the 1906 massacre.

The Dutch were left in control until World War II, when the Japanese occupied Bali. After the upheavals of the Japanese occupation, and Indonesia's declaration of independence in 1945, the Dutch again landed troops at Sanur in 1946, but their stay was comparatively short.

Today, with international travelers to Bali numbering one and a half million annually, and the government pumping in development funds to ensure that this number increases, southern Bali is becoming a tourist ghetto of sorts, unfortunately. Nevertheless, for those who prefer the comforts of home and the relaxation of the beach, this area is a good starting point. Many of Bali's interesting sites can be seen on day-trips.

Parasailing, Sanur Beach. **Sanur:** Sanur was little more than a tucked-away beach in the 1930s, with nary a hotel to its name. Today, the beach front is lined with hotels and bungalows, with access roads lined by so-called art shops. The only surviving home from those earlier times is that of the Belgian painter Le Mayeur, who moved to Bali in 1932 and lived there for 26 years. The **Le Mayeur house** – with its gardens full of statues, luxuriant gold and crimson carvings, and Le Mayeur's own paintings (many of his late wife, Ni Polok, a renowned *legong* dancer and famed beauty) is now a museum.

By the 1950s, the first cluster of bungalows in Sanur was built as a small hotel, attracting even more international travelers. The Grand Bali Beach Hotel, a Sukarno-era project, was opened in 1966, built with Japanese reparation money for World War II.

When the Grand Bali Beach first opened, it was a source of wonder to the Balinese. They came from all over the island to set eyes upon what, to the modern world, were everyday matters – running water, electricity and elevators. Bali's only high-rise structure, it burned

to the ground in 1992, but was rebuilt and reopened less than two years later. Meanwhile, dozens of other hotels have opened their doors along the beach. Today, Sanur is a prominent luxury resort area. The Bali Hyatt and Hotel Sanur Beach are the next largest hotels.

The building boom reached its peak for a Pacific Asia Travel Association (PATA) conference in 1974. Today, that boom has moved to the Bukit, the southern-most peninsula where the Nusa Dua resort complex sports a dozen hotels. (Construction here peaked, coincidentally, for the 1991 PATA conference.)

A wise government regulation forbidding buildings taller than a coconut palm (15 m/50 ft) has allowed Sanur to retain much of its village character. But while the rule remains on the books, new construction in the 1990s seems to have found creative ways around the law. Luxuriant vegetation quickly covers building scars, and moss transforms a new stone wall.

While the five-star hotel boom saturated the market with expensive rooms, the government has also encouraged bungalow-style hotels, based on the Balinese norm of many small buildings within a one-house compound.

Elegant triangular sails propel fishing *prahu* across the calm sea. These boats are called *jukung*, and many are for hire for trips along the shore. At low tide, great swathes of sand and coral stretch for hundreds of meters out into the reef.

At the south end of Sanur, in Belanjong, one can take a jukung to **Serangan** (**Turtle Island**), named for its turtle-breeding areas. On the island is **Pura Sakenan**, a temple with a *prasada* – a monolithic stone tower rarely found on Bali. The temple is a mixture of Javanese *candi* style and stone altars of early pre-Hindu design. In **Belanjong** is a temple with an inscription on an old pillar dating back to AD 913 – the oldest example of writing on archaeological finds in Bali.

For shopping, Sanur's beach-side shops offer the standard fare. Those at the **Sanur Beach Market** share their profits with the community; one can get **Downtown Kuta.**

158

a fine meal at the restaurant located there, as well.

The Kita Bookshop nearby sells magazines and newspapers from all over the world, and has a good collection of books on Indonesian culture at decent market prices.

Kuta: Sunsets make memories at the beach of Kuta, one of the island's loveliest coasts. People come from all over to watch the magnificence of the sun, which beats mercilessly down on this white-sand beach, and Indonesian tourists come to gawk at the international set, who erroneously assume that Kuta is for topless bathing, something quite offensive to Indonesian sensibilities.

Prior to 1990, the beach was peppered with countless children selling nearly everything. Today, however, one can relax in more solitude along cordoned areas of the beach, all the while getting a massage or corn-rows from one of the blue-hatted women. Some stationary umbrellas are planted in the sand – under which most vendors huddle – and other vendors rent canvas umbrellas.

Kuta Beach.

Unsightly beach bars have spring up along the beach, unfortunately for those seeking something more pristine.

The waters off of Kuta are among the best places to learn surfing; the waves are also perfect for body-surfing. Surfboards are available for rent, and for sale. It is said the goddess of the sea claims at least one victim each year at Kuta Beach – there is often quite a strong undertow.

Aside from its image as the surf-and-sun capital of Bali, Kuta is now a resort area filled with pubs and bars catering mainly to the drinking set, replete with "pub crawls". International cuisine is available at all sorts of restaurants; Made's Warung, on Jalan Pantai Kuta, the road down to the beach, is *the* place to be seen, as well as to people-watch. In fact, it was one of the first eating establishments around, when Kuta was still a sleepy haven for budget travelers in the early 1970s.

Early tourist days: The original villagers of Kuta were farmers, fishermen and metalsmiths, and, at first, they were

rather surprised at the great interest in their beach by foreigners. After all, traditional thought is that the ocean leads to the underworld.

But like many Balinese, they saw there was a profit to be made. For a small charge, they invited the travelers into their homes – clean, simple and cheap accommodation. Offering an economical alternative, home-stays are still popular with many travelers, despite the blossoming luxury resort hotels.

With all the development in Kuta, changes were bound to come. Many long-term residents (Balinese and foreigners alike) feel Kuta is an embarrassment, going there only for a quick swim and a fine meal. (Waikiki suffers the same domestic image in Hawaii.) Unregulated street hawkers are an increasing annoyance – not only in urban areas but even along jungle paths leading to white-water rafting trips.

Unfortunately, crime has escalated in southern Bali, especially in Kuta, and this once peaceful village is fast becoming a center for drugs, prostitution and muggings. (Don't walk or get romantic along the beach at night.)

Bukit and Nusa Dua: Connected to the mainland by a low, narrow isthmus, the limestone tableland of **Bukit Badung**, a peninsula 200 meters (660 ft) above sea level, is in striking contrast to the lush Bali mainland. Cacti grow upon this arid land, with some parts of the peninsula used for grazing cattle. **Udayana University**, Bali's main public university, moved many of its faculties here in the late 1980s.

A good surfaced road meanders across Bukit Badung to its western tip, where rocky precipices drop almost 100 meters (330 ft) to the ocean.

The famous sea-side temple of **Pura Luhur Uluwatu** balances picturesquely on the cliff's edge. Dating from at least the tenth century, it is one of the Sad Kahyangan, or Six Temples of the World, revered by all Balinese. The priests Empu Kuturan and Danghyang Nirartha helped to establish this temple, and it is said that Danghyang Nirartha achieved *moksa* – enlightenment – here.

Left, good fishing. **Below**, Uluwatu.

160

The temple's *candi bentar*, or split gate, is unusual in that the carvings are in the shape of wings. The entrance to the second courtyard (*jaba tengah*) is flanked by a statue of Ganesha, the elephant god, who is revered as the remover of obstacles.

The innermost sanctuary, *jeroan*, is off limits to those who are not praying here. However, one can still watch from an observation point off to the side.

Vantage spots along the peninsula's road afford breathtaking northern vistas of Bali rising to the peaks of distant volcanoes. This is also a beautiful spot to watch the sunset. (Plan well. It's one hour from Sanur.)

Down below this sacred site is Suluban, one of the best surfing sites in the world, but definitely not for beginners. Take the path just before the parking lot for Uluwatu. You'll then have to walk, as there's no road to the beach.

Resort enclave: Bali's latest resort area continues to develop, south of Jimbaran. The Four Seasons Resort and Bali Inter-Continental were the first international hotels to nestle around the lovely Jimbaran Bay, facing north toward the airport. Quickly, a number of smaller hotels and restaurants sprang up to fill in the gaps northward. The Ritz-Carlton is a spacious cliffside resort, further west of the bay.

Nusa Dua, a luxury hotel complex in the middle of a coconut grove, alongside a white-sand beach, caters to an upscale traveler – and to those seeking refuge from the ubiquitous hawkers found elsewhere, as they are banned in Nusa Dua. Indeed, in many ways, Nusa Dua seems a bit thin on local color.

A dozen luxury hotels wrap around the white-sand beaches, including Grand Hyatt, Hilton, Sheraton Laguna, Sheraton Nusa Indah, Melia Bali, Club Med, Amanusa, Putri Bali Nusa Dua Beach and Nikko Bali. If interested in architecture, take a look at the Nusa Dua Beach Hotel, which has incorporated traditional Balinese architecture into its basic design. A number of water sports are available here as well, including spectacular parasailing.

Resort at Nusa Dua.

CENTRAL BALI

Driving out of urban Denpasar, tranquil green seas of rice begin to contrast sharply with the boisterous sounds of the city. To the north, Gunung Batur rises over 1,700 meters, and should definitely be seen in the early morning before the fog rises. Palm-leaf carvings of Dewi Sri, the rice goddess, guard over the crops; small thatch huts dot the fields, giving shade to those who work them. Shrines and temples can be seen at every water source – the fields would not flourish without its nourishment. Women incessantly put out offerings of flowers, rice, incense and holy water, to appease destructive forces and please beneficent deities. Even with the great influx of tourism, village life still is centered on these centuries-old beliefs.

Almost every village along the way from Denpasar up to Ubud specializes in some kind of art form; numerous studios offer havens for artisans at work in their studios.

This region is that of Gianyar, extending like an elongated finger down the middle of southern Bali. From the fabulous views in Sayan to the bronze drum of Pejeng, from the *barong* dance in Batubulan to the *ikat* of Gianyar town, from the masks of Mas to the paintings in Penestanan, Gianyar impresses itself on all visitors to Bali.

What is it about Gianyar that distinguishes it from Bali's seven other regencies? It has no great beaches to speak of, and no mountain lakes. Yet it has a richness of the soil – the spring-fed, lava-enriched fertile paddy fields – that contributes to stunning panoramas and a history of cultural richness.

One day is not enough for the island's many delights: festive religious processions, exquisite vistas, warm smiles. Many of the places mentioned here make beautiful side trips. Morning walks through the villages lead to out-of-the-way retreats.

Batubulan: The soft tuft, or soapstone (*paras*), used for temple carving is just that: soft. The harsh weather of the tropics so wears down this stone that, every couple of centuries, these carvings must be renewed. Paras is found in the nearby ravines, and is used to create protective deities and demons for temples and households – and now for tourists. Men and boys carve side-by-side at roadside "factories", copying in stone what their ancestors had carved before them. Contrary to popular belief, many of the monstrous looking statues are not demonic at all; when placed in front of a temple or home, they scare unfriendly visitors of the otherworldly sort.

Aside from stone carving, Batubulan is most famous for the daily performances of the barong dance. More a drama, the story depicts the age-old struggle between that which is good and righteous – the path of Dharma, or right-doing – and that which seeks to destroy it. Barong is a mystical lion-dragon creature played in the dance-drama by two men. He is a benevolent fellow; the hairs of his beard are said to hold healing powers. His adversary is Rangda, queen of the underworld, who is equally feared and respected by the Balinese.

In the dance-drama, Rangda is never destroyed, for the Balinese believe that the balance between positive and negative must be maintained. Therefore, to kill Rangda on stage would be destroying one half of the life-force. Even though, to an outsider, this may seem like just a play, to the Balinese it is a serious portrayal of the struggle of life. (As an aside, it is interesting to note that even the most serious of Balinese staged dramas are imbued with humor. When watching the barong, don't be surprised to see bawdy portrayals of life-threatening situations. The Balinese love to laugh at themselves.)

Right before the barong-dance site is a turn-off for **Sekolah Menengah Karawitan Indonesia** (SMKI), or High School of Indonesian Performing Arts, and **Sekolah Seni Rupa Indonesia** (SESRI), or High School of Indonesian Fine Art. From the road, the schools look like a huge temple complex, with grand carvings and colored banners waving in the wind from the middle of the rice fields. Visitors are welcome to watch classes, held in the mornings. To enroll in SMKI, one must first audition, as this is essentially a teacher's training school. After graduation, students are expected to return to their villages to teach the traditional dances and music that they have learned here. Many of them continue on at Sekolah Tinggi Seni Indonesia (SKTI), the College of Indonesian Arts, in Denpasar, the college-level school for the performing arts of dance, music and puppetry.

Singapadu: If interested in masks, then a side trip to Singapadu is a must. Instead of turning right at the bend in the road bordering Batubulan and Celuk, continue straight for about one kilometer to a T-junction, with a huge banyan tree on the left and the *pura desa* (village temple) on the right. (Follow signs to the Taman Burung Bali Bird Park; the pura desa lies just beyond it.)

Just next to the temple is the main *puri* or palace of Singapadu, and one of the places where *barong* are made. Further on down the road is the home and workshop of I Wayan Tangguh, one of Bali's most prominent mask makers. The main prototypes of *topeng* dance masks are in his collection and are some of Bali's finest specimens. To see a mask evolve from a hunk of wood into an intricately-carved, and painted, piece of art is a fascinating process.

Singapadu, by the way, also has a barong dance performance, and some of the finest barong "legs" (men who play the front legs of Barong) are from here. Yet, not only does this tiny village produce barong dancers of high caliber, but the best *arja* singers and dancers on the island, as well. Arja is a genre of dance-drama that is closest to Western operetta. But it is losing popularity in Bali, and therefore is not performed as frequently as its masked cousin, the topeng dance-drama.

Just behind the *pura dalem*, down in the river gorge, is an amphitheater where *kecak* and fire-dance performances are conducted on Monday nights. While the performance is good, the setting is spectacular – a rock grotto provides the backdrop and the area is lit by torches.

Rice paddy, Batubulan.

The theater is a cooperative project between the village and the Taman Burung Bali Bird Park.

Taman Burung Bali Bird Park is a well-executed attraction, with more than 800 specimens of 125 bird species – a third of which are endangered in Indonesia or elsewhere in the world. Paved paths wander through gardens, leading to large aviaries in a natural setting. A breeding program preserves rare and endangered species. Endangered Bali starlings, the first born in captivity in Bali, are among examples of the program's success.

Celuk: Synonymous with silver and goldsmiths, Celuk has the second-highest per capita income of any village on the island. Every ten meters, it seems, there is another art shop beckoning visitors to view its wares: sterling silver and gold butterfly brooches, garnet-studded bracelets, earrings and ear-clips of all persuasions.

It's usually possible to see the workshops, usually a small room or area in the back with five to 20 workers, some not even in their teens. The intricacy and detail they can obtain with simple hand tools is amazing. Craftsmen use a tree stump with a protruding metal spike for an anvil, a bamboo stem to catch the filings and a manually-operated gas pump for heat. As with most Balinese crafts, smithing is largely an art passed down in a family.

Be sure not to miss the shops on the road just north and parallel to the main road, as many fine jewelers dwell here off the beaten track. Just past most of the art shops, on the left, is an asphalt road flanked by two small stone statues, which lead travelers to the back roads of Celuk and Batuan.

Sukawati: Across from the Wos River lies Sukawati village, an extremely powerful kingdom prior to the twentieth century. Once the seat of a powerful kingdom and the place to which many of the Peliatan and Ubud aristocracy trace their roots, Sukawati now sports a modern art market along with some of the best *dalang* (puppeteers) on Bali.

Many Balinese feel that *wayang kulit* – shadow puppetry – is the most difficult of the island's arts. Aside from having to learn how to manipulate different puppet characters, memorize hundreds of stories, sing, cue the musicians, and be able to create a variety of voices, a dalang must be clean in mind, body and soul. He is akin to a priest in many respects, and can even make the holy water so necessary for Balinese ritual (usually reserved for the domain of Brahmana priests). The stories of the wayang kulit are imbedded with innuendo and impart the values of daily life to the audience.

Often, these dalang make their own puppets, which are delicately-carved out of buffalo hide and then painted. In the *banjar* (neighborhood association) behind the food market live a number of dalang. If interested in seeing how the buffalo hide is carved into puppets, stop by the homes of puppeteers I Wayan Wija (just behind the food market, the first street to the left) and I Wayan Nartha (just south of the art market, on the other side of the street and in about 50 meters). Cowhide is also made into

Silver crafts, Celuk.

dance accoutrements in the village of Puaya, just north of Sukawati.

It is here that the production of traditional legong dance costumes - ornamented filigree leather headdresses, gilded clothes and beaded epaulets – can be seen. Even if not a dancer, it is fascinating to watch the process of cloth painting. If in the market for dance costumes, test the quality by rubbing the painted surfaces together. If it flakes off – don't buy it.

It is said that I Dewa Agung Made Karna, a ruling prince of Sukawati, ascended to heaven while meditating and saw the celestial nymphs dancing to the accompaniment of divine musicians. Awakening from his meditative state, he created the *legong* dance – an exquisite dance for two pre-adolescent girls – and music so well-known today.

The *pasar seni* or **art market** is a two-story building filled with woodcarvings, clothing and knickknacks, although an assortment of things such as ink drawings, gilded umbrellas, stone statues and bamboo flutes can also be found here. There are varying degrees of quality, but all are much less expensive than at the larger art shops.

If in Sukawati early, take a look at the *pasar pagi* or **morning market**, about a block behind the pasar seni. In this steaming, packed, warehouse-like barn, you will find, in bulk, every trinket that is on sale in Kuta, but for half the price. The market closes at mid morning.

Batuan: Most famous for its dense painting style, Batuan is also the site of some exquisite temple carvings and superb dancers. If lucky and in the area during a temple festival, it might be possible to see one of the three *gambuh* troupes. (There are less than a dozen on the entire island.) Moreover, some of the finest exponents of the topeng, or masked, dance-drama are from Batuan. Banjar Don Tiis, just up the main road, claims a club of *wayang wong* dancers.

Gambuh is considered by many scholars to be the precursor of classical Balinese dance. Currently, it is not a popular form among the Balinese, as the language used is archaic and not understood by many, and the jokes are few and far between. Nevertheless, it is in a period of revival. A stately form, it is unique in its movement style and for the accompanying gamelan orchestra, best known for its meter-long flutes.

A more modern dance genre with its roots here is the so-called frog dance. The instruments are unique: *suling* (flute) and *genggong* (Balinese-style jew's harp). This dance is often performed in the major hotels.

The dance most popular in Batuan is the topeng dance-drama, which chronicle the lives of Balinese kings and their subjects, as opposed to tales of Indian heroes and heroines. Studded with educational anecdotes, bawdy jokes and exquisite dancing, a good topeng troupe commands quite a crowd. Two of Bali's best topeng dancers and teachers reside in Batuan: I Ketut Kantor (son of the late I Nyoman Kakul, one of Bali's finest masters of dance) and I Made Jimat. Both have schools in their homes and will gladly teach foreigners.

Painters are as plentiful as dancers here, and the Batuan style is a rich one. There are many fine artists here. Don't leave Batuan without seeing the paintings of I Made Budi, who paints in the traditional Batuan style, which means he fills the canvas with color and imagery. Yet he adds a special touch to his work: tourists taking pictures, surfers, airplanes. To get to his house, go down the alley past the schoolhouse and turn right at the first crossroads. Another well-known Batuan painter is Ida Bagus Ketut Togog.

The *pura puseh* (village temple) in Batuan dates back to the eleventh century, with fine examples of temple carvings here. Head straight at the bend in the main road and up the little hill. It is directly across from the *wantilan*, or open-air pavilion.

Mas: Best known to the outside world for its intricate woodcarvings and masks, Mas was the home of the late Ida Bagus Nyana, who passed on his talent to his son, the late Ida Bagus Tilem. The son opened the Tilem Art Gallery, on the main road, a fine place to view some of the highest quality woodcarvings at some of the highest prices. Many of Ida Bagus

Nyana's innovative pieces are on display, along with those of his son. A third generation of the talented family manages the shop.

Carvings and masks can be found up and down the street, and in side alleys. Bring along a photograph or design of something you'd like carved, and place a special order. One of the best known artists for new designs in masks here is Ida Bagus Anom. He has carved masks for pantomimes, *commedia del arte* performers, as well as performance artists from all over the world. His yawning masks have been widely copied throughout the island.

The historical importance of Mas should not be overlooked. Primarily of Brahmanas, the priestly caste, Mas traces its roots back to Danghyang Nirartha, founder of **Pura Taman Pule** (which is just behind the soccer field). This great Brahmana sage created the system of the traditional village, or *desa adat*, whereby the village becomes, or rather is, a microcosm of the larger order of the cosmos. He also conceived the

padmasana, an open-roofed shrine found in every household and village temple, and dedicated to the omnipotent supreme god, Sanghyang Widi Wasa. At the Pura Taman Pule, performances of wayang wong are held all day and night on Kuningan (the Saturday after Galungan, every 210 days). One of the largest cockfights in Bali occurs in the early morning hours.

Traveling north from Mas, and just before the junction with a statue of a female dancer, is Tjokot and Sons – a home workshop of "primitive" woodcarvings. Natural tree roots are sculpted into grotesque figures that allude to the demonic.

If interested in woodcarvings, head north past the *bale banjar* (community hall) and stop at Wayan Pasti's house. Aside from being an amazing carver, he is also a traditional Balinese architect, as well as one of the finest makers of cremation bulls. His speciality is life-size horses and dogs – the realism will make you do a double-take.

Just behind the statue of the dancer at

Temple festival, Mas.

the junction lies the hamlet of **Teges Kawan**. This is a banjar of musicians and carvers. On Tuesday nights, they perform music and dance for visitors right here in the village square.

Peliatan: Continuing west is Banjar Kalah – a hamlet filled with artists specializing in the carving of small animals, fruits, giant flowers and banana trees. Hidden away among these carvers is an exquisite painter of the *wayang* style: I Ketut Madra. To get to his home, which is also a losmen, turn south onto the dirt road right at the next junction, and then left again. There's nothing for sale. To the contrary, one of Madra's paintings must be ordered well in advance, as it takes him many weeks to finish one.

A community of painters works in Dewa Nyoman Batuan's workshop, just west on the asphalt road and at the bend in the road. Dewa Nyoman began experimenting with painting mandalas in the early 1970s, and his paintings have a unique touch. One painting, which could extend up to 3 square meters (32 sq ft), may be worked on by many artists simultaneously. Aside from painting, Dewa Batuan's workshop manufactures painted, carved-wood mirror frames, boxes, and small cabinets, which has become a flourishing cottage industry, alongside basketry, in the village of **Pengoseken**.

Going back to the main road, the central village of **Peliatan** was famous in the 1950s for its legong dancers, who took New York by storm while on tour. Today, the daughters of these former legong dancers, along with their cousins and friends, continue the tradition. Every Friday night, at the hamlet square in Banjar Teruna, are some of Peliatan's finest exponents of music and dance performing the *tirta sari* gamelan.

Originally, these artists were all trained under the discerning and critical eye (and ear) of the late Anak Agung Gede Mandera, who died in 1987. For decades, Gung Kak (as he was affectionately called) groomed both dancers and musicians alike, and his legacy still lives today. A foundation is being estab-

Rice farmer.

lished in his memory by his family at his palace, Puri Kaleran, in the back of the Mandala Boutique. One of the few all-women performing gamelan (*gamelan ibu-ibu*) rehearses here; many of the members are relatives of Gung Kak. They perform every Sunday night with a dance troupe of children.

If wanting to study dance, music, painting or any other art form, find a style that appeals to you (by going to galleries and watching performances) and then approach the artist directly about lessons.

Even though Peliatan is literally a hop, skip and a jump from the relatively chaotic Ubud, a slower pace reigns here. With no glamorous hotels or restaurants, it remains a lovely rural area.

Blahbatuh: In this market village, **Pura Puseh Gaduh** is associated with Kebo Iwa, the legendary giant from Bedulu. He is honored in temples all over Bali, and here is no exception. Enshrined in a small pavilion is a massive stone head over a meter high, said to be a portrait of Kebo Iwa. Gajah Mada, the great minis-

ter of the Majapahit kingdom, realized he could never conquer Bali while Kebo Iwa lived. So he enticed him to Java, with the promise of a beautiful princess as a wife, and had him killed, thereby leaving Bali open to his conquest.

On the road from Blahbatuh to Gianyar is the village of **Bona**. If in the market for quality bamboo furniture, this is the village that makes it. Plain or fantastically carved, virgin or varnished – chairs, beds, tables – all are available here. At night, Bona offers a trance show for tourists. Three forms of trance dancing – *sanghyang dedari*, *sanghyang jaran* and kecak – are performed practically every day.

Up on the road from Bona is the Anoman Handicrafts Shop, the retail shop for their ikat weaving factory and featuring ready-made items of ikat and batik. The ikat process involves a complex tying and dyeing of white threads, resulting in incredible patterns. There are other weaving factory-showrooms in the capital of the regency, Gianyar.

A visit to I Made Gableran's gamelan

factory in Banjar Babakan, Blahbatuh, is a treat. Here, barefoot men blow bellows to stir up the heat for forging. They squat with large hammers, bending the bronze alloys into the desired shape for the metallophones used in Balinese gamelan. After they are cooled, the master, Gableran himself, tests the tuning by striking the key with a *tuding*, a bamboo tuning fork. Gamelan casings are assembled and painted here, and entire orchestras (worth well over $10,000) may be purchased – with enough lead time, of course.

Kutri: Atop a small hill off the main road, north of Blahbatuh in Kutri, is the temple of **Pura Bukit Dharma**. Found here is the famous statue of the goddess Durga, in the act of killing a bull possessed by a demon under her feet. In a fighting attitude, her four arms hold a spear, an arrow, a *cakra*, a shield, a bow and a winged conch shell. Durga is the wrathful aspect of Siwa's (Shiva) wife.

This statue is commonly thought to be Queen Gunapriyadharmapatni, the wife of King Udayana, as some people

believe that she is buried in the nearby village of Buruan. There are also two lingga or phallic symbols, and a small statue of Ganesha, offspring of Siwa and consort. This would suggest a temple dedicated to Siwa. Although the statue is now defaced, the fluid motion of the body defies the conventional pose of both Balinese and Javanese sculpture, especially of female figures, and is closer to Indian prototypes.

Gianyar: Once a powerful kingdom, Gianyar is now a sleepy, overgrown village. The speciality of this area is the ikat weaving the Balinese use in traditional wear. There are a number of factories that hold informal tours, and it's fascinating to watch the process of turning white threads – through a complex dyeing process – into stunning patterns of color.

Gianyar's open-air cafe-market, one block west of the puri, specializes in a Balinese delight: *babi guling*, or roast suckling pig. If you want to revel in the best of the pork dishes, do it here, but make sure your stomach is ready for it.

Following the road south of the puri, you'll come to **Lebih**, a fishing village. Men gather tiny tadpoles (*nener*), which are then sold to merchants, who in turn raise them in ponds in Java and sell them when they're mature. A view of **Nusa Penida**, or Bandit Island, delights the eyes, but don't go swimming. The undertow is treacherous and foreigners have already been "sacrificed" by the deities of the sea.

On the road to the west of Gianyar is the village of **Kemenuh**, the source of Bali's woodcarvings for generations. Prices are much cheaper here than in Mas. Stop in at the Komang Gallery.

From Gianyar, continue north. On a curve in the road near the village of **Sidan** stands a small, elegantly-carved temple – a particularly fine example of pura dalem, the temple of the dead. The *kulkul* drum tower is decked with reliefs showing tormented wrongdoers being punished by devilish giants. The gates are flanked by deities of death and transformation, who are associated with the pura dalem – particularly Durga, manifested as the witch-queen Rangda.

Left, prized fighting cock. **Right,** hard work in the fields.

UBUD AND SURROUNDINGS

From Peliatan, it's possible to walk to Ubud via the backroads. At the banyan tree in Peliatan, cross the street and follow the path until it dead-ends. Then turn right to the *pura dalem* (underworld temple). On Saturday nights, the *gunung sari gamelan* performs a star-studded show of traditional Balinese music and *legong* dance. Turn left (west) towards the center of town.

The main *puri* (court or palace) in Ubud lies in the northeast corner of the main crossroads, facing the modern two-story market building and the traditional village meeting hall.

Ubud has a myriad of shops. *Ikat* fashioned into wallets, backpacks and dresses is available in the small shops lining Ubud's main road, Jalan Ubud Raya, as are typical souvenirs such as silk-screened T-shirts, baskets, colorful batik clothing and linens. Antiques (or at least old-looking things) are sold in shops along Jalan Wanara Wana, as is every craft, garment and eccentricity being produced for the export and tourist trade in Bali.

Ubud is a picturesque township, and visitors have been attracted by its charm and beauty for decades. In the 1970s, Ubud was a sleepy haven with a few losmen. Now, it is a mecca for foreign artists and business people alike, with hundreds of inns, cafes and restaurants to soothe the weary traveler. The streets are paved and sidewalks line the major thoroughfares. It has a post office, telegraph and telephone office, and business centers that will take messages, send and receive mail, book an airline ticket, pack goods for shipping and type letters. Ubud is home to a few international hotels, including the distinctive Amandari and Four Seasons, and a wealth of quaint cottages set among the rice fields. Despite its growth and the large influx of foreigners passing through, Ubud still retains its charm.

The name of Ubud comes from the word *ubad*, Balinese for medicine, stemming from the healing properties of a certain herb growing near the Campuhan River. Many of Ubud's aristocrats were (and some still are) renown for their healing powers. Yet their powers went beyond health. Even into this century, and long after the Dutch invasion of Bali and Indonesia's independence, Ubud's royal families have commanded great respect from the people.

If tired of urbanity, virtually any of the major paths out of Ubud leads through smaller villages and acres of paddy fields. Bali Bird Club's ornithologists lead daily walks through the island's central foothills around Ubud. During a four-hour trek through rice fields, birders are guaranteed to see about 50 varieties of birds, including the striking turquoise Java kingfisher and scarlet-headed flowerpecker.

One of the many unique things about Ubud is the establishment of the Yayasan Bina Wisata, or Ubud Tourism Information Foundation. The creed of Bina Wisata is the preservation of Ubud's natural and cultural beauty. Instead of

Left, modern colors. **Right**, gamelan orchestra leader.

simply encouraging tourism on a grand scale, they are striving to unify the needs of both visitors and locals.

Visitors are asked to respect the local ceremonies, wear traditional clothing when appropriate, and, in general, learn more about the Ubud people. There is a message board detailing festivals, ceremonies and cremations in the area. The staff is helpful in answering questions and plotting journeys – definitely worth a visit if only to discover the week's special happenings. It's 500 meters east of the market.

On *pasah*, which takes place every three days, Ubud market is packed. Produce, dry-goods and linens are sold, and even traveling medicine men appear here. The activity is for early-birds; after two o'clock, the market is quiet.

Just down from the market is the **Puri Lukisan** (Museum of Painting). Established in 1954, it is dedicated to showing the work of local painters, and is an excellent place to get an overview of the stylistic differences between artists. Other museums are the Lempad Museum, near Puri Lukisan, Neka Museum in Campuhan, and the Agung Rai Museum of Art (ARMA) in Peliatan.

One short walk is to the **monkey forest**. At the main crossroads, take the southern road, Jalan Wanara Wana, all the way to the woods. It's best to do this walk in the early morning or late afternoon, as the midday sun beats down unmercifully. Once in the forest, hold onto all belongings – the monkeys are fast and eager to run off with anything snatchable, usable or not.

Continue up out of the monkey forest and turn east (right). A lovely view of the rice fields is just behind the modern rice mill.

An art form utilizing bright and festive colors are the paintings of **Penestanan**, in a style influenced by Dutch-born artist Arie Smit, who is still in residence in Ubud. This tiny village is just past the Campuhan bridge and up the steep stairs to the left.

Down by the Campuhan River ("place where three rivers meet") is a small temple built by Mpu Narada. A bamboo

Trail through monkey forest.

spout pours out pure spring water, and many Balinese come here to bathe in the evening. A place to get sweets (and maybe even a sweetheart, as it's the place to be seen) is the Lotus Cafe, in the middle of town. Just past the market, sit outside by the large lotus pond and sip cordials while chatting to visitors from all over the world. For Indonesian and Balinese food, try Ibu Satri's, behind the *bale banjar* of Ubud kelod. There are so many places to choose from that you could spend all your time eating.

If looking for solitude, head up the hill at Campuhan and bear left (south) to **Sayan**, the former home of composer Colin McPhee and still home to a spectacular view of gorges and palms and rice fields. Take any of the small paths on the right side of the road to get to the ridge, and then walk along it. There are a number of small losmen along here.

Backtracking north along the ridge (via the main road) leads to **Kedewatan**, another village privy to an outrageous view. More upscale accommodation is available along the ridge in all ranges,

from Villa Indah, near the Kedewatan intersection, to Puri Bunga and The Cedi (complete with spa), further north toward Payangan. Stop by the market in Payangan, with a rather large gathering of vendors but not nearly as commercial as the Ubud market. There are also vanilla and coconut plantations nearby.

Coming back down the hill to Campuhan, drop in for a quick dip (for a nominal fee) at the Hotel Campuhan's swimming pool. This hotel was *the* luxury hotel in the area years ago, and its rustic charm still remains. It has lost its luster, however. Artist Walter Spies used to live here, in the 1930s.

In the Ubud area are numerous temples, and festivals occur frequently throughout the year. One interesting ritual is in the village of **Kutuh**, just north of Ubud. The people here originally fled from the area of Singaraja, on the north coast, when their kingdom (also called Kutuh) was defeated. At the village's *pura dalem alit* festival is a special ritual called *Mesiram Agni*, or Bathing the Fire, which is held on every

other Anggara Kasih (a Tuesday) in the week of Prangbakat. Sacred *baris* dances from both Kutuh in Singaraja and the local Kutuh are performed nightly during this celebration.

Petulu is known for many things, but most spectacular are the *kokokan*, or white herons. Every morning at dawn, and in the afternoon around four or five o'clock, they circle the trees in flocks. To get there, head north out of Peliatan, past the statue at the Ubud intersection. After about one and a half kilometers, there is a sign for Petulu on the right; on the left is a wide road – follow that to the village. It's impossible to miss the birds, but note that it's a long walk from Ubud or Peliatan. Nearby accommodation ranges from the large but quaint Merpati Inn to the deluxe Banyan Tree Kamandalu and spa.

Seven kilometers (4 mi) further north are the villages of **Pujung** and **Sebatu**. This is where the Balinese themselves go to buy exquisitely-carved and painted garuda birds.

Returning to Peliatan, travel east past the statue of the dancer. About 500 meters up the road, on the right, are two small stone statues marking the *banjar* of **Teges Kanginan**.

This banjar has one of the few remaining *semar pegulingan* gamelan in Bali; Tirta Sari, in Peliatan, is the only one around for miles. Most clubs have *gong kebyar*, which are distinctly different in sound, and a delightful stage space in front of the main temple complex to watch performances. Here in Teges Kanginan, young girls still dance the traditional legong. The *seka* (club) also does its own version of the *kecak* monkey chant, which Sardono Kusuma, nationally-known choreographer from Java, set on this group in the mid 1970s.

Just a few miles from Ubud sits the former capital of Bali, **Pejeng**, and around it the most densely-packed area of antiquities on the entire island.

Goa Gajah: East of Peliatan, past the statue of the dancer, is Goa Gajah, the Elephant Caves. There are no elephants here and no one knows for sure why it was accorded this appellation. There is **Private retreats outside Ubud.**

a reference in the 1365 *lontar* (palm-leaf manuscript) Nagarakertagama to a Balinese place called Lwa Gajah (Elephant Water, or River), which was a dwelling place of a Buddhist priest. This may refer to the Petanu River running just next to the cave.

Goa Gajah, which dates back to at least the eleventh century, was excavated in 1922. A monstrous head with a gaping mouth (the cave's entrance) appears to be pushing apart the entrance with its hands. All around are fantastically-carved leaves, animals, waves and humans running from the mouth in fear. (Some say that this all represents humanity's helplessness in the face of natural danger.) Inside is a 13-meter-long (43-ft) passage stopping at a junction, 15 meters (49 ft) wide. This inner sanctum contains several niches, which could have served as sleeping compartments for ascetics. At one end of the passage is a four-armed statue of Ganesha, and at the opposite end is a set of three *lingga*.

As Ganesha (elephant-headed deity) is the son of Siwa (Shiva), and lingga are generally attributed to Siwa-worship, one might conclude that Goa Gajah is a temple. But the sleeping niches and Buddhist ruins just outside the cave suggest otherwise. The sculpted face of the cave wears large earplugs, and is therefore a woman; many interpret her as a Rangda-type witch figure, which could be linked to Tantric Buddhism or Bhairavite Siwaism.

Another theory is that this cave is being pushed apart and split into two – just as Siwa pushed apart the great cosmic mountain and created Gunung Agung and Gunung Batur. There is a symbiotic relationship between these two sacred mountains: Gunung Agung is the male, Gunung Batur the female. Often, ceremonies propitiating the deities in the temple of one must be held in the other as well to complete the ritual.

In front of the cave is a statue of Hariti, a Buddhist demoness-cum-goddess. She used to devour children, then changed her ways to those of a good Buddhist, becoming the protector of children. This statue dates back 1,000

Entrance to Goa Gajah.

to tilt his head back, and so his eyes fell on the bestial head of the king. Dalem Bedulu was enraged by this act of defiance and wanted to kill Gajah Mada. Yet according to Balinese custom, one cannot disturb even one's enemy during a meal. One version of the story has it that the king literally burned up in a flaming rage at Gajah Mada's impudence. Another version, based more on historical evidence than whimsy, says that the king died of sadness after Gajah Mada's troops killed his beloved son. The Pejeng dynasty finally fell in 1343 to Majapahit forces.

Centuries prior to this, Bedulu was the center of another meeting at the **Pura Samuan Tiga**, which means the temple "of a meeting of three parties," and is at the junction of three roads coming together as well. During the reign of Queen Gunapriya Dharmapatni and King Udayana (988–1011), Balinese religion had no cohesiveness, no basic tenets to follow.

Instead, there were a number of separate sects, each with their own codifications of religious law. Small battles were beginning to break out, and the safety of the people was threatened. Therefore, six holy men (including the great Mpu Kuturan) gathered at Pura Samuan Tiga to try and simplify the existing religion. Out of this exceptional meeting emerged the key tenets of Balinese Hinduism today: the three elements of manifestation of Sanghyang Widi, or the Absolute God, being Siwa, Brahma and Wisnu; the triune temple system in each village; and the concept of *desa adat*.

Pejeng: There are literally hundreds of old shrines and sacred springs in Pejeng, and probably hundreds more waiting to be discovered.

One of the most impressive antiquities in this area – and in all of Indonesia for that matter – is the Moon of Pejeng, in the **Pura Penataran Sasih** (to the right, east, off the main road from Bedulu). Actually a large (190 cm/75 in) bronze kettle drum, the Moon of Pejeng dates back to Indonesia's Bronze Age, which began in 300 BC. It is the largest drum in the world to be cast as a single piece. Shaped like an hour glass,

the kettle drum is of a rare type decorated with eight stylized heads. Decorations on both the heads and body suggest that this kettle drum had its origins in northern Vietnam, dating back to Dong Son times. The Chinese rulers of northern Vietnam, or Tonkin, attempted a takeover of Vietnam in the early centuries, which led to indigenous revolts. It is theorized that the Tonkin aristocrats escaped to Southeast Asia, bringing with them, among other things, the kettle drums.

Why does this artifact carry the name Moon of Pejeng? Legend says that the drum used to be a wheel of the chariot that drives the moon on its nocturnal journey through the sky. This illuminated wheel fell from the heavens and landed in a tree near the Penataran Sasih temple, where it has been housed since. One night, a thief broke into the temple and was annoyed at the brilliant light that revealed his deeds. So he climbed a tree and peed on the wheel, whereby the wheel lost its shine and the man lost his life. Since then, no one has dared touch

Going to *odalan* festival.

182

the drum; it is kept locked up in this temple and given daily offerings. This temple was the main religious center of the old Pejeng kingdom, and therefore Balinese from all over the island make pilgrimages here.

Pura Arjuna Metapa (Temple Where Arjuna Meditated) is just south of Pura Pusering Jagat (Temple of the World's Navel). Arjuna is an epic hero throughout South and Southeast Asia, and a warrior supreme.

In this story, Arjuna is meditating on a mountain top, gathering up his energies for an upcoming battle with the evil ogre demon Niwata Kawaca. Pictured here with this divine hero are his two attendants, Tualen and Merdah, trusted servants who never leave his side. The gods test Arjuna's powers of concentration by sending down two celestial *bidedari*, or nymphs, to rouse him out of his ascetic state. But Arjuna is not disturbed by the celestial beauties and passes the gods' test, marrying the bidedari much later in heaven after he defeats the ogre king.

In **Pura Pusering Jagat** there are dancing figures called *catuhkaya,* statues carved with a figure on all four sides. Like the Pejeng giant, these are demonic with large, open eyes and sneering mouths.

The Pejeng Vessel, also called Naragiri, or Mountain of Man, is a remarkable cylindrical vessel that represents the "churning of the ocean" when the gods produced the elixir of immortality from the bottom of the sea.

Pura Kebo Edan (Temple of the Mad Bull) is in the rice fields south of **Intaran**. Take the first left (west) off the main road after arriving in Pejeng. On this site is a statue over three meters (11 ft) high, locally called the Pejeng Giant. Restored in 1952, this giant is a male figure in a dance posture standing on a wide-eyed human (perhaps a corpse). A stone mask covers his face, which curiously has no face of its own, only abstract designs, horns and fangs. Scholars say that this giant symbolizes Bhairava, a Tantric Buddhist manifestation of the Hindu god Siwa.

Temple relief, Pejeng.

EAST BALI

Neither as developed nor as rich as the southern part of the island, East Bali has a different ambience in its archaic rituals, lava-strewn landscapes and high, bare hills ribbed with ancient terracing. The coastal strip along the eastern shore consists primarily of coconut and banana groves, although it is rapidly turning into a tourist destination of its own. Coral is gathered for making into lime used in construction, but the coral reefs are being destroyed, which has caused irreparable erosion.

Partly hidden by the eastern coastal ranges is the colossal cone of Gunung Agung, which on clear days soars high above the countryside.

From Gianyar, follow the main road to Klungkung, which is the capital of the Klungkung regency. East of Klungkung, the landscapes are still blackened by the lava streams of the 1963 eruption, which isolated this area from visitors for several years. To see the east, it's better to plan a night or two in Manggis or Candi Dasa, and do it in two or three days – the first day to Klungkung and Besakih, and the second to Tenganan, the seacoast and other points in the Karangasem area.

Klungkung: As the seat of the Dewa Agung, nominally the highest of the old Balinese rajas, Klungkung holds a special place in the island's history and culture. As artistic centers, the palaces of Klungkung's rajas and noblemen supported and developed the styles of music, drama and the fine arts that flourish today.

The capital was shifted to Klungkung from nearby Gelgel in 1710, and a new palace built. Probably towards the end of that century, the original **Kerta Gosa**, or Hall of Justice, was erected. An exquisite example of the Klungkung style of painting and architecture, the present justice hall, at the town's main intersection, is beautifully laid out within its moat. Problems were brought here for resolution only if they could not be settled among families or individual villages, as the Kerta Gosa was the

island's highest court of justice, and by far the strictest.

The paintings here depict the story of *Bima Swarga* (Bima in Heaven). One of the great Pandawa heroes, Bima went looking for his parents in heaven and in hell. As the Balinese believe in reincarnation, they strongly believe in *karma phala*, whereby one is punished or rewarded for one's actions, either in this lifetime or a subsequent one. Therefore, if one were a miserly king in one lifetime, for example, then he might be a pauper in the next, so that he would learn about the true value of material wealth. These paintings show the good and bad consequences of our deeds. The style of these paintings is called *kamasan*, named after the village where this style of painting still exists; they date back to the eighteenth century.

The **Bale Kambang**, the Floating Pavilion, is likewise decorated, used by the attending royal family as a place to rest. Pan Semaris and Mangku Mura, both from Kamasan, directed the restoration of the paintings in 1945. This

Preceding pages: Eka Dasa Rudra, Pura Besakih. **Left,** Kerta Gosa, Klungkung. **Right,** salt extraction.

structure is all that is left of the old palace, which was destroyed by the Dutch during a fierce battle in 1908.

Two kilometers south, between Klungkung and Gelgel, lies the village of **Kamasan**, the present-day center of the kamasan style, which draws its main themes from Old Javanese classics; the figures look like *wayang* puppets.

In 1973, Nyoman Mandra started a painting school, where young artists imitate the master's stroke. Kamasan is also a famous center of gold and silver work. In the shops of Klungkung, one can buy modern and antique Klungkung-style paintings, carvings and silks.

Gelgel: For history buffs, a four-kilometer (2.5 mi) side trip south to Gelgel, the former capital, is recommended. In the 1400s and 1500s, the Dewa Agung (a title given to the current king of the time meaning, literally, Great God) of Gelgel held immense power. However, in the seventeenth century, with the decline of his power, he lost both battles as well as allegiances.

It was said that a curse had befallen the palace during the rule of Gusti Sideman. As a consequence, the palace was moved to Klungkung. However, small conflicts and jealousies broke out among the kings, causing many small rajadoms to emerge. The eight regencies of today are based upon the last eight kingdoms.

Pura Jero Agung, or Great Palace Temple, is the ancestral shrine of the local palace. Just to the east is another temple, **Pura Dasar**. Families of the royal caste from all over Bali come here for the temple festival.

Kusamba: Colorful outrigger *prahu* line the black-sand shores of Kusamba, a fishing village that also engages in salt-making. Kusamba lies directly across from Nusa Penida, an island of 40,000 people. The strait between Bali and Nusa Penida is filled with fish.

Twice a day, fishermen set out for Nusa Penida with cargoes of peanuts, fruit and rice; a dry island, Nusa Penida is only sparsely cultivated. The sailors of Kusamba boast that their large prahu can carry up to one and a half tons of

Left, Kusamba's black sand. Below, roadside greeting.

cargo. They also carry passengers who wish to visit the coral gardens and white-sand shores of Nusa Penida.

Where the road nears the sea, rows of brown, thatched roofs emerge from the sands. These huts are small factories for making salt. Wet sand is gathered from the sea and spread along sand banks on the beach. After drying, it is dumped into a large bin inside the hut. Slowly, a water with a high salt content drains through the sands, and is then poured in bamboo troughs to evaporate in the sun, leaving salt crystals. The entire process takes two days, and if the weather is good, the salt panner can make five kilograms (11 lbs) of salt, which he sells in the market of Klungkung.

Nusa Penida: A trip to this island is for the traveler who can appreciate out-of-the-way places lacking comforts. Originally a penal colony for the Klungkung kingdom, Nusa Penida remains a dry and austere place, and to the Balinese, it is an island of mystery and magic. The legendary sorcerer, Jero Gede Mecaling, is from here, sending his invisible hench-men to Bali to claim victims. The natives of this island are considered to be quite expert in black magic, and therefore are treated with great kindness by the Balinese. The way most inhabitants of Nusa Penida make their living is by fishing, trade and cultivating seaweed. There is little or no infrastructure on the island, although it is a fine place to hike. Ratu Gede Mecaling has his own temple, **Pura Peed** (pronounced *pehd*), three kilometers west of Toya Pakeh. On its day of *odalan*, Balinese from the mainland come to pay homage. Sebuluh waterfall, near Batu Madeg, is quite beautiful, as is the spring at Sakti.

To the northwest of Nusa Penida are two islands, **Nusa Lembongan** and **Nusa Ceningan**. Here, one can snorkel, dive, fish and surf; the main attractions are the stunning coral reefs. The easiest way to get here is to book in Kuta, or arrange a boat from Padang Bai, Kusamba, Sanur or Benoa.

Goa Lawah: The road continuing east from Kusamba runs parallel to lovely seascapes with a full view of Nusa

Outrigger to Nusa Penida.

Penida. It passes close to **Goa Lawah**, the walls of which vibrate with thousands of bats – their bodies packed so close together that the upper surface of the cave resembles undulating mud. An extraordinary phenomenon, Goa Lawah is considered holy, and a temple with shrines protects the entrance. The cave is said to extend all the way back to Pura Besakih, and may continue to an underground river that comes up, it is said, at Pura Goa within the Besakih complex. (Besakih is a temple associated with the mythological *naga* or serpent Basuki, who is also honored at Pura Goa Lawah, where a snake is supposed to live, feeding on the bats.)

Gunung Agung: According to mythology, when the deities made mountains for their thrones, they set the highest peak in the east, a compass point that is a place of honor to the Balinese. In every temple in Bali, a shrine is dedicated to the spirit of Gunung (Mount) Agung. The tapering form of cremation towers, *meru*, and even temple offerings bear the shape of a mountain, mirroring the people's reverence for this holy volcano. Here, on the slopes of Gunung Agung, lies **Pura Besakih** – the Mother Temple, so called as it houses ancestral shrines for all Hindu Balinese. A cluster of temples, Pura Besakih is the pinnacle of the sacred to the Balinese.

To get to Besakih, go east to Klungkung and then turn north, passing through the astonishing landscapes of **Bukit Jambul**. Once in the village of Besakih, climb up to the temple. Non-worshippers are not allowed into the temple, but can see the layout quite easily from the open gates. Do *not* enter into the temple grounds.

In February 1963, devotees of this temple were busily engaged with last preparations for the *Eka Dasa Rudra*, the greatest of Balinese sacrifices that occurs once every 100 years. Suddenly, a glow of fire shone from the crater and Gunung Agung began to rumble. A priestess interpreted the ashes of the volcano as a sacred portent sent to purify Besakih, and the people continued with their festival arrangements. By the

Bats at Goa Lawah.

time the great sacrifice was held in March, thick columns of dark smoke were surging from the summit. Shortly after, Gunung Agung exploded, destroying hundreds of homes and killing over a thousand people.

Westerners might say it was a remarkable coincidence, for the volcano had been dormant for centuries. To most Balinese, of course, the eruption did not occur by chance, but was chastisement for having offended the gods. The volcanic ash destroyed most of the crops on the island. The ceremony was held again in 1979, after priests decided that they had been wrong in their calculations.

Besakih originated most probably as a terraced sanctuary in the eighth century, where worship and offerings were made to the god of Gunung Agung. Over a period of a thousand years or more, it was enlarged until it grew into the present complex of over 80 temples, with 22 main temple complexes. Many of the structures were added from the fourteenth through the eighteenth centuries. According to inscriptions kept here, an important event of some sort took place here in 1007. It can only be guessed that this was associated with death rituals for Queen Mahendradatta, Udayana's co-ruler who died the previous year. In the fifteenth century, it was the state temple of the Gelgel-Klungkung dynasty, which built a series of small temples in honor of its deified rulers. Now, it is the state temple for the provincial and national governments, which cover all the temple's expenses.

Within the Besakih complex, the paramount sanctuary is **Pura Panataran Agung**, with its lofty meru on a high bank of terraces. Steps ascend in a long perspective to the austere split gate. Inside the main courtyard are the three shrines enthroning the three aspects of God: *Siwa*, God as creation; *Pramasiwa*, god without form; and *Sadasiwa*, God as half male and half female. Many interpret this trinity to be Wisnu (Vishnu), Brahma and Siwa. Three sacred colors are associated with this shrine: red, black and white. Red symbolizes the earth as lava and is associ-

Meru at Pura Besakih.

ated with Brahma; white is light and is associated with Siwa; black is both water and heaven and is associated with Wisnu. During festivals, the shrines are wrapped in colored cloth. Often one will see yellow as well, which symbolizes compassion.

Besakih's main temple festival is held in the fourth lunar month of the Balinese calendar (March or April), in a ritual called *Bhatara Turun Kabeh* (The Gods All Descend Together). Balinese from all over the island come during this month-long festival to pay homage to their gods and deified ancestors.

Besakih can be reached from both the south and the east. Usually visitors come through Klungkung, continuing north. A nice trip is this northern route, and then continuing east through Selat. One can then continue on to the coast through Bebandem, or turn right after Selat and return to Klungkung. Either road offers spectacular views of terraced rice fields.

Taking the eastern route (left at Rendang) provides a chance to explore seldom-visited villages of the beautiful east. One of the first villages is **Muncan**, where a unique ritual occurs the day before *Nyepi* (mid-March), the Day of Silence. Here, Jero Ding and Jero Dong – represented by two tree trunks, one with a natural hole in it, the other with a protruding stick attached to it – are used to re-enact an old fertility ritual. After they have been mated, the figures are taken to the river, where they are discarded; it is believed that the surrounding rice fields are fertilized by this river water after this ritual. Beyond Selat, make a right turn southwards.

Iseh, a mountain village where people grow rice and onions, was chosen in 1932 by the German artist Walter Spies as a site for a country house, which has an uninterrupted view of Gunung Agung. The massive slope is cut by deep ravines, forming serpentine shadows descending to a wide valley of rice fields. Hues vary from luminous yellow to the opulent light green of mature rice, to red-stemmed stalks before harvest.

A little further south is **Sideman**, where every household is engaged in

Village girls prepare for temple dance.

some aspect of textile weaving. This is one of the centers of *ikat* weaving, and from the road, one can hear the *click-click-click* of looms. *Songket* cloth (cotton and silk with an overweft of silver or gold threads) is also produced here.

There are four home-stays here, each owned by one of the four wives of the local prince. If looking for an isolated place to stay, to stroll through the rice fields and drink in the view, then this is it. Another unique aspect about this village is a school of cultural arts. Here, adolescent students can study traditional literature, painting, dance, music, and Balinese language, in addition to the regular school work.

Backtrack north and make a right at the main road. Turn right at the turn-off for **Putung**, a lookout point that also has small bungalows and a restaurant. A little further on the main road leads to **Sibetan**, home of the famous *salak*, a small and tart fruit with a snakeskin-like outer peel.

Padang Bai: To the east, a perfectly-shaped bay is cradled in the hills. The harbor of Padang Bai is the main port of transit to the neighboring island of Lombok, with passenger and cargo vessels departing each morning. International shipping lines making stopovers in Padang Bai anchor to the left of the bay; visitors and cargo are ferried to the pier. An area enclosed by white-sand coves and turquoise sea, the small harbor makes a good visit for yachts sailing to Bali. There are a few bed-and-breakfast places here, and the beach is fine for playing the complete beach bum.

The history of this coastal village is connected with those eventful years that saw the deaths of Mahendradatta and Udayana, at the beginning of the eleventh century. At that time, a priest of great stature, Kuturan, lived here, now remembered for his reforms of Padang Bai's organization. **Pura Silayukti** at Padang Bai was built on the site of his former hermitage, sometime around the eleventh century.

Manggis: Named after the delectable mangosteen fruit, Manggis is primarily a fishing village; some of the best *prahu* are made here. Down the road, **Balina Beach** now boasts a few high-class hotels, along with lower budget losmen. Take the turn-off to the right for **Puri Buitan**. The sparkling white-sand beach is inviting and unspoiled by art shops and beach vendors.

For a quiet, relaxing spell at the beach, stop in **Sengkidu**. Here, there are a couple of losmen on the beach, along with a fancy, sterile hotel. Erosion has not been as bad here, and at low tide, one can stroll the beach.

Tenganan: Further east is the turn-off for Tenganan, a Bali Aga village. Even though there are numerous Bali Aga villages scattered around the northern part of Bali, the most famous is here in Tenganan, near Candi Dasa. Within the bastions, all living compounds are identical in plan and are arranged in rows on either side of the wide, stone-paved lanes that run the length of the village.

There is some evidence that the people of Tenganan originally came from the village of Bedulu. The legend of how they acquired their land dates from the fourteenth century: the mighty King

A few scattered ducks.

Dalem Bedulu lost his favorite horse, and so sent the villagers of his kingdom in all directions to search for it. The men of Tenganan traveled east and found the corpse of the horse. When the king offered to reward them, they requested the land where the horse was found, that is, all the area in which the carcass of the dead horse could be smelled. The king sent an official with a keen sense of smell to partition the land.

For days, the chief of Tenganan led the official through the hills, yet still the air was pungent with the odor of the dead horse. At last, the tired official decided this was enough land and departed. After he had left, the Bali Aga chief pulled from his clothing a smelly remnant of the horse's flesh.

Tenganan still owns, communally, these larger tracts of well-cultivated land and is one of the richest villages on the island. Traditionally, the men of the *krama desa*, or elders' association, were not permitted to work in the fields with their own hands. So they hired out their land to men of neighboring villages.

The aristocratic Tenganese went to the fields chiefly to collect *tuak*, a popular palm wine. The women of this village weave the famous "flaming" cloth, *kamben geringsing*, which supposedly has the power to immunize the wearer against evil. Through double ikat, an intricate process of weaving and dyeing known only in Tenganan, a single cloth can take up to five years to complete. Only the finest geringsing pieces are worn by Tenganan people, for ceremonial dress. The imperfect ones are sold, since they are much in demand throughout Bali. A large piece can cost well over a thousand dollars.

During ceremonies here – the most spectacular occurring in January and June – girls from the age of two wrap their bodies in silk, don multicolored scarves and flowered crowns of beaten gold. The geringsing cloth tends to shimmer in the sunlight. Men play the *gamelan selunding*, an archaic orchestra of iron-keyed metallophones, which are only allowed to be played at specific ceremonies. The National Arts College **Guest houses, Candi Dasa.**

has made a replica, and young composers have adapted the traditional melodies to make up their own "fusion" music. Gamelan selunding accompanies the *rejang* dance, a ritual-offering dance composed of slow, elegant and simple movements.

The Fight of the Pandanus Leaves, at Tenganan, takes place only once a year during a festival called *Usaba Sambah*. To the accompaniment of the sacred gamelan selunding, two men – each with a round, plaited shield – attack each other with bunches of bound pandanus leaves, with thorns down either side of the leaf. The favorite tactics are to rush and clench the opponent. The clench has one disadvantage, however. While one man rubs this thorny weapon across his opponent's back, he is rather open to the same treatment. After battles, wounds are treated with a mixture of tumeric and vinegar, which leaves no scars. During this festival, creaky ferris wheels are set up on the rising terraces of the village. The unmarried girls of the village are turned in these as part of

Palace at Ujung, 1930s.

ancient rites; the turning represents the unification of the earth with the sun.

Candi Dasa: Just past Tenganan is Candi Dasa, not a village at all, but a resort area that has seen drastic development in the past five years. Most of the accommodations here are at the low end of the scale, although there are a few upscale hotels and more are being built. Further east is less densely packed.

The beach at Candi Dasa has been marred by T-form jetties protruding into the water, intended to stop the erosion from years of coral blasting. These structures make it impossible to walk more than 50 meters on the beach, once a truly lovely landscape. In any case, now the beach is only visible at low tide.

For serious students of culture, a visit to Ibu Gedong's **Gandhian Ashram** is suggested. Started in the 1970s as a self-sufficient community based on Gandhian principles, the *ashram* was once the only structure along this isolated beach. There are now bungalows for rent, or one can stay in simpler accommodations while volunteering

here. (There are strict rules on behavior.)

Just east of Candi Dasa lies the village of **Bugbug**, more like a Bali Aga village in structure. Here, once every two years on the full moon of the fourth month (October), *Perang Dewa* (War of the Gods) takes place on top of a hill. Villagers from four surrounding villages gather here, carrying offerings of suckling pig, which they hang in the trees. They also bring their gods (as *pratima*), which then battle each other; many of the men go into trance during the ritual.

Amlapura: Crossing a wide, solidified lava flow that is slowly being brought back to cultivation (this area was ravaged by the volcanic eruption in 1963), the road enters Amlapura, the main town of Karangasem regency.

The former kingdom, founded during the weakening of the Gelgel dynasty late in the seventeenth century, became, in the late eighteenth and early nineteenth centuries, the most powerful state in Bali. **Puri Agung Karangasem** long served as the residence of these kings, who extended their domain across the

eastern straits to Lombok. During the Dutch conflict at the turn of the century, the raja of Karangasem cooperated with the European army and was allowed to retain his title and autocratic powers. **Puri Kanginan**, the palace where the last raja was born, is a twentieth-century creation of designs from Europe, China and Bali.

The main building, with a large veranda, is called *Bale London*, as its furniture bears the royal crest of England. The wooden paneling appears to be Chinese, while *Ramayana* reliefs, on the adjacent tooth-filing pavilion, retain a Balinese flavor.

The photograph over the entrance to Bale London portrays the late king, Anak Agung Anglurah Ketut, whose pleasure it was to make fantastic moats and pools. Eight kilometers (5 mi) south, on the beach at **Ujung**, he helped design a palace with a moat, opened in 1921. Unfortunately, two earthquakes – in 1963 and 1978 – destroyed most of the standing structures. The lack of funds has kept it in ruins.

In 1948, he built **Tirtagangga** (6 km/ 4 mi north on the road to Culik) as a retreat, with a series of pools decorated with unusual statuary. Tirtagangga, with its commanding hilltop view of the surrounding rice fields and its isolation, is a wonderful place to spend a few days. Accommodations and fare are simple, but the mountain air and the fresh-fed swimming pools are refreshing.

Seraya, a village perched on the slopes of Gunung Seraya (l,175 m/3,855 ft), offers a fabulous view of Lombok. Further on, after a long and tortuous drive, is **Amed**, a small fishing village that also has excellent snorkeling.

Tulamben: Some of the most spectacular scenery is to be found in the regency of Karangasem. One can continue up north through Culik and on to Tulamben, with the scenery drastically changing to dry hills covered with scrub. Diving or snorkeling is good at the site of the USS *Liberty* shipwreck. Diving and snorkeling gear are available for rent and teachers can be hired. One can drive up around the seacoast to Singaraja, but check road conditions first.

Left, Pools of Tirtagangga. Right, morning market.

NORTH TO BATUR

A complex of rock-hewn *candi* and monks' cells, **Gunung Kawi** overlooks the Pakrisan River, in a valley near Tampaksiring. There are 10 candi in all – the main group of five on the east of the river, a group of four west of the river, and one by itself at the southern end of the valley.

Legend has it that Kebo Iwa, the powerful prime minister for the king of Bedulu, was a man magically-endowed, carving out all the monuments with his fingernails. Dating back to the eleventh century, the candi are remarkably preserved. People mistakenly say that the candi at Gunung Kawi are tombs, but that is not correct. Rather, they are monuments commemorating the royal family of the Udayana dynasty, or at least that is what the latest research indicates.

In Bali, the development of royal funeral cults – in which kings, queens and consorts were deified after death – began around the eleventh century.

One theory says that the main group of five candi honored Udayana, his queen Mahendradatta, his concubine and his two sons, Marakata and Anak Wungsu. Another theory suggests they honored Anak Wungsu (king of Bali in the eleventh century) and his royal wives, with the next group of four candi enshrining his concubines. The 10th candi, which stands alone, honors a high official.

Tampaksiring: The sacred spring of **Tirta Empul**, in Tampaksiring, is revered by all Balinese. They say that it was created by the god Indra when he pierced the earth to create a spring of *amerta*, the elixir of immortality (and with which he revived his forces who were poisoned by the evil king Mayadanawa). Be that as it may, the bathing place was built under the rule of Sri Candrabhaya Singha Warmadewa in the tenth century.

The waters are believed to have magical curative powers, and every year, people journey from all over Bali to purify themselves in the clear pools. After leaving a small offering of thanks to the deity of the spring, men and women go to opposite sides to bathe. (Please remember that it is offensive and rude to photograph the Balinese while they are bathing.)

On the full moon of the fourth month (October), the villagers from nearby Manukaya bring a sacred stone, which is housed in the Pura Sakenan, in Manukaya, to be cleansed at Tirta Empul. Early this century, the old inscriptions on this stone were deciphered for the first time by a Dutch archaeologist. The inscriptions read that on the anniversary of the construction of Tirta Empul, falling on the full moon of Kartika (the fourth month), the stone would be purified at the wells. It was dated AD 962. The villagers had been performing this ritual for over a thousand years without having been aware of the meaning on the inscriptions.

South of Tirta Empul, on a line that joins it with Gunung Kawi, is **Pura Mengening**. There is a definite connection between Tirta Empul, Gunung Kawi, and Pura Mengening. At the lat-

Preceding pages: temple idol. **Left**, Rangda image at village pura dalem. **Right**, temple stone carving.

opposite Trunyan at Toya Bungkah, are hot springs, which the locals use for bathing. Few people bathe in the lake itself, although it is not forbidden.

There are a number of starting points down by the hot springs for climbing Batur; the journey takes less than three hours round-trip. (From Purajati, two hours.) Leave quite early in the morning so as not to get heatstroke, and wear sunscreen; there are plenty of guides waiting to take visitors up.

Formerly, the people of this area lived relatively unperturbed at the base of the volcano. In 1917, Batur violently erupted, destroying 65,000 homes and 2,500 temples, and taking more than a thousand lives. Lava engulfed the village of **Batur**, but miraculously stopped at the foot of the village temple itself. The people took this as a good omen and continued to live there. In 1926, a new eruption buried the entire temple except the highest shrine, dedicated to the goddess of the lake. The villagers were then forced to resettle on the high cliffs overlooking Batur. They brought the surviv-

ing shrine with them and began rebuilding the temple, **Pura Ulun Danu Batur**.

An ambitious project, the majority of the 285 planned shrines of the temple are yet to be completed. Two august gateways, severe in contrast to the elaborate split gates of South Bali, open onto spacious courtyards laid with black gravel. Rows of meru towers silhouette against the sky, in full view of the smoking volcano.

The *bale gedong*, a storehouse of precious relics, contains a bell of solid gold. As the story goes, the bell was presented to the treasury of the temple by a king of Singaraja in atonement for his having insulted the deities. There is also a *gamelan gong gede* here, which accompanies the stately sacred dances of the *baris gede* and the *rejang* during the grand temple festival here.

The ritual in this temple is closely linked with the veneration of Danau Batur (Lake Batur) and supplication for the blessing of irrigation water. Here, once a year, heads of all the local subak gather to discuss the distribution of water **Danau Batur.**

to their rice lands, and to pay homage to Dewi Danau, goddess of the lake, and her consort Wisnu, who rules over water. The mountain lakes help regulate the flow of water to the fields and villages through the many natural springs lower down the slope.

Bali Aga: The mountain areas are known as the home of the Bali Aga villages – places relatively untouched by Hinduism, and where ancestral rites take precedence. Here, the arts are not as developed, and ceremonies tend to be simpler. In the Batur area, **Trunyan**, across the lake, is perhaps the most well-known Bali Aga village, named after a *taru menyan* (fragrant tree), which grows in the cemetery outside the village. There is no cremation here, and the cemetery is where the dead are left for vultures to feast upon. According to Trunyanese, the bodies do not decompose normally and there is no odor of rotting flesh, due to the fact that they are placed under this sacred tree.

The Trunyanese have been isolated for centuries from mainstream Balinese, and are quite reticent about sharing their culture. Secretive and protective about the customs exclusive to their community, the people keep hidden Bali's largest statue – four meters (13 ft) high and of Ratu Gede Pancering Jagat, patron guardian of the village. Once a year, the Berutuk ritual is performed for him, where dancers dress in coconut-husk masks and shredded palm and banana leaves. They represent a group of witches who follow Ratu Gede Pancering Jagat.

To get to Trunyan, take a boat from Kedisan (set the round-trip price beforehand) or Toya Bungkah, or else walk around the lake in a rather long journey. Trunyan is also one of the few villages in Bali where begging is condoned; as soon as visitors step off the boat, villagers beg for money. Most domestic and foreign tourists avoid going to Trunyan, as it is not what one would call a pleasant excursion.

Kintamani: Inscriptions from the tenth century indicate that Kintamani – a high mountain district that takes its name from the ancient, wind-blown town at 1,500 meters (4,920 ft) – was one of the earliest known kingdoms in Bali. Every third morning, on *pasah* of the Balinese calendar, the main street becomes a bazaar for all the surrounding villages. There are several losmen for an overnight stay while exploring the area.

Penulisan: The main road continues its ascent to a hillside in the clouds, where the symbol of modern civilization, Bali's television aerial, claims its place beside a long flight of steps rising to the mountain sanctuary of **Pura Tegeh Koripan**. The highest temple in Bali at 1,745 meters (5,725 ft), Pura Tegeh Koripan is actually a complex of temples at which a circle of surrounding villages worship. The sparsely-adorned *bale* shelter sculptures of kings, queens and divinities, and lingga. Several statues bear dates of the eleventh century, and another of the fifteenth century.

On a clear day, the view from Penulisan encompasses half the island, from the crest of Gunung Bratan in West Bali to the Java Sea. A paved road at **Sukawana** leads to Pinggan, on the north side of the crater.

Highland produce, Kintamani.

NORTH BALI

On the other side of the volcanic peaks from the populous south, the scenery is drastically different. Instead of terraced rice fields, there are orchards of citrus fruits, vanilla, coffee and cocoa, and fields of strawberries. The latest cash crop is red grapes, which thrive in the dry heat of Buleleng regency. The countryside is golden in the north, due to the scarcity of rain.

The feudal rule of local rajas in North Bali ended in 1848, when the Dutch gained control here 60 years prior to control in the south. Many descendants of the rajas became officials for the Dutch, and as a result of the European influence, the way of life in North Bali is more Westernized than in most of the communities in the south.

In Singaraja, the former Dutch capital, the *banjar* system of communal responsibility is not so institutionalized; instead, the social order centers more around the individual family. Nor is the caste system so stringent as it is in the south, where the aristocracy continued to rule until 1908.

The art of North Bali is also distinctive. The intricate sandstone carving found in the southern temples is more restrained than that of the northern temples, where tall gates have a dynamic, flaming ascendancy and are covered with luxurious designs.

The pink sandstone that is used in the north, and which is quarried near Singaraja, is extremely soft, enabling the northern carvers to give full vent to their creative imaginations, an advantage that often leads to humorous Rabelaisian scenes. Burlesque caricatures of well-fed European officials appear in cartoon reliefs along the walls of some northern temples.

Offerings here differ and are not as elaborate as in other parts of the island. The holy days of Galungan and Kuningan don't achieve the same intensity as in the south. Instead, the holy day of Pagerwesi is more venerable a day to the northerners.

Singaraja: From the highest point on the road from the south over the mountains, 1,220 meters (4,000 ft) above sea level, a spectacular descent ends on the northern coast at Singaraja, capital of Buleleng regency. A strip of land that stretches along the whole northern coast of Bali, Buleleng is open to the sheltered waters of the Java Sea.

Throughout history, Buleleng has indeed been more open than the rest of Bali to the world. A province before and after Majapahit conquest, Buleleng rose to prominence at the beginning of the seventeenth century under Raja Panji Sakti, who conquered the eastern tip of Java, among other successes. In 1604, he built a new palace called Singaraja, on fields where the grain known as *buleleng* was grown.

In 1814, a British military expedition stayed several months in Singaraja. The British left, and then the Dutch came, at first with demands, and later bearing arms and accusing the rajas of raiding wrecked ships. First attempts of the Dutch to subdue the north ended in

Preceding pages: grapes going to market, Lovina. Left, black sands of Lovina. Right, cocoa plant.

defeat. After a long, fierce battle in 1849, a reinforced expedition captured the Buleleng stronghold of Jagaraga.

The Dutch imposed direct colonial rule upon Buleleng and Jembrana in 1882. Singaraja became the capital and chief port, and was the colonial government seat for the old Lesser Sunda province until 1953.

As an important shipping center, Singaraja has a cosmopolitan flavor about it. The population of 150,000 comprises many ethnic and religious groups, and it is not unusual to see an Islamic procession pass before a Chinese temple flanked by office buildings of European design. The city houses a historical library, **Gedong Kirtya**, on Jalan Veteran. The library is the storehouse of some 3,000 Balinese manuscripts, including *lontar* – leaves of the lontar palm cut in strips and preserved between two pieces of precious wood, or even bamboo. Subjects covered in these ancient works include literature, mythology, historical chronicles and religious treatises. Some works are rela-

tively new, while others are almost a millennium old, although they have been constantly recopied. Miniature pictures, incised on the leaves with an iron stylus, are masterpieces in the art of illustration. *Prasasti*, metal plates inscribed with royal edicts of the early Pejeng-Bedulu dynasty, are among the earliest written documents found in Bali.

South of Singaraja is **Gitgit**, a splendid waterfall and a good place to kick back. You'll need your own transportation to get there, as it's about 10 kilometers (6 mi) south of Singaraja, on the road to Bedugul.

Sangsit: East of Singaraja are some of the finest examples of northern Balinese temples. Instead of the small shrines and *meru* towers of southern temples, a single pedestal built on a terraced stone base furnishes the inner courtyard. Often, the pedestal supports a *padmasana*, throne of the sun god, and sacred places to store relics and serve as a resting place for deities during temple festivals.

Compared with the classical lines of southern decoration, North Balinese

Northern Bali temple style.

carving is forcefully baroque. Every crevice of the temple proper is gaily carved in curves, flames, arabesques and spirals, cascading a light ebullience nearly everywhere.

Pura Beji in Sangsit is a *subak* (irrigation association) temple dedicated to Dewi Sri as Ratu Manik Galih, the goddess of rice. Built in the fifteenth century, this temple sports many *naga*, symbols of earth and fertility. Naga snakes form the balustrade of the fine gateway, and fantastic but imaginary beasts and devilish guardians peer from the entangled flora, their heads deliberately cocked at an angle to throw the facade slightly off balance. Jawless birds, fierce tigers and sunflowers project from every part of the pedestal. Rows of stone towers jut up from the terraces, forming a labyrinth of pink sandstone. To counterbalance the overpowering decor, the courtyard is spacious and decorated with a few frangipani trees.

Jagaraga: This village is famous for a bloody battle between the Balinese and the Dutch, in 1849. However, its main attraction today is its **Pura Dalem**, where Siwa (Shiva) in his manifestation as dissolver presides. Here, reliefs portray two smug Europeans in a Ford Model T taken unaware by an armed bandit, flying aces in aircraft plunging into the sea, and a Dutch steamer signaling an SOS upon being attacked by a crocodilian sea monster. Even the wicked Rangda and fertility statues – a dazed mother buried under a pile of children – are skillfully hewn with a delightful sense of humor.

To the south is **Sawan**, a village with a gamelan gong-casting industry, a talented bamboo *gamelan angklung* orchestra, and an interesting night market.

Kubutambahan: Along the main road further east is **Pura Maduwe Karang**, a temple dedicated to dry-land (as opposed to wet-irrigation) agriculture. It was built in 1890 and has many fertility themes, including erotic portrayals of love. Outside the temple are statues depicting characters from the *Ramayana*. Pura Meduwe Karang literally means Temple of the Owner of the

Pura Beji, Sangsit.

WEST BALI

The western districts of Tabanan and Mengwi were once powerful and warring rajadoms. The days of absolute rule by the rajas ended with the Dutch conquest of southern Bali, in 1908. Unlike the raja of Karangasem, however, the raja of Tabanan did not have an agreement with the Dutch, and so lost the rights to his lands, which were then redistributed among the councils of individual villages. Now with their own land, the communities thrived, and Tabanan is today a prosperous area, due almost entirely to its fertile rice land.

Although the rajas were deprived by the Dutch of political power, they remained leaders among their people. Palaces continued to serve as centers of the arts, and royal families retained their essential role of presiding over devotions at temples. Residents throughout Mengwi still participate in the *odalan* at Pura Taman Ayun, the old kingdom's state temple. In jungles near the peak of the volcano Batukau lies the mountain sanctuary of Pura Luhur, also a royal temple. The gigantic forests that surround the sanctuary are uninhabitable wilderness, yet thousands have journeyed there to pay homage.

The western uplands of Batukau are famed for magnificent landscapes. The view from the mountain village of **Jatiluwih** takes in the whole of southern Bali. Perched on a high terraced slope, Jatiluwih deserves its name – Truly Marvelous.

The central mountains extend to the western tip of Bali, rising through the darkest and most mysterious regions of the island, now a national wilderness park. Here dwell the ghosts of Pulaki, a legendary city destined to sink into the earth. Deer, crocodile and wild hogs roam these dense bushlands. Some even say the last tiger of Bali stalks here, though no one has seen it for some years. The Balinese starling, on the verge of extinction, makes this forest its home.

Kapal: The most important temple in this area is **Pura Sada**, an ancestral

sanctuary honoring the deified spirit of Ratu Sakti Jayengrat, whose identity remains uncertain. The temple's original foundation may be as old as the twelfth century. The temple itself was rebuilt during Majapahit times by one of the early kings of Mengwi, perhaps in the sixteenth century. The oldest of the Mengwi state shrines, predating Pura Taman Ayun, Pura Sada was destroyed in the great earthquake of 1917 and restored in 1950. A large brick *prasada*, ornamented with modern statues, dominates the complex. Seven saints adorn the body of this structure, and at the top are the nine gods – the lords of the eight directions and of the center.

There are two versions of what the temple's 54 stone seats represent. They are the wives and concubines of the king, or else they are the retainer servants of three royal leaders.

Canggu and Seseh: If following the road from Dauh Pangkung, just south of Kapal, toward the beach, turn right at Klutulang to Seseh, a black-sand dune that currently sports a tiny shrine to the

Preceding pages: Pura Ulun Danu Bratan. <u>Left</u>, harvesting the rice. <u>Right</u>, rare Bali starling.

memory of Ratu Mas Sepuh. This extremely powerful and charismatic man came from Blambangan, Java, centuries ago and was famous for his magical abilities. (It is said he could pop corn and fry eyes with only his clothing.) The raja of Mengwi was alarmed by his popularity and so had him murdered. After that, apparently, the royal houses of Mengwi were plagued with bad luck. At the turn of this century, the raja went to the grave of Ratu Mas Sepuh, begged forgiveness and built the current mausoleum, where all people from Mengwi now come to pray – and the palace's luck has changed for the better.

Mengwi: A turn-off toward the mountain leads to the principality of Mengwi, which, until 1891, was the center of a powerful kingdom going back to the Gelgel dynasty, whose kings continue to be venerated in temples of Mengwi, in particular, **Pura Taman Ayun**.

Taman Ayun was founded by the raja of Mengwi, I Gusti Agung Anom, in the seventeenth century. The small doors of the shrines here are beautifully carved.

The surrounding moat gives the impression of a garden sanctuary in the middle of a pond, explaining the name *taman*, or garden. This temple is a *penyawangan*, or place to worship other sacred sites or temples. Here are shrines to Bali's mountain peaks of Agung, Batukau, Batur and Pengelengan, as well as to Pura Ulun Siwi and Pura Sada. There are three main courtyards that represent the three realms of the earth spirits, humans and the gods. The entire complex symbolizes the holy mountain of Mahameru floating in a sea of milk.

Across from the temple is the **Manusa Yadnya Museum**, where ritual artifacts used in life-cycle rites are on display. The most interesting are the cremation tower and wooden bull sarcophagus. One can also charter performances of *kecak* and other Balinese dances here.

Sangeh: Rawana, the villainous giant of the *Ramayana* epic, could die neither on earth nor in air. To kill him, the monkey general Hanuman devised a plan to suffocate the giant by pressing him between two halves of the Hindu

Sculpture, Pura Sada.

holy mountain, Mahameru, a destruction between the earth and air. When Hanuman took Mahameru, part of the mountain fell to the earth in Sangeh, along with a group of monkeys from his army, whose descendants remain on the island to this day.

Such is the legendary origin of the Bukit Sari **monkey forest**, a cluster of towering trees and home of hundreds of rude monkeys. The forest is sacred, and for many years, no one was permitted to chop wood there. A moss-covered temple lies in the heart of the woods, a familiar hideout for the nimble inhabitants. Peanuts are sold to feed the monkeys, but be sure to keep items such as glasses, dangling earrings and cameras out of temptation's way. These monkeys are tourist-savvy, and they demand considerable remuneration for their antics.

Pura Bukit Sari was originally built during the seventeenth century as an agricultural temple. It has been restored several times, most recently in 1973. In the central courtyard, a large statue of a garuda, an old carving of uncertain date, symbolizes freedom from suffering and the attainment of *amerta*, the elixir of life. The forest of surrounding nutmeg trees was presumably planted deliberately a long time ago, and is a unique grove in Bali.

A separate route linking Sangeh directly with Denpasar begins at Jalan Kartini, a short trip. A side-road joins Blahkiuh, just south of Sangeh, with Mengwi, which can also be reached by returning to Denpasar and heading west. An asphalt road, in stages of repair and disrepair, links Sangeh with Ubud.

A number of roads run north and south through the western part of Bali. North from Taman Ayun is the village of Marga, important historically and socially to the Balinese.

Marga: In 1946, the commander of Indonesian troops in Bali, Lt. Col. I Gusti Ngurah Rai, and his company of guerrilla fighters were killed in the Battle of Marga. Surrounded and outnumbered by Dutch forces, and under bombardment from the air, the small band of 94 men refused to surrender. They attacked the enemy positions and died to the last man – a *puputan* reminiscent of the royal puputan carried out 40 years earlier, also in defiance to the Dutch. In Marga there stands a monument honoring these soldiers, inscribed with a famous letter written by Ngurah Rai refusing surrender until the cause was won. A Heroes' Day is held on the anniversary of Ngurah Rai's death, 20 November, where many of Bali's finest musicians and dancers perform to pay tribute, and Bali's international airport and a university are named in his honor.

Bedugul: Leaving the southern plains, the landscape changes from flowing tiers of rice to motley patches of onion, cabbage and papaya growing in the cool climate of the highlands. The clusters of farmhouses along the way are no longer the familiar thatched huts of the south, but instead are sturdy cottages made of wood and tile to withstand the steady downpour of heavy rains. The earth, saturated by mountain streams, is smothered with thick moss and creepers. The road climbs and winds its way around

Coconut cooler.

steep cliffs covered with ferns, wild flowers and elephant grass.

Up into the mountains, the air becomes clearer, crisper and cooler. Bedugul lies 1,300 meters (4,300 ft) above sea level. Bedugul is the name of both a small town and mountain lake resort area, which for decades locals have used for weekend retreats.

In jungle terrain lies the serene **Danau Bratan**, a lake often veiled with mist and filling the ancient crater of **Gunung Bratan**, in Candi Kuning. Because the lake is an essential water source for surrounding farmlands, the people of Bedugul honor Dewi Danau, goddess of the lake, in the temple Ulun Danu, on a small promontory on the lake. It is peaceful and cool.

Near Bedugul is the market of **Bukit Munggu**, popularly called Candi Kuning, where wild orchids and brilliant lilies are sold, along with temperate and tropical vegetables grown in the fertile soil here.

Just south of the market is a **botanical garden**. This is a sprawling lawn filled with local and imported species of flora, but it is not an admirable cross-section of the flowers and trees of Indonesia. Just past Pancasari is the Bali Handara Kosaido Country Club, with one of the most magnificent 18-hole championship golf courses in the world. There is also a hotel and restaurant on the country club grounds.

Returning south to the town of Tabanan, turn west at Pacung and stop at the town of **Penebel**. This mountain village has a *pura puseh* with a *lingga-yoni,* an ancient fertility symbol of both a penis and vagina, representing Siwa and his consort Uma.

Tabanan: Together with Badung and Gianyar, the district of Tabanan forms the island's most prosperous region – the rice belt of the southern plains. Kept in impeccable order by the *subak* associations, the fertile fields stretch from the foothills of Batukau volcano to the south coast. Farmers adhere to no special season for planting and harvesting; cycles of growth vary with individual plots, and planting continues throughout the year.

Tabanan became a separate and powerful kingdom during the shake-up of political domains in the seventeenth century. It has long been the home of famous gamelan orchestras and dancers, among them the great male dancer I Ketut Mario. Born at the end of the nineteenth century, he was already dancing at the age of six. Somewhat later, he developed and perfected the spectacular solo dances of *kebyar duduk* and *kebyar trompong*, which began in northern Bali during World War I. Mario's grace and movement enraptured European audiences who saw him dance in the 1930s. When Mario was shown his photograph in Covarrubias' book, he exclaimed, "That man is a good dancer. How is it that I have never seen him?" and laughed with amazed delight to discover it was himself.

Tabanan, like the capitals of the other regencies, is left behind by Denpasar. However, it is a spirited town, its shops in the hands of Chinese merchants.

From Tabanan, head southwest to this region's most famous, and most photo- **Temple shrines.**

graphed, temple. At the crossroads of Kediri, a side road branches to the sea, ending on a green hill sloping down to the beach, and to the remarkable temple of **Pura Tanah Lot**, balanced on a huge rock offshore. Set apart from the land by a stone basin, the rock has been carved by incoming tides. Tanah Lot, with its solitary black towers and tufts of foliage spilling over the cliffs, recalls the delicacy of a Chinese painting. In one of the shrines, just outside the temple, dwell two striped sacred snakes, discreetly left undisturbed by Balinese.

Erosion along the base of the temple forced the government to build concrete reinforcements, which have marred the beauty of this much-photographed holy spot. Only worshippers are allowed into the temple, but visitors can get a dramatic view from the adjacent hill, particularly fine at sunset.

Although a small sanctuary, Pura Tanah Lot is linked to a series of sea temples along Bali's south coast: Pura Sakenan, Pura Uluwatu, Pura Rambut Siwi and Pura Petitenget. These tem-

Pura Tanah Lot.

ples are related to the principal mountain sanctuaries: Besakih at Gunung Agung, Pura Batur at Gunung Batur and Pura Luhur at Gunung Batukau.

The upland temples are for the veneration of the deities associated with mountains and mountain lakes, while rituals at the sea temples include homage to the guardian spirits of the sea. These main temples are often listed with the Sad Kahayangan, the six holy "national" temples, which exact tribute from all Balinese.

The chronicles attribute the temple at Tanah Lot to the sixteenth-century priest Nirartha Danghyang. During his travels, he saw a light emanating from a point on the west coast. When he came to this spot, he stopped and meditated. A local spiritual leader's followers became entranced with Nirartha and began studying with him. This so angered the local priest that he challenged Nirartha. Not to be bothered, Nirartha simply moved the spot upon which he was meditating to the middle of the ocean, and it became known as Tanah Lot, or Land in

the Middle of the Sea. Returning back to Kediri, stop in at **Pejaten** village, famous for its pottery. Built with foreign-aid money, the factory was opened to train the local youth. It is now a booming industry.

Tabanan's coast is developing into tourist resorts, even though the coastal waters are quite rough and dangerous, and there is little reef to protect the beach. At the end of every side road to the coast lies a long, deserted black-sand beach, with surf that sometimes breaks over three meters high.

The undertow and currents here can be quite treacherous, and drownings are not uncommon.

If it's more of the village ambience that you're looking for, then stay at one of the two *puri* in **Krambitan**. Belonging to the royal family of Tabanan, these two palaces have been showcasing their *tektekan gamelan* ensemble (bamboo split-drums and wooden clappers) for over two decades, along with their local cuisine. For a fair amount of money, anybody can participate in one of these chartered evenings, which include either a *joged* (flirtation dance accompanied by a bamboo gamelan) or a *calon arang* trance performance, complete with buffet dinner. If it's just the surroundings you're after, then you can rent rooms here as well.

Taking the northern route out of Krambitan, continue up the road until it dead-ends at **Pura Luhur**, on the slopes of **Gunung Batukau** (2,278 m/7,474 ft). The closest village is Wongaya Gede.

As one of Bali's most venerated temples, every other temple in West Bali has a shrine dedicated to Pura Luhur, located within solitary grounds far above the populated farmlands. The forest and the green moss everywhere are Pura Luhur's modest decorations – there are no ornate carvings or gilded shrines to be found in this mountain sanctuary.

A single, seven-tiered *meru* exalts Mahadewa, the deity associated with Batukau. As this was the state ancestral temple of the royal family of Tabanan, each of the shrines also represents one of the deified ancestors. This seven-

Temple to Gunung Batukau deities.

tiered shrine is also the home of Di Made, a ruler of the Gelgel court in the late seventeenth century. The three-tiered shrine is to the former king of Tabanan. The adjacent stone shrines (*prasada*) are similar to those at Kapal and Serangan.

Not far from the temple itself, a square lake recalls the moat of Pura Taman Ayun, at Mengwi. Both temples are classed as *pura taman*, a temple with a garden pond and maintained by a king. Lakes are also related to mountain sanctuaries; the rituals here include veneration of lakes and a blessing for irrigation water. At Pura Luhur stand shrines for the three mountain lakes within its catchment: Bratan, Buyan and Tambelingan.

Near Pura Luhur is the holy spring **Air Panas**, where hot water surges from the river bank. All strange, natural phenomena are believed to be frequented by spirits, and so Air Panas is graced by a small temple where people make prayers with offerings.

Jembrana: The most western regency of Bali, Jembrana – or **Negara** as it is usually called – is a rugged strip of land on the southwest coast of Bali. Legend has it that, in Java, a great priest banished his unruly son to the western coast of Bali. Drawing his finger across the land, he (literally) cut his son off – geological records show that Java and Bali were once connected at Bali's northwestern tip. Tourism is minimal here, and development is slow, offering a more rustic experience to travelers. Negara has many things to offer, most of them for nature lovers. A national wildlife park takes up most of this regency, once the home of Bali's tigers.

Because of a civil war started by the sibling rivalry of two royal brothers, court culture in Negara was never as developed as in the neighboring regencies. Many of its inhabitants are Muslim seafarers; there are even two villages that are predominantly Christian: Palasari is Catholic, while Belimbingsari is Protestant.

On the coastal road out of the Tabanan region lies a tranquil temple on a spectacular length of beach, **Pura Rambut**

Buffalo races, Jembrana.

Siwi, founded by the priest Nirartha Danghyang in the sixteenth century. Story has it that during his wanderings, he stopped at the village of Yeh Embang, where people began to worship him. He presented them with a gift of his hair, thus the name of the temple, Worship of the Hair (*rambut*). This is a wonderful place to stop and rest, even have a picnic lunch on the beach.

To the west is **Pura Gede Prancak**, which marks the spot of Danghyang Nirartha's entrance to Bali. Carved out of white stone, this shrine overlooks the Prancak River. It is not that easy to find. At Tegalcangkring, turn left off the main road to an intersection with a monument in the middle of it, then turn right. The temple is nine kilometers (6 mi) down the road.

The most exciting event in Negara is the *mekepung*, or water-buffalo races, a secular entertainment that began less than a century ago. Possibly it developed from the custom of carrying home harvested rice by bullock cart, or it may have been introduced from Java or Madura, where the sport is strong. Dressed up in silk banners with painted horns and enormous wooden bells, the bulls parade before the crowd of spectators. The course is a four-kilometer-long stretch of road; the teams are judged for speed and style. There are two main races: the Regent's Cup Championship, held on the Sunday before Indonesian Independence Day (17 August), and the Governor's Cup Championship held in September or October. It is remarkable to see such ordinarily docile creatures thunder down to the finishing line at speeds up to 50 kilometers an hour (30 mi/hr). The agile charioteers often drive standing up, twisting the bulls' tails to give them spunk.

If fortunate enough to be in Bali during the bull-racing season, usually between July and October, head west.

One of the most unique things about this area is the music, which is quite different from the standard gamelan music heard elsewhere on the island. *Jegog* is a musical ensemble entirely of bamboo instruments, and giant bamboo at that. Some have likened its sound to roaring thunder; it can be heard – and felt – from quite a distance. Jegog accompanies the standard traditional dances and has some of its own repertoire as well. The instruments may be seen up close at a privately-run museum, Sangkar Agung, three kilometers east of Negara, just off the main road near Pangintukadaya.

National park: The northwestern area of Bali that is **Taman Nasional Bali Barat** (West Bali National Park), said to be the home of the people of Pulaki, who were voluntarily "banished" to be invisible by the god Indra. Now it is home to the Bali starling (*Leucopsar rothschildi*), a small white bird with brilliant blue streaks around its eyes, and black-tipped wings.

Other animals gracing the land are deer, civets, monkeys and the wild Javan buffalo. For those interested in nature, or backpacking and hiking, this is the place, where 25,800 hectares (63,700 acres) of rain forest, palm and mangroves are protected by the government. Park headquarters are located at **Cekik**, on the west coast, at the intersection of the roads from Singaraja and Denpasar. Opened only in 1984, the park has limited facilities.

To go hiking, one must obtain a permit at Cekik, or from the Department of Forestry, on Jalan Suwung, Sesetan, in Denpasar. One must also hire a guide, available in Cekik for a few dollars a day. To stay overnight, bring necessities such as bedding, utensils, food and water. Tents can be rented at the park. Day-trips are also possible, with simple guest-house accommodation available in **Labuan Lalang**.

It is from Labuan Lalang that one commences on an underwater adventure. Here, hire a boat and snorkeling gear, and sail to **Pulau Menjangan** – Deer Island – where coral reefs extend to the ocean floor. Rarely will the deer for which the island is named be seen.

Further west in **Pemuteran** is comfortable accommodation. Most notable is the availability of dive gear for hire, and boat arrangements for reaching Pulau Menjangan can also readily be made from here.

Rain forest.

LOMBOK

Lombok is often called Indonesia's island of 1,000 mosques. Of all Indonesian Muslims undertaking the *haj* to Mecca, the greatest percentage in the nation – and Indonesia has the world's largest Islamic population – is in Lombok. Yet it is a culturally-diverse island. Buginese dominate the coasts, and there is a Javanese-style aristocracy. Arabs and Chinese are the merchants and sell just about anything.

Lombok, which means chili peppers in Javanese, is an island of roughly 4,700 square kilometers (1,800 sq mi) off the eastern tip of Bali. Dominating the landscape is a mountain range of 13 peaks, anchored by the volcanic Gunung (Mount) Rinjani, at 3,726 meters (12,224 ft) the third-highest peak in Indonesia.

Most of western Lombok is green and looks like Bali, but to the east and south the island becomes progressively drier, until wet-rice agriculture turns to dry-rice cultivation. The Wallace Line, named for naturalist Sir Alfred Wallace, runs between Bali and Lombok, demarcating climatic, zoological and botanical distinctions within the region; the Bali side is more like Asia, the Lombok side is more like Australia.

Mataram, Lombok's main city, is the provincial seat of Nusa Tenggara, which includes Lombok and its eastern neighbor, Sumbawa. The majority ethnic group, the Sasak, comprise about 94 percent of Lombok's population of over 2.5 million. The remaining six percent consists of Balinese, Buginese, Chinese, Javanese and Arabs.

Lombok retains many traits and customs similar to those of Java and Bali, and the Sasak language is closely related to Javanese and Balinese. However, Sasak culture sharply contrasts with Java and Bali in several aspects, due to historical events.

The Sasak, a Malay race inhabiting Lombok for at least 2,000 years, probably settled on coastal areas as long as 4,000 years ago. For much of the last 1,000 years, Lombok was a feudal state with many small kingdoms, some of which followed animistic beliefs, while others combined animism with Hinduism or Buddhism. The primary Sasak kingdom was Selaparang, in eastern Lombok, at first a Hindu kingdom in the thirteenth and fourteenth centuries, falling in a decline before arising again as an Islamic kingdom in the sixteenth and seventeenth centuries.

Over the centuries, Java influenced Lombok in varying degrees. East Java conquered Lombok, incorporating it into the Majapahit empire in the fourteenth century. Several small kingdoms on Lombok were ruled by Javanese nobles, who had been exiled to Lombok; today's Sasak aristocracy still claims Javanese ancestry. Java introduced both Hinduism and Islam to Lombok, but religious and political influence had waned by the seventeenth century. Islam gradually spread through eastern and central Lombok, while Balinese – and thus Hinduism – influence began dominating western Lombok.

The Balinese entered Lombok from

Preceding pages: perfect beach; Lombok village and rice fields. **Left,** Lombok aristocrat. **Right,** sacred Balinese-Hindu stone.

Karangasem, ruling the island for 150 years until 1894. Balinese influence was always centered in the west, where today Balinese constitute ten percent of the population. Here, they cleared forests and engineered irrigation systems and terraces, creating extensive wet-rice agriculture under the system of *subak*, the water-use cooperative.

The last king, Anak Agung Ngurah Gede Karangasem, managed to gain extensive influence over eastern Bali as well during the mid 1800s. Overseeing development of the arts and the construction of an impressive number of temples, he also restricted the land rights of the Sasak aristocracy, introduced an inflexible taxation system and demanded forced labor of Sasak peasantry. Revolts erupted several times in the nineteenth century, with Islam becoming the rallying cry among Sasak.

In the early 1890s, Sasak leaders approached the Dutch for help in overthrowing Balinese rule. The Dutch, mistakenly believing Lombok was rich in gems, assisted the Sasak. The Balinese eventually revolted and war broke out in 1894. The Balinese were eventually, and soundly, defeated, and many temples and palaces were destroyed. Many of the final confrontations ended in *puputan*, the mass suicides of palace nobles, and their families and followers.

The Sasak leaders believed they would have the right to rule, but, instead, the Dutch colonized the island, banishing the king and his remaining family, and offering only minor government positions to Sasak and Balinese leaders. Colonization intensified land use and taxation until the Japanese conquered the island in 1942. When the Japanese left in 1945, the Dutch returned briefly but were repelled by guerrillas.

There are two main groups among the Sasak: Wetu Lima and Wetu Telu. The Wetu Lima are orthodox Sunni Muslims, while the Wetu Telu are nominal Muslims, who combine the first tenet of Islam – belief in Allah with Muhammad as Prophet – and some Islamic observances with a mosaic of ancestor worship, Hinduism and Buddhism.

Lake atop Gunung Rinjani.

While Wetu Lima ("five times") indicates the Wetu Lima should carry out the five daily prayers and fulfill the five tenets of Islam, Wetu Telu ("three times") suggests that the Wetu Telu should pray at three different periods and acknowledge three types of ceremonies: life-cycle rites (birth, marriage, death), Islamic ceremonies (Maulid, Lebaran), and cyclical rites associated with agriculture. The Wetu Lima have adopted the emerging Islamic identity of Muslims throughout Indonesia, while the Wetu Telu are generally uninterested in the world at large, focusing instead on their strong ties to ancestral lands. Many fought beside the Balinese against the Dutch and Wetu Lima, in 1894, to retain their way of life.

Wetu Telu rituals have declined to the point where few identify themselves as Wetu Telu. Wetu Lima religious leaders (*tuan guru*), on the other hand, are very active with thousands of followers, demanding that all Sasak Muslims observe Islamic religious practices.

The local government supports preservation of traditional arts, maintaining Sasak cultural identity and history. But these arts, even those associated with religious practice, are often considered as traditional, rather than religious. Lombok's most important traditional, yet religious, festival is the annual *Pujawali* at Lingsar, in West Lombok. Although primarily a Balinese festival, Sasak attendance is considerable.

Efforts to retain traditional arts is paying off. Tourism is rising in Lombok, now adding substantially to the economy of rice, coffee, tobacco, fisheries, livestock, mining, and textiles.

Visitors to Lombok should not expect the overwhelming cultural experience of Bali, but they can expect a great sense of adventure. The so-called dark-time, when religious leaders banned all traditional arts and cultural activities not considered Islamic, is over. Today, artists and young people are rediscovering cultural influences—Javanese, Balinese, Malaysian, and Islamic.

The locals are very interested in visitors and, for the most part, polite and

At the morning market.

friendly. If respect is shown toward their religious practices and expectations of dress and behavior, they are quick to respond positively.

West Lombok: Three main towns in West Lombok – Ampenan, Mataram, and Cakranegara – meld together to create what is, for Lombok, a large urban sprawl. **Mataram** is the administrative center of the political and cultural life of Lombok, with provincial government offices, banks, mosques, bookstores, the main post office, and Mataram University downtown. The provincial tourist office is near Mataram, on Jalan Langko.

The **National Museum** in Mataram houses historical and cultural artifacts from Lombok and Sumbawa, and occasionally hosts special exhibits. The cultural center, **Pusat Budaya**, on Jalan Pariwisata, presents traditional music and dance nightly.

Just west of Mataram is **Ampenan**. With its numerous shops, cheap hotels, dusty roads, plentiful horse-drawn *dokar*, Islamic bookstores, and its Arab quarter, Ampenan is easily the most colorful town of Lombok. The Arab traders were drawn to Ampenan when it was the only harbor for incoming and outgoing ships. Nowadays, however, most shipping arrives at Lembar, and Ampenan is used only for fishing, and for shipping cattle.

The beach at Ampenan is occasionally used for performances of the dance *gandrung*, or for the shadow play *wayang Sasak* on special holidays. Sometimes both go on simultaneously, while young people flirt or create mischief on the beach.

Cakranegara, to the east of Mataram, is the main market center. It is also home to many Chinese and Balinese, who make up over 50 percent of its population. Much of Lombok's weaving and basket industries is located in Cakranegara. The baskets, in particular, are sold in Bali at many times the Lombok price.

Several important Balinese temples are in Cakranegara. **Pura Meru**, the largest temple with its giant *meru* for the

Left, odalan, Pura Meru. Right, priest at Pura Narmada.

Hindu trinity – Siwa (Shiva), Wisnu (Vishnu), and Brahma – is the "navel" temple for most of the Balinese, and its annual *Pujawali* festival, held over five days during the September or October full moon, is the biggest Balinese event in Lombok. **Pura Mayura**, built in 1744, was the court temple of past kingdoms. The temple sits behind the sedate Mayura water gardens and is adjacent to a public swimming pool.

The structures and pool at **Pura Narmada**, 10 kilometers (6 mi) east of Cakranegara, were reportedly built in 1805 as a replica of Gunung Rinjani and Segara Anak, the lake within its caldera. An elderly king did not like undertaking the long and mandatory annual trek to Segara Anak, where he was to throw crafted gold pieces into the lake as offerings. So he had Pura Narmada built instead. There is still an annual pilgrimage and offering at Segara Anak, and the festival at Pura Narmada coincides with this pilgrimage during the full moon of either October or November. Some of the other pools at Narmada are available for swimming (modest suits please), popular with local kids. The gardens at Narmada are splendid and are the site of special performances of *gandrung, kendang belek* and other traditional dances on special occasions.

Pura Suranadi, a complex of three temples located a few kilometers north of Narmada, is the oldest of the Balinese temples in Lombok, founded by the legendary Pedanda Wawu Rauh to obtain the proper holy water for cremations. **Pura Lingsar**, comprising two temples, is the mother temple of Lombok, not only for the Balinese but also for the Wetu Telu. This is the temple where even local Chinese, Buddhists, Christians, and occasionally Wetu Lima come to pray for prosperity, rain, fertility, health, and general success. The temple is associated with irrigation and rice, and the annual festival there features a ritualized war, *perang topat*, which acts as an offering.

While the main courtyards of both temples symbolically unite the deities of Bali and Lombok, the second court-

Royal pool, Pura Narmada.

yards, called *kemaliq*, contain sacred pools and unique altars of rocks, reminiscent of ancient megalithic worship. Both Pura Suranadi and Pura Lingsar have sacred spring-fed pools within the temple grounds, home of large freshwater eels. Visitors are welcome to feed the eels hard-boiled eggs, which can be purchased at nearby stands.

A festival, held during the November or December full moon, brings together sacred Balinese performing arts, such as *gamelan gong kuna* and the *canang sari* dance, along with sacred Sasak arts, such as the *gamelan tambur* ensemble and *batek baris* dance. This is the only event that ties together the Balinese and Sasak, and it is the second-biggest event in Lombok.

Other traditional Sasak rites include the *alip* and *gawe* festivals. Rare today, these celebrations occasionally occur in Bayan in the north, Lenek in the east, and Sembalun Bumbung, next to Gunung Rinjani. These villages are known for their Wetu Telu traditions and customs.

To the North: About 10 kilometers (6 mi) north of Ampenan, **Senggigi** has become the main tourist area of Lombok. With its beautiful beaches, picturesque views of Gunung Agung in Bali, good coral for snorkeling and diving, and millions of dollars invested for tourism, Senggigi is an attractive place to stay, with several deluxe hotels.

Batulayar, near Senggigi, has an important ancestral grave, *makam*, where nominal Muslims come to picnic, and to pray for health and success. There are many makam all over Lombok, as the graves of all important religious leaders become shrines. The makam at Batulayar is near **Pura Batu Bolong**, an interesting Balinese temple on a cliff facing Bali, beside the large rock with a hole, from which the temple gets its name.

North of Senggigi, toward Bayan along the hilly coastal road, is a variety of terrain and villages. First is **Pamenang**, then further west, **Bangsal**, which has a beautiful beach. Boats depart here for the three islands with the best diving and snorkeling in Lombok: *Kecodak dance.*

Gili Air, **Gili Meno**, and **Gili Trawangan**. There are many home-stays, the best of which seem to be on Gili Trawangan, the furthest island from Pemenang and the most difficult to reach.

There is no fresh water on the Gili islands. Problems with cholera during the dry season (May–October), and malaria and dengue fever during the wet season (November–March) have been recorded. Drink only bottled water, eat only cooked food and choose accommodation with mosquito nets.

South-facing **Sira Beach**, along the peninsula north of Bangsal, is beautiful, pristine and, for the moment, unblemished. A golf course has been built on this point of land, so things are due to change. Around the point, in **Medana Bay**, is a luxury Oberoi resort.

Tanjung is another interesting village, in which live Sasak Muslims, Balinese Hindus, and Sasak Buddhists, known as *Boda*. Tanjung has an interesting Sunday market, Pasar Minggu.

West of Godang is **Tiu Pupus waterfall**, a 20-minute walk beyond the end of a poorly marked, rocky road. While the spring-fed falls are disappointing during dry season, they still flow into a deep, swimmable pool. The trek through a traditional Sasak village, **Kerurak**, makes the effort worthwhile.

The dusty village of **Segenter** provides a glimpse into the harsh reality of life on the island's dry side. The 300 villagers in this northern interior village eke out a living raising corn and beans – yet they welcome visitors with a smile and proudly share their simple life.

Bayan, a source of early Islam, maintains old dance and poetic traditions, as well as *kemidi rudat*, a theater based on the Thousand-and-One Nights fables. One of the most important Wetu Telu mosques is in Bayan. Nearby, Sendang Gila waterfalls are among the island's most spectacular, even after climbing the 200 vertical steps down to see them.

Central and East Lombok: Well-known as a source of traditional Sasak music and dance, Lenek also offers *tari pakon*, a medicinal trance dance. Pak Rahil has established an organization to reinvigorate the performing arts in Lenek. Visitors are welcomed for a rustic, though healthy, stay at the facilities.

Other villages in East Lombok are strongly Islamic. Although transportation and lodging are difficult, several are worth visiting: Lendang Nangka, known for its blacksmith industry; Labuhan Haji, with its beautiful beach; and Labuhan Lombok, a friendly harbor with ferries running to Sumbawa.

Another village, **Tetebatu**, is a cool mountain retreat with beautiful rice terraces at the foot of Gunung Rinjani. **Kotaraja**, just south of Tetebatu, still produces some of Lombok's best handicrafts. **Bonjeruk**, in Central Lombok, is a village of numerous *dalang*, or puppeteers, for the shadow play *wayang Sasak*; many of the puppets are made here.

Sembalun Bumbung is located in a high, cold valley beside Rinjani, along with a neighboring village, **Sembalun Lawang**. There are many *haji* (those who have gone to Mecca) in both villages, but Sembalun Bumbung has retained the older traditions, such as

Hobby-horse used in *kecodak* dance.

tandang mendet, a men's martial dance, and a unique version of *wayang wong* theater based on the Amir Hamza stories of world Islamification. In contrast, Sembalun Lawang has become an orthodox village banning most arts.

Sembalun Bumbung has an old tomb that holds the remains of a Majapahit ancestor. It is also the site of the phenomenal *alip* festival held about once every three years.

Climbing **Gunung Rinjani** from the south is usually done via Sembulan, and it should only be undertaken during the dry season, due to slippery paths during the rainy season. An active, though momentarily dormant, volcano, Rinjani is a worthy climb. There is a lake within its crater, and a number of hot springs. The best route is actually from the north, by Bayan through Batukok to Senaru. Travelers should carry most of their own provisions, but equipment rental, porters and guides are available.

To the South: Close behind Senggigi in development is **Kuta Beach**, an expansively beautiful white-sand beach in southern Lombok, about 45 kilometers (30 mi) from Cakranegara. The big hotels here are very expensive, the homestays fairly dirty, and the villagers not particularly friendly. There is a lot of petty theft in Kuta, and unaccompanied women are often accosted (as everywhere else in Lombok).

The biggest event in Lombok – *Bau Nyale*, the seaworm-catching ritual – is held in Kuta and other southern beaches, in early February. This event, which is primarily a secular gathering, attracts over 100,000 young people who flirt and strut while watching the seaworms spawn. They may also find time to sing improvised *pantun* poetry, and to watch a dance-drama based on the Sasak *putri nyale* myth, in which a princess, unable to choose between suitors, throws herself off a cliff into the ocean, where she transforms into seaworms.

Seaworms are associated with fertility, and today farmers catch them, grind them up, then place the result in irrigation channels to help assure fertility.

On the road to Kuta is **Sukarare**, a village specializing in traditional Sasak weaving and clothing, and **Gunung Pengsong**, the hill the Balinese aimed for in the mythic account of their initial arrival in West Lombok. They built an unusual temple on the hill with a wonderful view of Lombok and Bali, and monkeys all around. The festival there includes a sacred procession with a water buffalo up to the temple, where it is ritually sacrificed.

Gerung, near Lembar, is the village of the famous *cepung*, a men's social dance where they read and sing from the *Lontar Monyet* (Monkey Manuscript), drink *tuak* (palm wine), dance, and vocally imitate gamelan instruments.

In 1988, New Zealand initiated a joint venture with local craftsmen to improve the quality of the locally-produced pottery, with the aim of making it commercially viable. Three villages – **Banyumulek, Masbagik Timur** and **Penujak** – are now the pottery-producing centers of Lombok. Using very simple tools, potters turn out exquisite pots of natural earthen clay, dug from the slopes of Gunung Sasak.

Left, Kuta Beach. Right, beach near Malimbu.

INSIGHT GUIDES
Travel Tips

FOR THOSE
WITH MORE THAN
A PASSING INTEREST
IN TIME...

Before you put your name down for a Patek Philippe watch *fig. 1*, there are a few basic things you might like to know, without knowing exactly whom to ask. In addressing such issues as accuracy, reliability and value for money, we would like to demonstrate why the watch we will make for you will be quite unlike any other watch currently produced.

"Punctuality", Louis XVIII was fond of saying, "is the politeness of kings."

We believe that in the matter of punctuality, we can rise to the occasion by making you a mechanical timepiece that will keep its rendezvous with the Gregorian calendar at the end of every century, omitting the leap-years in 2100, 2200 and 2300 and recording them in 2000 and 2400 *fig. 2*. Nevertheless, such a watch does need the occasional adjustment. Every 3333 years and 122 days you should remember to set it forward one day to the true time of the celestial clock. We suspect, however, that you are simply content to observe the politeness of kings. Be assured, therefore, that when you order your watch, we will be exploring for you the physical—if not the metaphysical—limits of precision.

Does everything have to depend on how much?

Consider, if you will, the motives of collectors who set record prices at auction to acquire a Patek Philippe. They may be paying for rarity, for looks or for micromechanical ingenuity. But we believe that behind each $500,000-plus

bid is the conviction that a Patek Philippe, even if 50 years old or older, can be expected to work perfectly for future generations.

In case your ambitions to own a Patek Philippe are somewhat discouraged by the scale of the sacrifice involved, may we hasten to point out that the watch we will make for you today will certainly be a technical improvement on the Pateks bought at auction? In keeping with our tradition of inventing new mechanical solutions for greater reliability and better time-keeping, we will bring to your watch innovations *fig. 3* inconceivable to our watchmakers who created the supreme wristwatches of 50 years ago *fig. 4*. At the same time, we will of course do our utmost to avoid placing undue strain on your financial resources.

Can it really be mine?

May we turn your thoughts to the day you take delivery of your watch? Sealed within its case is your watchmaker's tribute to the mysterious process of time. He has decorated each wheel with a chamfer carved into its hub and polished into a shining circle. Delicate ribbing flows over the plates and bridges of gold and rare alloys. Millimetric surfaces are bevelled and burnished to exactitudes measured in microns. Rubies are transformed into jewels that triumph over friction. And after many months—or even years—of work, your watchmaker stamps a small badge into the mainbridge of your watch. The Geneva Seal—the highest possible attestation of fine watchmaking *fig. 5*.

Looks that speak of inner grace *fig. 6*.

When you order your watch, you will no doubt like its outward appearance to reflect the harmony and elegance of the movement within. You may therefore find it helpful to know that we are uniquely able to cater for any special decorative needs you might like to express. For example, our engravers will delight in conjuring a subtle play of light and shadow on the gold case-back of one of our rare pocket-watches *fig. 7*. If you bring us your favourite picture, our enamellers will reproduce it in a brilliant miniature of hair-breadth detail *fig. 8*. The perfect execution of a double hobnail pattern on the bezel of a wristwatch is the pride of our casemakers and the satisfaction of our designers, while our chainsmiths will weave for you a rich brocade in gold *figs. 9 & 10*. May we also recommend the artistry of our goldsmiths and the experience of our lapidaries in the selection and setting of the finest gemstones? *figs. 11 & 12*.

How to enjoy your watch before you own it.

As you will appreciate, the very nature of our watches imposes a limit on the number we can make available. (The four Calibre 89 time-pieces we are now making will take up to nine years to complete). We cannot therefore promise instant gratification, but while you look forward to the day on which you take delivery of your Patek Philippe *fig. 13*, you will have the pleasure of reflecting that time is a universal and everlasting commodity, freely available to be enjoyed by all.

Should you require information on any particular Patek Philippe watch, or even on watchmaking in general, we would be delighted to reply to your letter of enquiry. And if you send us

fig. 1: The classic face of Patek Philippe.

fig. 4: Complicated wristwatches circa 1930 (left) and 1990. The golden age of watchmaking will always be with us.

fig. 6: Your pleasure in owning a Patek Philippe is the purpose of those who made it for you.

fig. 9: Harmony of design is executed in a work of simplicity and perfection in a lady's Calatrava wristwatch.

fig. 2: One of the 33 complications of the Calibre 89 astronomical clock-watch is a satellite wheel that completes one revolution every 400 years.

fig. 5: The Geneva Seal is awarded only to watches which achieve the standards of horological purity laid down in the laws of Geneva. These rules define the supreme quality of watchmaking.

fig. 10: The chainsmith's hands impart strength and delicacy to a tracery of gold.

fig. 7: Arabesques come to life on a gold case-back.

fig. 11: Circles in gold: symbols of perfection in the making.

fig. 3: Recognized as the most advanced mechanical regulating device to date, Patek Philippe's Gyromax balance wheel demonstrates the equivalence of simplicity and precision.

fig. 8: An artist working six hours a day takes about four months to complete a miniature in enamel on the case of a pocket-watch.

fig. 12: The test of a master lapidary is his ability to express the splendour of precious gemstones.

✦

PATEK PHILIPPE
GENEVE

fig. 13: The discreet sign of those who value their time.

your card marked "book catalogue" we shall post you a catalogue of our publications. Patek Philippe, 41 rue du Rhône, 1204 Geneva, Switzerland, Tel. +41 22/310 03 66.

Reality check. Call home.

—— *AT&T USADirect® and World Connect®. The fast, easy way to call most anywhere.* ——

Take out AT&T Calling Card or your local calling card.** Lift phone. Dial AT&T Access Number for country you're calling from. Connect to English-speaking operator or voice prompt. Reach the States or over 200 countries. Talk. Say goodbye. Hang up. Resume vacation.

American Samoa **633 2-USA**	**Korea** **009-11**	**Taiwan*** **0080-10288-0**
Australia **1800-881-011**	**Macao** ■ **0800-111**	Thailand♦ 0019-991-1111
Cambodia ■ **1800-881-001**	**Malaysia*** **800-0011**	
China, PRC♦♦♦ **10811**	**Micronesia** ■ **288**	
Cook Islands ■ **09-111**	New Zealand 000-911	
Fiji ■ **004-890-1001**	**Palau** ■ **02288**	
Guam **018-872**	**Philippines*** **105-11**	
Hong Kong **800-1111**	**Saipan**† **235-2872**	
India♦ **000-117**	Singapore..........................800-0111-111	
Indonesia† **001-801-10**	**South Africa** **0-800-99-0123**	
Japan*■...............................**0039-111**	Sri Lanka...............................430-430	

AT&T
Your True Choice

You can also call collect or use most U.S. local calling cards. Countries in bold face permit country-to-country calling in addition to calls to the U.S. World Connect® prices consist of USADirect® rates plus an additional charge based on the country you are calling. Collect calling available to the U.S. only. *Public phones require deposit of coin or phone card. †May not be available from every phone. ♦Not available from public phones. ♦♦♦Not yet available from all areas. ■ **World Connect calls can only be placed *to* this country. ©1995 AT&T.

For a free wallet sized card of all AT&T Access Numbers, call: 1-800-241-5555.

Getting Acquainted

Time Zones

There are three time zones in Indonesia. Bali follows Central Indonesian Standard Time, which is **8 hours ahead of Greenwich Mean Time**. Bali is on the same time zone as Singapore and Hong Kong.

Climate

As Bali is quite close to the equator, its temperatures vary between 21°C and 32°C (70–90°F), with an average temperature of 26°C (78°F) and only two seasons: dry and rainy. The dry season lasts from May to November, with July being the coolest month of the year. The rainy season lasts from November to April, with January being the wettest month of the year. Humidity is 75 percent year-round.

The People

Culture & Customs

To the Balinese, the world is their home and its travelers their guests. Decades of tourism have somewhat dimmed this positive attitude, but the Balinese remain remarkably friendly and courteous. They also remain staunchly conservative, for tradition is the backbone of their highly civilized culture. Please try to respect their traditions and attitudes. The Balinese are a very polite people and smiles are an island-wide characteristic. Shaking hands on introduction is the usual thing nowadays for both men and women. The use of the left hand to give or to receive something, however, is considered taboo (the left hand is used for hygienic purposes), as is pointing with the left hand. Crooking a finger to call someone is impolite.

When buying something, settle all prices in advance. Don't ask the price or make an offer unless you intend to buy. When bargaining, generally start at half the asking price and then work

out a compromise. Remember that Rp. 500 can mean the difference of a day's meals to them; to you it is nothing. It is silly to quibble over small sums because of principle. Don't display large sums of money – in a place where the average annual income is under US$500, tourists' wallets seem and are fat. The Balinese have a strong pride and consider temptation an affront, suspicion an insult.

Wear a shirt when not on the beach and don't walk around outside the beach or pool area in a swimsuit. What may seem like a quaint beach-side alley may be the courtyard of a house or holy temple. Nude bathing is illegal and impolite. Before entering a private house, leave your shoes outside on the steps. Shoes and a collared shirt or modest skirt and blouse must be worn when visiting government offices.

It is compulsory for anyone visiting temples to wear a waist sash. Any material will do, although the Balinese admire colorful brocades or woven cloths. By an ancient law, menstruating women and anyone with a bleeding cut are asked not to enter temples. This is based on a general sanction against blood on holy soil.

Begging is not a tradition in Bali and the annoying beggars in Kuta are not Balinese. If you freely hand out money, you will only be encouraging people to ask again. The only exception is a small contribution at the entrance to a temple. This is used to offset the cost of maintenance, so give what you can afford, as you would for a church or house of worship in your own country. At temple festivals or dance performances, the Balinese are relaxed around a camera, providing the photographer does not interfere by standing directly in front of the priest or the kneeling congregation. According to custom, one's head should not be higher than that of a priest or village headman. Therefore, it is rude to climb on the walls of a temple. Likewise, do not remain standing when the people kneel to pray. Move to the back and wait quietly until the blessing has been completed. The same pertains to a procession. If local bystanders kneel in veneration, you should always move to the side.

The Balinese are not performing for the benefit of tourist cameras, but are performing a sacred ritual.

The Economy

Agriculture was once the main economic activity of the people in Bali, who grow rice for personal consumption. Tourism is now the largest income source per capita. Their main sources of agricultural income are coconuts (for copra) and the sale of cattle and pigs. Coffee and tobacco are also sold to wholesalers for export.

The Government

Bali is one of 27 provincial regions of the Republic of Indonesia, each of which is ruled by a governor. The governor of Bali lives in Denpasar. The province is divided into eight *kabupaten* (counties or regencies), each headed by a *bupati* (regent) under the governor. There is further subdivision into 51 *kecamatan* (subdistricts) under a *camat*. There are 564 incorporated villages, each ruled by a *perbekel* or village head. There are another 1,456 *desa adat* (traditional villages) sub-divided into 3,627 *banjars* (hamlets or wards), each administered by a *klian* (banjar head).

The banjar system is unique to Bali. Essentially, every married male is a member of a banjar and must attend meetings held every 35 days, when issues pertinent to the well-being of the village are discussed. If someone is having a ceremony, then all the members (both male and female) are obligated to help; conversely when they have a ritual, they have the right to ask their neighbors to assist them. It is said that the family planning program in Indonesia is the most successful because of this system of *gotong royong* (mutual assistance) and the way news spreads through these monthly meetings. Each banjar also has a youth club, the *seka teruna-teruni*, which often holds fund-raising events and helps in keeping the village grounds clean.

Planning The Trip

What to Bring

Travel as lightly as possible, as there are many great things to buy in Bali to take home, and never enough luggage space in which to put them. Essentials are insect repellent, a flashlight (as roads and even paths to your hotel room can be dark), sunscreen, prescription medicines and an extra set of prescription glasses (or at least the prescription, which often can be refilled here quickly and for less than in the west).

Electricity

In most places, 220 volts, 50 cycles – but check first, as 110 volts is still used in some areas. Be warned that power failures are common except in the large hotels, which have their own backup generators. The plug is two-pronged round.

Converters should be bought abroad, as they are difficult to find in Bali, although one can buy voltage regulators with a 110-volt outlet.

What to Wear

Indonesians are quite concerned with how they present themselves, and clothing is definitely a part of this. The nonchalant hippie look is not well-accepted by locals; in fact, wearing ragged clothing can hamper your chances of getting good service, particularly at government offices. Singlets, halter tops, shorts and miniskirts are frowned upon and should be left at home. Government offices may post dress codes: trousers and shirt with sleeves for men, and dress or skirt with blouse, again with sleeves, for women. As the climate is quite humid, it is best to bring all-cotton sundresses, short-sleeve shirts, etc. Bali has a thriving garment industry and clothes made out of fabulously hand-dyed and hand-woven fabrics are readily available everywhere. Sandals or footwear that can be slipped off easily are a good idea, especially if planning to visit locals' homes, as shoes are always taken off before going into a house. However, avoid rubber thongs or slippers. Suits and party dresses are rarely worn. For formal occasions, men wear *batik* or *ikat* (dyed off the loom) shirts and trousers; women modest dresses. A light jacket or sweater is necessary for visits to mountain spots – and if spending a lot of time in air-conditioned lounges.

Entering a temple: one must be dressed modestly, in *pakaian adat* (the full native dress of a *kain, kebaya* and sash for the women, and *udeng* (head-cloth) *kain, saput* (overskirt), nice shirt and sash for the men. Throwing a sash on over shorts just won't do; make sure you have a sarong handy as well. It's best to wait outside the temple if there is a festival going on. Remember that temple ceremonies and other rituals are sacred to the Balinese and appropriate clothing should be worn.

Entry Regulations
Visas & Passports

Visitors from 46 countries will automatically be issued a two-month tourist visa: Argentina, Australia, Austria, Belgium, Brazil, Brunei, Canada, Chile, Denmark, Egypt, Finland, France, Germany, Greece, Hungary, Iceland, Ireland, Italy, Japan, Kuwait, Liechtenstein, Luxemburg, Malaysia, Maldives, Malta, Mexico, Monaco, Morocco, Netherlands, New Zealand, Norway, Philippines, Saudi Arabia, Singapore, South Korea, Spain, Sweden, Switzerland, Taiwan, Thailand, Turkey, United Arab Emirates, United Kingdom, United States, Venezuela and Vietnam.

Visitors from all other countries must obtain a tourist visa from their local Indonesian consulate or embassy. Make sure your passport is valid for six months upon entry into Indonesia, otherwise you'll find yourself on the next plane out. You also must have proof of onward passage (ie., a ticket out of Indonesia). Tourist, social and business visas can be obtained from any Indonesian embassy or consulate abroad. To obtain a visa, submit two application forms with two passport photographs, the appropriate fee and proof of onward passage. Employment is strictly forbidden on a tourist visa, visa-free entry, social visa or business visa.

You will fill out a white, disembarkation/embarkation document, half of which should be retained and returned upon departure. Don't lose this card. **Immigrations offices** are near Ngurah Rai Airport, Tel: 751-038, and at Jl. Panjaitan, Tel: 227-828.

Extending a tourist visa is impossible; one must leave the country and come back in again. But this is a simple matter of going to Singapore and coming back the same day. Extending business and social cultural visas involves more paperwork, but can easily be done. See your local Indonesian consulate/embassy for details.

In Singapore, the Indonesian Embassy (Kedutaan Besar Republik Indonesia) is at 7 Chatsworth Road, Tel: (65) 737-7422.

Animal Quarantine

Bali, unlike its neighbors, is rabies-free. Bringing in a dog or cat (or monkey, for that matter) is close to impossible. You will need an official letter from your veterinarian stating that the animal is disease-free, but that won't guarantee non-quarantine. Contact your local Indonesian consulate/embassy for details.

Customs

Regulations prohibit the entry of weapons, narcotics and pornography as well as radio-cassette players (yes, an odd thing to prohibit but rarely enforced) and anything written in Chinese characters. Fresh fruits, plants, animals and exposed films and videos may be checked. To prevent rabies, the import of dogs, cats and monkeys is restricted.

A maximum of 1 liter of alcohol, 200 cigarettes, 50 cigars or 100 grams of tobacco, and a reasonable amount of perfume may be brought into the country. Photographic equipment, typewriters and radios are admitted provided they are taken out on departure. They must be declared; a customs declaration form must be completed before arrival. There is no restriction on the import or export of foreign currencies and travelers' checks. However, the import and export of Indonesian currency exceeding Rp. 50,000 is prohibited. Upon leaving, limited quantities of duty-free purchases and souvenirs are exempt from taxes, but the export of "national treasures" is severely frowned upon. Tortoise shell, crocodile skin and ivory are not allowed to be taken out.

Airport Customs, Tel: 751-037

Left Luggage

As in most airports, file a claim at the airlines' office. In theory, they will bring your luggage to your hotel when it has arrived, but it may be quicker for you to check at the airport after the next scheduled flight has landed.

Health

International health certificates of vaccination against smallpox, cholera and yellow fever are required only from travelers coming from infected areas. Typhoid and paratyphoid vaccinations are optional, but still advisable. If you intend to stay in Bali for a long time, gamma-globulin injections are recommended by some doctors; they won't stop hepatitis, but many physicians believe that the risk of infection is greatly reduced. For Hepatitis B, you can get the series of three shots (manufactured from yeast, not blood products) in Denpasar at less than half the price it costs abroad. But it is a six-month series of shots.

Most people traveling through Bali get the infamous "Bali Belly" at some time or other. Taking Lomotil and Imodium will stop the symptoms, but it keeps the infection inside. At the first sign of discomfort (diarrhea and cramping), drink strong, hot tea and avoid all fruits and spicy foods. Taking charcoal tablets (Norit is the brand name) will help alleviate the cramping. If you get a fever along with the above symptoms, then get to a doctor who will prescribe antibiotics. Oralite (mineral replacement salts) for dehydration are available at every local pharmacy. You should drink as much liquid as possible. **Malaria** is not a significant problem in Bali.

Any cut or abrasion must be treated immediately. Betadine, a powerful non-stinging, non-staining, broad spectrum antiseptic, is available in solution or ointment at any drugstore.

You may want to bring along a tube of antihistamine cream for relief of itches, a triple antibiotic cream (such as Neosporin), an ointment for fungoid skin infections, a good prickly-heat powder (Purol, available in Indonesia, works well), some insect repellent, and aspirin. All water, including well-water, municipal water and water used for making ice, MUST be made safe before consumption. Bringing water to a rolling boil for 10 minutes is an effective method. Iodine (Globolien) and chlorine (Halazone) may also be used to make water potable. All fruits should be carefully peeled before eating, and no raw vegetables should be eaten, except at the fancier eating establishments. Ice in all eateries is safe, as it is manufactured at a government factory, but often it is dumped in front of the restaurant on the dirty sidewalk and then only perfunctorily washed. Watch what and where you eat, and wash your hands with soap.

Protect yourself against the **sun**. As in all tropical areas, the sun can be quite intense around noon. Use a protective sunblock and protect your head, perhaps with a Balinese-style straw hat, sold everywhere.

Promiscuity is not a cultural trait of Indonesians. However, **sexually-transmitted diseases** (especially gonorrhea and herpes) are on the increase in Indonesia, and AIDS and HIV infection, although still rare, are a harsh reality. Please act responsibly and use condoms. If you have not brought your own, they are available over the counter at pharmacies (*apotik*). Indonesian and imported brands are for sale. Popular brands include the government-approved brand used in the Indonesian Family Planning program, Simplex and Durex.

Prostitutes are not checked for STDs (sexually-transmitted diseases) and the Bali Cowboys or local gigolos have multiple female, mostly foreign, partners from all over the world. For those of you who hope for a little tropical romance during your travels, here are a few reminders: Some of the men (gay and straight) and women you may find yourself involved with are at least semi-professional and may ask for money "after the fact". Be warned.

Money Matters

Currency & Exchange

The **rupiah** is the basic unit of money, normally abbreviated to *Rp* followed by the value. Often travelers call rupiah *rupee*, which makes little sense to Indonesians.

Smaller denominations, Rp. 5, 10 and 25 are quite rare; Rp. 50 and 100 are in the form of coins, and larger ones – Rp. 100, 500, 1,000 – in coins or bills. Bills are only available for Rp. 5,000, 10,000, 20,000 and 50,000. Values below Rp. 50 are rarely seen except in the supermarket, where they are used as change. Don't be surprised when totals are rounded up in the seller's favor and small change (under Rp. 100) given in sweets instead of coin. Change or *uang kembali* for high-value notes is often unavailable in smaller shops and stalls. In view of this, it's a good idea to carry a handful of coins or Rp. 100 notes, especially when traveling in outlying areas. It is best not to exchange large sums of money if you plan to be in Indonesia for a long period of time.

The postal service offers **cek pos**, a kind of postal travelers check. You can exchange your cash for these checks from a main post office and use them throughout Indonesia as travelers checks, or cash them at any post office. Travelers checks cannot be accepted by individuals; when you sign them at money changers, you need to put your passport number and a second signature on the reverse.

Changing Money

Foreign currency, in bank notes and travelers checks, is best exchanged at major banks or authorized money changers. Hotels generally give rates way below what a money changer will offer. Always be sure to keep receipts. Wherever you change currency, calculate and verify the amount according to the given exchange rate. Money changers in Kuta and at the airport have been known to use quick fingers to short-change travelers. Get a receipt for your transaction, too.

Travelers checks are accepted at all major hotels and at some shops. Money changers are much quicker than banks when it comes to changing travelers checks and the rates are about the same. The best rates are to be found in Kuta; Ubud rates are generally 3–4 points below market rates. Rupiah may be converted to foreign currency when leaving the country.

See the World with a different eye.

The world's leading series of full-colour travel guides

★ More than 300 titles

★ Three distinct formats tailored for individual needs

★ Spectacular photography and award-winning writing

INSIGHT GUIDES
alaska

INSIGHT POCKET GUIDE
Bali

INSIGHT COMPACT GUIDE
London

APA INSIGHT GUIDES

FLY SMOOTH AS SILK TO EXOTIC THAILAND ON A ROYAL ORCHID HOLIDAY.

Watching exquisite cotton and silk umbrellas being hand-painted in Chiang Mai. Lazing in the shade in sun-drenched Phuket. This

is what holidaying in Thailand is all about. Book the holiday of your choice now, flying Thai. Smooth as silk.

ROYAL
ORCHID
Holidays

Let your message travel with Insight Guides

Credit Cards

Today, many shops, large and small, accept plastic, with the proviso that an additional 3 to 5 percent is added onto the bill.

Cash advances can be obtained in all the major tourist resorts – Denpasar, Kuta, Sanur, Ubud. Automatic teller machines (ATM) are popping up all over the place, especially at shopping centers and bank branches. Many are connected to international banking networks, so you can look for those affiliated with your own ATM network. Bank Bali handles Cirrus cards and has five locations: Jl. Dewi Sartika, Jl. Sulawesi 1, Jl. Legian 118 (opposite The Bounty), Matahari Department Store at Kuta Center, and Galalel Supermarket at Sanur.

American Express offices are at the Pacto Travel agency at the Grand Bali Beach Hotel (Tel: 288-449, 288-511 ext PACTO), and at Jl. Ngurah Rai, Tel: 288-247; and Galleria Nusa Dua Shop A5 Unit 1-3-5, Nusa Dua, Tel: 773-334, Fax: 773-306; Pan Indonesia Bank, Jl. Legian 80X, Kuta, Tel: 751-058, Fax: 752-815.

The **Diners Club** office is on Jl. Diponegoro 45, Denpasar, Tel: 235-559, 235-545, and in Kuta on Jl. Legian, Tel: 754-045.

The **Visa** office is in Bank Duta, Jl. Hayam Wuruk 165, Denpasar, Tel: 226-578/9.

Receiving Money/Transfers

Trying to have money sent quickly to you from home can be a real headache. If you can't bring it all with you in travelers checks, then there are two options: have someone send you a **telex transfer** (money wire) to one of the banks listed below, or an **international money order** from a major bank (those from Bank of America and Chase Manhattan are readily accepted). The bank at home should send you money via a telex transfer to a specific bank, with your name, address and passport number on the telex. Make sure that the bank also sends approval of the money transfer at the same time they send the money; otherwise, you'll be waiting, sometimes for months, for your money to be cleared. There are no foreign banks in Bali yet, although a number of

them operate out of Jakarta. What sometimes happens is that if you ask your home bank to send money to Bank A in Bali and they don't have a direct line to that bank, then your home bank will use whatever bank they do have relations with in Bali. Trying to trace your money can then be a bit difficult.

Bank Dagang Nasional Indonesia, Jl. Diponegoro 45, Denpasar, Tel: 238-041, Fax: 237-876, Tlx: 35713 BDNI DP IA; Jl. Raya Legian, Kuta, Tel: 745-546, Fax: 751-250, Tlx: 35693.
Bank Danamon, Jl. Gunung Agung 1A, Denpasar, Tel: 436-490, Tlx: 35232; 35696IA.
Bank Harapan Sentosa, Jl. Diponegoro 134, Denpasar, Tel: 263-963/9, Fax: 263-970, Tlx: 35627 HABANK IA.
Bank Negara Indonesia (Persero), Jl. Raya Puputan, Renon, Denpasar, Tel: 263-304, Tlx: 3650 BNIWIL IA.
Bank Utama, Jl. Gajah Mada 112-114, Denpasar, Tel: 423-091/3, 436-156/9, Fax: 423-094, Tlx: 35174; 35569 UTMDPS IA.
Panin Bank, Jl. Legian 80X, Kuta, Tel: 751-076, Tlx: 35278 PIB DPR IA.
Tamara Bank, Jl. Diponogoro 153, Denpasar, Tel: 262-538, 362-860/1, 222546, Fax: 262-859, Tlx: 35697.

There are branches of major banks at the leading hotels and in Ubud and Kuta. If you have an account in one of the branches, then you can have the money sent directly. Bank Central Asia in Ubud gives excellent service.

Public Holidays

Religion is a way of life in Indonesia, and throughout the entire archipelago people enjoy and celebrate Buddhist, Hindu, Muslim and Christian holidays. (Every Indonesian must declare one of the five official religions as their own: Hinduism, Buddhism, Islam, Protestantism or Catholicism.)

New Year's Day (January 1) is observed throughout the country. Although celebrations vary from area to area, it is often celebrated with street carnivals, fireworks, special entertainment and shows. **Chinese New Year's** is timed according to the lunar calendar, usually in February or March.

The Balinese New Year, **Nyepi** (Day of Silence) is also a national holiday. It

is a Hindu holiday of retreat and spiritual purification; no lighting of fires (including electricity), no work and no travel may occur on this day. You are confined to your hotel or losmen on this day. (It is best to choose a hotel which has dispensation from the government to use electricity after dark.) If you arrive at the airport this day, there are no taxis available and only designated hotel buses are allowed on the roads. Hitch a ride, stay at one of these hotels or walk.

The most important Muslim celebration is **Idul Fitri** (Grebeg Sjawal), on the first day of the 10th month (Sjawal) of the Islamic calendar, symbolizing the end of the fasting month of Ramadan. All over the country, mass prayers are held in mosques and town squares, and everyone wears new clothes and visits relatives seeking forgiveness for past transgressions. It is a two-day public holiday, and in Bali is secular, as few Muslims live on the island. Other public Muslim holidays occur throughout the year, including **Mohammad's birthday** and the day of sacrifice, **Idul Adha**, but as they are based on a lunar calendar.

Check the schedules for holidays during your visit (your local Indonesian consulate will have that information), or a Balinese calendar (any day marked in red is a holiday).

The Buddhist day of enlightenment, **Wisak**, is a public holiday. **Good Friday**, which usually falls in April, is a national holiday, as is the Ascension of Christ, the 14th day after the resurrection. April 21 is **Kartini Day**, a national holiday commemorating the birthday of the late Raden Ajeng Kartini, the pioneer for the emancipation of Indonesian women at the turn of the century. Everywhere, women appear in national dress.

August 17 is the Indonesian national **Independence Day**, celebrated throughout the country with organized sports events, puppet and shadow plays, traditional cultural performances and carnivals.

October 5 is **Armed Forces Day**, the anniversary of the founding of the Indonesian armed forces with military parades and demonstrations of the latest achievements of the army, navy, air force and police.

A national public holiday, **Christmas** is celebrated with candlelight gatherings and religious ceremonies, although most of the Christian holidays are pretty much overlooked by the Hindu Balinese.

Getting There

Unless otherwise stated, all telephone numbers are preceded by the **area code 0361** and prices are in US$.

By Air

Bali's **Ngurah Rai International Airport**, which straddles the narrow Tuban Isthmus in the south of the island, is served by many daily flights from Jakarta, Yogyakarta, Surabaya and various other cities in Indonesia, as well as a growing number of international flights from around the world. Many airlines fly only as far as Jakarta, where you must then transfer to a domestic Garuda flight to reach Bali.

Flights to Bali from Jakarta's Soekarno-Hatta International Airport are frequent throughout the day, and you can generally make an on-going connection if you arrive in Jakarta before 5pm. The flight is pleasant and it takes only 90 minutes, and includes an incredible view of several volcanoes from the starboard (right) windows.

By Rail

From Jakarta, Bandung or Yogyakarta, travel first to Surabaya's Gubeng Station. A first-class night train, *Mutiara Utara*, connects Jakarta with Surabaya everyday. It departs from Jakarta's Kota Station in the late afternoon and arrives in Surabaya early the next morning. In Surabaya, choose from two daily departures from Gubeng Station, at 11am and 9.30pm, for the 8-hour trip on the *Mutiara Timur*, a non-airconditioned train bound for Banyuwangi, at Java's eastern tip. In Banyuwangi, catch the ferry to Bali. A bus takes you across the straits on the ferry and over to Denpasar, an extra 4 hours (although sometimes you have to wait quite a while for the ferry).

Overland

By Bus

With improved roads, the *bis malam* (night bus) from Java to Bali is now faster than the train, although some say more dangerous as well (drivers like to go fast). There are air-condi-

tioned buses from Surabaya (a 10- to 12-hour trip) to Denpasar and from Yogya (15–16 hours) to Denpasar. This is the way most Indonesians travel, although one's tolerance for cigarette smoke and noise must be high, as there are no nonsmoking buses and videos are blared to keep passengers entertained. Do not sit in the first row, which is dangerous in case of an accident. Be sure to specify A/C (air-conditioned) to avoid inhaling the noxious diesel fumes spewed out by trucks and buses en route. Meals included.

One of the best Jakarta-Bali buses is the **Lorena**, which for a little more includes deluxe services and a toilet. Contact any travel agent or their office in Jakarta: Jl. K.H. Hasyim Ashhari 15 C2-C3, Tel: (021) 231-3166, 345-8111. In Bali: Jl. Hasanudin 6 or Jl. Diponegoro 11/12, Tel: 237-660, 221-937, 235-010.

The buses leave Jakarta at 10am, 1.30pm or 2.30pm and arrive in Denpasar 24 hours later. (Bali departures: 6.30am and 4pm.) The fare is about $30. The complete route is Bogor-Jakarta-Semarang-Surabaya-Malang-Denpasar. Non-somnambulists will want to stop over along the way to Bali. If anywhere, you should stop in Yogyakarta, the cultural center of Java. The bus from Yogya to Bali (I5–I6 hours) is about $20, and about $11 from Surabaya. Some buses will go all the way to Kuta or Sanur, where you can walk to the nearest hotel room and crash.

The same buses leave Denpasar from the Ubung terminal for Yogyakarta, Surabaya, or Jakarta. Companies have an agent around Jl. Hasanudin; tickets are available from **Agung Transport**, Jl. Hasanudin 97, Denpasar, Tel: 222-663.

Otherwise, those with much luggage will need to charter a **minibus** on arrival, which is readily available. You should refuse to pay over $6 to go to the beach areas (Kuta-Legian) from Denpasar.

Minibuses

Families or small groups can also charter a private minibus (colt), with driver, between Bali and all cities in Java, at about $30–$40 per day plus fuel. Going to and from Java this way costs about the same as flying, but you get to see a lot more. Some minibuses are

air-conditioned. Stopovers and side-trips can be planned, and this is the ideal way to see Java.

By Car

You can rent your own car in Java and drive to Bali, but the cost will be about the same as hiring a driver and car, and then there is the added hassle of returning the car. If using your own transport, you need to get to **Banyuwangi** in East Java and take the ferry over to Bali.

As of 1996, you can drive your own car across from Asia or Australia, travel cross-country and re-export it. Several restrictions apply. Check with an Indonesian embassy or consulate if you are considering this route.

By Ferry

There are both private and state-run ferry services that operate between Java and Bali. Visitors who have traveled overland from Java will have to take this 25-minute trip that runs at intervals of 15–25 minutes to get to Bali. This is a pleasant trip, but be warned that you might have to wait several hours before boarding, especially if it is a holiday.

Special Facilities

Children

Children are so loved in Bali that it'd be a shame not to bring any along with you. Babysitters are available at all major hotels, and even the owners of the smallest inn would be happy to look after kids for a day. Disposable diapers are not widely available here. Bring your own or else cloth ones (the disposables get dumped in the river). Baby food is available at the supermarkets for exorbitant prices. Remember to bring sunhats and sunscreen. Soybean-based formula is only available at Tiara Dewata supermarket, and is expensive. Many larger hotels now have kid's clubs and children's programs. Ask when booking.

Matahari Department Store, Jl. Legian, Legian, has an amusement center packed with interactive and video games guaranteed to amuse the young and young at heart for a couple of hours, for a sum.

The Gay Scene

Male homosexuality is tolerated to a certain degree in traditional Balinese society, but the people involved are expected to eventually marry and have children. Due to AIDS, gay men are regarded in a different light these days – flagrant displays of romance are considered distasteful. (This applies to heterosexuals, as well.) There are no real gay hangouts, although there are a few pubs in Kuta where gay behavior is more accepted, such as Gado Gado. Note that the Campuhan Hotel, in Ubud, is no longer a gay haven.

Disabled

Balinese tend to believe that all physical and mental disabilities are due to behavior in a past life; that imperfections of any kind are punishment for how we acted in the past. Because of this, people with disabilities are often laughed at (but not without a heavy dose of compassion); any blemish we have will be remarked upon in front of us. There is very little consciousness in Indonesia about the special needs of the disabled. It would be very difficult for one to maneuver in a wheelchair, for example.

Language Teachers

Learning the language is the best way to learn about a culture. It makes communication possible and enhances human relationships. Balinese have their own language, but the national language (Bahasa Indonesian) is what is used in commerce, schools and in the media. Balinese is a very complex language and one that, if spoken incorrectly, can deeply offend. Indonesian, on the other hand, is an easy language to learn. There are no schools for learning Indonesian; you must find private tutors. At Udayana University in Denpasar, tutors are available for a hefty price; out in the villages, it's much cheaper. Be wary of those too willingly to teach; trained language teachers are few and far between.

Those who do teach and have been trained are: Anak Agung Gede Dwiputra, Puri Kapal, Banjar Kalah, Peliatan, Ubud, Tel: 975-180, 298-831.

I Wayan Sidakarya, c/o Mudita Inn, Peliatan, Ubud, Tel: 975-179; Putu Swasta, Kompleks Biaung Indah, Blok D. I3, Denpasar, Tel: 235-715.

Language and Culture Programs

A novel way to immerse oneself in Bali is through courses in language, dance, cooking, art, etc.

Agung Ray Museum of Art (ARMA), Ubud, TelL 976-659, 975-742, 96495, Fax: 974-229, offers lessons in music, art, and dance with masters. Accommodation available.

Pusat Saraswati, Center for Studies in Balinese Art & Culture; Jl. Goa Gajah, Teges, Peliatan, Ubud, P.O. Box 60 Ubud, Tel: 96303. Courses in Balinese dance, gamelan music, woodcarving, painting, shadow-puppet making, palm-leaf decorations. Guesthouse lodging available.

Sua Bali, Language in Culture Center, Desa Kemenuah, Gianyar, P.O. Box 574, Denpasar, Tel: 941-050, Fax: 941-035. An international award-winning facility, offers intensive courses in Indonesian language covering politics, economy, socio-geographical development, religions, arts and handicraft. Strives to bring Bali to visitors and integrate visitors into Balinese ways. Accommodation available.

Useful Addresses

Tourist Information Centers

Ngurah Rai International Airport, Tel: 751-011.

Badung Government Tourism Office, Jl. Surapati 7, Denpasar, Tel: 234-569, 223-602. Hours: Monday–Thursday, 7am–3pm, Friday until noon.

Bali Government Tourism Office, Jl. S. Parman, Renon, Tel: 222-387. Hours: Monday–Thursday 7am–3pm; Friday until noon.

Department of Tourism, Post and Telecommunications, Jl. Raya Puputan, Niti Mandala, Denpasar, Tel: 225-649, 233-474, Fax: 233-475.

Tourist Information Office, Jl. Benasari 7, Legian Kelod, Tel: 754-146.

Tourist Information Office, Jl. Veteran, Singaraja, Tel: 233-32.

Ubud Tourist Information Service, Jl. Raya Ubud, Ubud, Tel: 962-85. Hours: 8am–9pm.

Tour Operators

Bali Ekawisata Tours (BEST), Jl. Ciung Wanara V/5A, Renon, Tel: 238-260, 231-202, Fax: 238-259.

Bali Indonesia (BIL), Jl. Danau

Tamblingan 186, Sanur, Tel: 288-464, Fax: 288-261.

Carefree Bali Holiday, Jl. Bakungsari, KCB Building Kuta, Tel: 751-140, Fax: 753-053.

Golden Kris Tour, Jl. Bypass Ngurah Rai 87X, Sanur, Tel: 229-225, Fax: 289-228.

Jan's Tour, Jl. Nusa Indah 62, Denpasar, Tel: 234-930, 232-660, Fax: 231-009.

Kuta Cemerlang Bali (KCB), Jl. Raya Kuta No 79, Kuta, Tel: 751517/8, Fax: 752-777.

Genta Bali Tours, Jl. Danau Tamblingan 65, Sanur, Tel: 289-477.

Natrabu, Jl. Bypass Ngurah Rai 58X, Sanur, Tel: 288-660.

Nitour, Jl. Veteran 5, Denpasar, Tel: 236-096; counter at Grand Bali Beach Hotel, Sanur, Tel: 288-562.

Pacto, Jl. Bypass, Sanur, Tel: 288-247/8, Fax: 287-506; counter at Grand Bali Beach Hotel, Sanur, Tel: 288-511.

Rama Tours, Jl. Bypass Ngurah Rai 1, Kuta, Tel: 752-321, Fax: 752-863; also a desk at the Grand Bali Beach Hotel, Sanur, 288-511.

Satriavi Tours, Jl. Danau Tamblingan 27, Tel: 287-074, Fax: 287-019.

Tunas Indonesia, Jl. Danau Tamblingan 107, Sanur, Tel: 288-056.

Vayatour, Jl. Hayam Wuruk 124A, Denpasar, Tel: 223-757.

Airline Offices

Indonesian Carriers:

Garuda, Kuta Beach Hotel, Kuta, Tel: 751-179; Sanur Beach Hotel, Sanur, Tel: 287-915; Grand Bali Beach Hotel, Sanur, Tel: 288-511 ext 130; Jl. Melati No 61, Denpasar, Tel: 225-245. Ticketing hours: Monday–Saturday 8am–4.45pm, Sunday & holiday 9am–1pm. Airport: 751-178/4, 751-273; 24 hour reservations Tel: 227-825.

Mandala Airlines, Jl. Diponegoro 98, Kerthawijaya Plaza D/23, Tel: 231-659, 222-751, 232-986.

Merpati, Jl. Melati No 51, Denpasar, Tel: 235-358. Ticketing hours: 7am–7pm daily, reservations 7am–9pm; Hotline: 722-740, 722-741.

Bouraq, Jl. Sudirman No 7A, Denpasar, Tel: 223-564, 237-420. Reservations hours: 8am–9pm.

Sempati, Jl. Diponegoro, Komplek Diponegoro Megah, Blk B/No. 27, Tel: 237-343. Reservations and ticketing 24 hours daily.

International airlines with offices at Grand Bali Beach Hotel, Sanur; can be reached through the hotel operator at Tel: 288-511.
Air France, Tel: 287-734, Fax: 2870-774;
Ansett Australia, Tel: 289-636;
Cathay Pacific, Tel: 287-774;
Continental, Tel: 287-774;
Japan, Tel: 287-577, 287-576;
Korean, Tel: 289-402, 281-074;
Lufthansa, Tel: 287-069;
Malaysian, Tel: 285-071;
Qantas, Tel: 288-331;
Thai, Tel: 288-141;
SAS, Tel: 288-141;
Singapore, Tel: 261-666.

Airlines with offices at Wisti Sabha Building at Ngurah Rai International Airport, airport operator Tel: 751-011.
Air New Zealand, Tel: 756-170;
China, Tel: 754-856;
Eva, Tel: 756-488, 757-295;
KLM, Tel: 756-124, 756-126;
Royal Brunei, Tel: 757-292.
Others: LTU, Ambarah Building, Jl. Kuta Raya 88R, Tel: 757-552, 757-556.

Practical Tips

Emergencies

Security & Crime
Be warned! Bali, once blissfully free of theft and petty crime, is now something of a haven for petty thieves. Carelessness on the part of foreign visitors has a lot to do with this.

Points to remember: Don't leave valuables unattended. Lock up your room securely and make sure that your windows are locked at night – no matter how hot it is. Put all valuables in the hotel's safe or lock them up in a cupboard in your room. Straight off the plane and the first night in a new place are times to be extra careful. Be extra careful with purses, wallets and backpacks at crowded festivals or in the back of a bemo. It's usually when you are hot and flustered that the pickpocket strikes.

There are two scams that are frequently used on public transportation. You will be flanked by two friendly, usually English-speaking young men – one will engage you in conversation and distract you while the other picks your pocket. The other scam is to get you distracted and take your wallet and put it under a large package on the pickpocket's lap. This is usually just a piece of plywood wrapped in brown paper, but looks like a painting. They might ask you to change a large bill to see how much money you're carrying.

Don't fall asleep on a bemo, and don't get on an empty one leaving a bus station (they never leave until full and you might be taken for a ride, literally). Don't lend money unless you don't mind not getting it back.

It has recently become unsafe to walk alone along Kuta Beach at night and along the Kuta-Legian road. Sanur Beach is still relatively quiet and its hotels are patrolled.

All thefts should be reported immediately to the police, even though there is little chance of recovering stolen belongings. This applies especially to passports and other official documents. Without a police report, you will have difficulty obtaining new documents and leaving the country. It's a good idea to keep photocopies of your passport, ticket and driver's license in a separate place from the originals. If you have an old or expired passport, throw it in the bottom of your suitcase when traveling. This will be a handy identification tool in case your valid passport is lost or stolen.

All narcotics are illegal in Indonesia. The use, sale or purchase of narcotics results in long prison terms – even death – and/or huge fines. This is one area in Indonesia where bribery can't help. Be aware that a lot of planting goes on in the Kuta area. Don't keep or carry packages for people that you don't know.

Medical Services
Ambulance: 118 (it is often quicker to hire a taxi)

Every major village has a small government clinic called **puskesmas** (open from 7am–3pm), but for major problems visit one of the hotel clinics or one of the public hospitals in Denpasar. The major hotels have on-call doctors and well-stocked clinics.

For parasite, hepatitis, pregnancy or a myriad of other **tests**, the reliable **Prodya Laborotorium**, Jl. Diponegoro No 172, Tel: 227-194, 236-133, open daily 7am–10pm.

HOSPITALS
Rumah sakit means hospital. If you have a real life-threatening emergency, get thee to Singapore. If your insurance policy covers SOS or medical evacuations, you're in luck (but you have to have proof of this). If not, you need to put up $30,000 for the special jet to Singapore, and this is paid in cash (or credit card). Your consulate should be able to help you.

SOS representative in Jakarta, Tel: (021) 725-811.
Asia Emergency Assistance (AEA) is handled by Bali Tourist International Assist, Jl. Hayam Waruk 40, Tel: 228-996, 227-271, 231-443.

If you intend to seek medical treatment locally, the major hospitals' emergency rooms have English-speaking staff, but the quality of service is not up to Western standards. Pregnant women can go to the **maternity hospital** (*Rumah Sakit Kasih Ibu*).

Rumah Sakit Umum Sanglah (public hospital), Jl. Diponegoro, Sanglah, Denpasar, Tel: 227-911, 227-912, 227-913.
Rumah Sakit Wongaya (public hospital), Jl. Kartini, Denpasar, Tel: 222-142.
Rumah Sakit Angkatan Darat (army hospital), Jl. Sudirman, Denpasar, Tel: 226-521.
Rumah Sakit Dharma Usada (private), Jl. Sudirman No 50, Denpasar, Tel: 227-560, 234-824.
Rumah Sakit Kasih Ibu (maternity hospital), Jl. Teuku Umar No I20, Tel: 223-036, 237-016.

Psychiatric clinic: Dr I Gusti Putu Panteri, Rumah Sakit Bina Atma, Jl. HOS Cokroaminoto 30, Tel: 425-744.
Emergency dental treatment: Dr Indra Guizot, Jl. Patimura 19, Denpasar, Tel: 222-445, 234-375.

SPECIALISTS
The following specialists in Denpasar all have open clinics from 4–7pm daily, except Sundays and holidays. No ap-

pointment is needed, although some will take your name over the phone or in person and put you on a list.

PEDIATRICIANS

Dr Hamid, Jl. Diponegoro 126, Tel: 227-605.

Dr Widya, c/o Rumah Sakit Kasih Ibu, Jl. Teuku Umar No 120, Denpasar, Tel: 223-036.

INTERNISTS

Dr Tuti Parwati, Jl. Diponegoro 115A, Denpasar, Tel: 227-911 (5–7pm).

Dr Moerdowo, Jl. Melati No 24 (no phone).

SURGEONS

Dr Otong Wirawan, Jl. Danau Poso, Sanur, Tel: 287-482 (Monday–Saturday 8am–noon).

Dr Ketut Budha, Jl. Gunung Kidul No 53, Tel: 437-896.

OPHTHALMOLOGIST

Dr I Gusti Nyoman Tista, Jl. Sutoyo 50, Tel: 233-941.

OBSTETRICIAN/GYNECOLOGIST

Dr Suwanda Duarsa, Jl. Sumbawa No 24, Tel: 261-914.

Dr Gede Surya, Jl. Diponegoro 204, Tel: 223-736.

DENTISTS

Dr Retno Agung, Jl. By Pass Sanur, Sanur, Tel: 288-501. Also has an open clinic every weekday at Rumah Sakit Kasih Ibu (mornings).

Dr Indra Guizot, Jl. Patimura 19, Tel: 222-445, 226-445.

PSYCHIATRIST

Dr I Gusti Putu Panteri, Jl. Nakula, Tel: 437-462.

Dr Robert Reverger, Bangli, Tel: (0366) 91074; Jl. Nangka 12, Tel: 234-453.

DERMATOLOGIST

I Gusti Ayu Sumeda Pinda, Jl. Diponegoro 115A, Tel: 262-186.

GENERAL PRACTITIONERS

Dr AA Made Djelantik, Jl. Hayam Waruk 190, Tel: 262-186.

Dr Conny Pangkahila, Jl. Bypass Ngurah Rai 25X, Sanur, Tel: 288-128; Jl. Danau Buyan 74, Sanur, Tel: 288-626.

PHARMACIES

Most pharmacies or *apotik* are open daily 8am–6pm. Late at night on Sundays and holidays, there is a rotation system in Denpasar. Check the *Bali Post* newspaper or ask your hotel.

Kimia Farma, Jl. Diponegoro 123-125, Denpasar, Tel: 227-812.

Ria Farma, Jl. Veteran 43, Denpasar, Tel: 222-635.

Bali Farma, Jl. Melati 9, Denpasar, Tel: 223-132.

Dirga Yusa, Jl. Surapati 23, Denpasar, Tel: 222-267.

Farmasari, Jl. Banjar Taman, Sanur, Tel: 288-062.

Apotik Maha Sandhi, Jl. Raya Kuta, Kuta, Tel: 751-830.

Smaller "drugstores" are also found on many streets, selling film, toiletries, etc.

Weights & Measures

Indonesia employs the metric system of measurement. One kilometer is equal to 0.6 miles; one meter is equal to 3.3 feet; one kilogram is equal to 2.2 pounds; one liter is equal to 0.3 US gallons or 0.2 imperial gallons. To convert Celsius to Fahrenheit, multiply by 1.8 and add 32; to convert Fahrenheit to Celsius, subtract 32 and multiply by 0.56.

Business Hours

Indonesians like to get their work done in the morning to avoid working in the heat of the day, so if you need to visit a government office, try to get there between 8am and 11.30am. This also applies to banks and private businesses. Government offices close early on Fridays and Saturdays. Generally, offices are open from 7am–3pm Monday–Thursday, 7.30am–noon on Friday, closed Saturday and Sunday.

Tipping

At most of the larger hotels and restaurants, a government tax and service charge of up to 21 percent is added to the bill automatically. Tipping is not usual and do not feel compelled to tip at restaurants. If you've hired a taxi and liked the driver, then a tip of 10–I5 percent would be appreciated. If

you're traveling in a group, then a tip to drivers and guides is a good idea. An airport or hotel porter expects Rp. 500–1,000 per bag depending on the size and weight of the bag. Always carry small change with you, as taxi drivers are often short of change – or so they claim. Rounding up the fare to the nearest Rp. 500 is standard.

Religious Services

There are a number of churches and mosques in Bali. They are mainly in Denpasar, Sanur or Nusa Dua. A church is presently being built in Andong in Ubud.

Churches

CATHOLIC MASSES

Grand Bali Beach Hotel: Saturday 5.30pm;

Bali Hyatt Hotel: Saturday 7pm;

Bali Sol Hotel: Sunday 6pm.

INTERDENOMINATIONAL SERVICES

Nusa Dua Beach Hotel, Sunday 6pm, sponsored by Youth with a Mission;

Grand Bali Beach, Sanur, Sunday 6.30pm, Tel: 237-058;

Catholic Church, Jl. Kepundung, Denpasar, Tel: 222-729. Sunday 7am, 9am, 5.30pm;

Church of St Francis Xavier, Jl. Kartika Plaza, Kuta/Tuban, Saturday 7.30pm;

Mary Mother of All Nations Church, Nusa Dua, Saturday 5pm;

Protestant Maranatha, Jl. Surapati, Denpasar;

Protestant Bali, Gang Menuh, off Jl. Legian, Kuta, Sundays 10am;

Seventh Day Adventist, Jl. Surapati, Denpasar;

Pentecostal, Jl. Karna, Denpasar;

Evangelical, Jl. Melati, Denpasar.

Mosques

Raya Mosque, Jl. Hasanudin, Denpasar;

An-nurr Mosque, Jl. Diponegoro, Denpasar;

Al-Hissan Mosque, Grand Bali Beach;

Taqwa Mosque, Jl. Supratman, Denpasar.

Newspapers & Magazines

There are three English-language papers published in Jakarta: the *Jakarta Post*, the *Indonesian Times*, and the *Indonesian Observer*. These are available at all major hotels, most bookstores and the magazine kiosks in Sanur, Kuta and Denpasar. *Time*, *Newsweek* and the *International Herald Tribune* are also available at these places. The deluge of Indonesian magazines includes many devoted to the private lives of film stars and pop culture heroes. *Bali News* is a bimonthly newspaper dedicated to culture and the arts. *Bali Advertiser* lists items for sale, properties for rent and "job wanted" ads. *Bali Kini*, *Bali Echo*, and *Bali Tourist Guide* are among local tourism-oriented publications.

Radio & Television

Radio is a vital force in the dissemination of Bahasa Indonesia and a vehicle for aural aspects of Indonesia's diverse cultural traditions. Besides the government radio, Radio Republik Indonesia, (RRI 93.5 FM), which plays a lot of traditional Indonesian music and also has morning and evening programs in English, there are two local Denpasar stations broadcasting in English: Bali FM, FM 100.9 and Casanova, 101.5 FM. Many other FM stations play Western pop and rock music. For those who must keep up with the world they left behind, the BBC and the Voice of America both broadcast in Indonesia on shortwave. Check the times and frequencies in newspapers.

Indonesian television has a good portion of the broadcasting time is devoted to news. There are two stations run by the government: TVRI and TPI, which is educational. The three private channels are SCTV, Indosiar and RCTI. There is a half-hour, locally-produced English news broadcast, "Bali Vision", daily at 6.30pm.

Postal Services

There are post offices in every major town and village; Monday–Thursday 8am–2pm, Friday 8am–noon, Saturday 8am–1pm, and in some places (such as Ubud) Sundays 8am–noon.

The **central post office** in Denpasar, Jl. Raya Puputan, Renon, is open daily 7.30am–8.30pm, 8am–8pm on Sundays. Other main post offices: in Sanur, Jl. Danau Buyan; in Kuta between Jl. Raya Kuta and Jl. Tanjung Sari; and in Ubud, Jl. Jembawan, just off the main road. Letters and parcels take 2–3 weeks to arrive from abroad.

Poste restante, akin to general delivery, is available in Denpasar 80000, Sanur 80228, Kuta 80200, Singaraja 81110, Nusa Dua 80316 and Ubud 80571. When picking up letters, take identification. Letters should be addressed: Recipient's Name, c/o Poste Restante, City, Post Code, Indonesia.

If mailing anything crucial and important, use the international couriers: **DHL**, Jl. Hayam Waruk 118, Tel: 222-526, Fax: 234-489 **ELTHEHA**, Dipenogoro, Kompleks Dipenogoro Megah, Tel: 222-889, Fax: 235-261 **VIP**, Jl. Dipenogoro B27, Tel: 237-343, Fax: 236-131 **TNT Express Worldwide**, Jl. Teuku Umar 88E, Tel: 238-043, 222-238, Fax: 238-043 **Federal Express**, Jl. Bypass Ngurah Rai 100X, Jimbaran, Tel: 701-727, Fax: 701-725. Ary's is the local DHL agent for receiving and sending express mail in Ubud, Tel: 975-053, Fax: 975-162.

More and more individuals and businesses now have telephones. However, not everyone is used to "telephone culture", so you must exercise great patience.

Numerous government and private **Telkom Wartel** (*warung telekomunikasi*) offices dot the streets, from where you can place local and international calls, send and receive faxes, purchase telephone cards, etc. A list of 52 Telkom Wartels appears in the front of the Denpasar telephone directory.

The **main office** (including IDD, fax, telex and telegram services) in Denpasar (Jl. Teuku Umar 6, Fax: (62-361) 236-021) is open 24 hours a day. There are branches in Gianyar, Kuta and Sanur. The Ubud branch in Andong is open from 7am–7pm every day (Fax: 62-361-95120).

You can receive faxes which will be delivered within 24 hours, provided you have specified the complete delivery address. There is a service charge of Rp. 600 per page.

Ary's Tourist Services, Jl. Ubud Raya, Ubud, also has an incoming fax service; the number is (62 361) 975-162 and the cost is Rp. 1,000 per page. You must collect your own fax.

Pay phones are few and far between, and most of them are not in working order. But those that do work cost Rp. 50 for a two-minute call; this is much cheaper than making a local call from a phone office. Pay phones which operate with a phone card, which may be purchased from post offices, wartels, airports, supermarkets, etc., are increasingly abundant and a handy way to make international calls, especially from larger hotels, which slap hefty surcharges and taxes on calls made from the room.

Internet: For internet addicts and business people who travel with laptops, there are numerous local internet service providers in Bali. America Online has a Bali node, CompuServe has access through Infonet and Sprintnet, via Jakarta. Lines do not always hold well and you may have trouble getting hotel staff to understand that you are trying to bypass the PBX, even when there are modem outlets in larger hotel rooms.

Australia: Jl. Prof. Moch Yamin 51, Renon, Denpasar, Tel: 235-092, 235-093, Fax: 235-146.

French (Honorary): Jl. Tambaksari 5, Sanur, Tel/Fax: 287-383.

German (Honorary): Jl. Pantai Karang No 17A, Sanur, Tel: 288-535, Fax: 288-826.

Italy (Honorary): Jl. Cemara, Semawang, Sanur, Tel: 288-896, Fax: 227-642.

Japan: Jl. Raya Puputan 1, Denpasar, Tel: 234-808, Fax: 231-308.

Netherlands (Honorary): KCB Travel, Jl. Raya Kuta 99, Kuta, Tel: 751-517, Fax: 752-777.

Norway & Denmark: Jl Jayagiri VIII/10, Denpasar, Tel: 235-098, Fax: 234-834.

Sweden & Finland: Jl. Segara Ayu (c/o Segara Village Hotel), Tel: 288-407, Fax: 287-242.

Switzerland & Austria (Honorary): c/o Swiss Restaurant, Jl. Pura Bagus Teruna (Jl. Rum Jungle) Legian Kelod, Tel: 751-735, Fax: 754-457.

United States (Consular): Jl. Hayam Wuruk 188, Renon, Tel: 233-605.

Getting Around

On Arrival

If arriving late at night, it might be best to just go to Kuta for one night to rest. You can get taxis to Ubud and Sanur as well; there is a taxi stand just outside the customs area. If not carrying much luggage, walk some distance out of the airport parking lot and charter a minivan or sedan for much less than the official price, but bargain.

Orientation

Though one can circumnavigate Bali in a single day, some claim that you will see more by standing still, thus allowing the island to come to you. While in principle this is true, not all of us have the time to wait, and the opportunity for serendipitous encounters certainly increases when on the move.

Don't try to go everywhere. The real Bali is all around, not in some remote village on the other side of the island.

The main tourist hub is in the southern triangle formed by Sanur, Kuta and Nusa Dua. Half-day outings are best, leaving the other half of the day to relax on the beach, stroll through a nearby village or sit in a cafe. If a sun lover and prefer the comforts of home and the relaxation of the beach, then stay at Kuta (a wild and crazy kind of place). If you prefer something quieter, there are the sister beaches of Legian and Seminyak up the road to the north, Candi Dasa on the east coast, Canggu and Yeh Gangga in the west, Sanur in the south or Lovina.

If a culture lover, stay in Ubud, where outlying villages offer everything from basket-making to woodcarving and dance-drama. There is no reason to stay in Denpasar, which has little of interest. (If on business, stay in Sanur and commute the 7 km/4 miles to town). Balinese roads are a parade ground, used for escorting village deities to the sea, funeral cremation processions, filing to the local temple, or

the performances of a trans-island *barong* dance. They are also increasingly crowded, and the increase in traffic has been dramatic over the past two decades.

From the Airport

There is a taxi service from the airport, with the fixed rates for airconditioned and non airconditioned cars posted at the counter. Pay the cashier at the desk and receive a coupon that is to be surrendered to your driver. The fixed rates range from $3.50 to Kuta to $20 to Ubud. Refuse offers from informal "guides" loitering in the airport.

Note that rather than taking a taxi from the airport, you can walk about a kilometer out to the main road (if traveling light) and catch a local bemo to Kuta (Rp. 1,000) or Denpasar (Rp. 1,700). There are also "wild taxis" in the parking lot that will take you to your destination a bit cheaper than the taxis (but you have to bargain).

Taxis are hired by the car, not per person, and generally by the half- or full-day, not the hour.

Domestic Travel

From Kuta to:
Denpasar: Hop on a bemo at "bemo corner" going to Tegal Station. Either walk into Denpasar or jump on a three-wheeled bemo to get into town.
Ubud: Go to Tegal, transfer to Kereneng station, get on a bemo to Batubulan station and then another one to Ubud.
Sanur: Go to Tegal, transfer to Kereneng, then get a Sanur bemo. Sometimes you'll be able to get a Sanur bemo at Tegal.
Singaraja: Go to Tegal, to Kereneng, then to Ubung station. From there you can get buses and vans to all points north and west.
Lovina: From Singaraja bus station.
Teluk Terima: From Singaraja.
Tanah Lot: Go to Ubung first, then get a van going to Kediri. At Kediri, get a bemo to Tanah Lot.
Candi Dasa: Go to Tegal, Kereneng, Batubulan, then get on a van going to Klungkung, transfer to an Amlapura van. Sometimes there are direct vans from Batubulan station.

From Ubud to:
Denpasar: Bemo to Batubulan station, transfer to Kereneng. Walk into town or get on a three-wheeler to Gajah Mada.
Kintamani/Gunung Batur: Go to Sakah, hop on a bemo to Bangli, then on one to Kintamani.
Candi Dasa: Go to Sakah, then to Gianyar town where you can pick up a van to Klungkung. There get on a bus/van going to Amlapura (which passes through Candi Dasa).
Besakih: Get to Klungkung, then transfer to Besakih.
Points west: Batubulan, then Ubung.

By Bemo

Balinese travel by *bemo*, which are minivans with two benches facing one another in the back. They are hot, dusty and full of diesel exhaust, but are a great way to meet the local people. Buses go longer routes and are not as common. Mini-buses (called colt) are very popular now and go all over the island. You don't need to go to a "bemo stop" to get on a bemo; just flag them down and yell "stop" when you want to get out.

The **major bus terminals** are at Tegal (in Denpasar going to Kuta, Sanur airport and Nusa Dua); Kereneng (in Denpasar going to Batubulan, Sanur and in the city); Ubung (going to all points north and west, including Java); Batubulan (going north and east) and in Singaraja (going to Java and Denpasar).

Intercity buses leave for Java from Ubung Terminal, and the bus companies have their offices in town on Jl. Hasanudin, near Jl. Sumatra, as well as at the Ubung Terminal. Within Denpasar, you have to travel a distance to cross town, as the city is full of one-way streets. Sometimes it's quicker to walk.

Chartering a Minivan/Car

Walking down the street, inevitably you will be approached by young men waving their arms in front of them as if turning a wheel and yelling, "Transpor? transpor?" It is easy to charter a minivan with a driver (and a guide if through a tour agency or hotel) for an hour, day or month. There are also shuttles from Kuta and Ubud, and from major resorts and Lombok. For quick, fixed-price transportation without the hassles of a bemo, check with:

Ganda Sari Transport, Jl. Legian, Kuta, Tel: 754-383
Perama Tourist Service, Kuta, Tel: 751-875, 751-170
Cahaya Sakti Utama Tour, Ubud, Tel: 975-520.

Renting a car and driver can be done by the half-day or full-day. It is only courteous to give your driver money for a meal if you pause for lunch or dinner. If pleased with the driver, a tip (Rp. 10,000 is sufficient) is appropriate.

Water Transport

Most large ships sail out of Surabaya Bay, but a few go out of Bali (Padangbai and Benoa). You can sometimes find a yacht which will take on an extra person or two – just ask down at the ports.

Indonesia's national shipping line, **PELNI** (Tel: 228-962), offers travel to many islands in the archipelago. There are five classes of rooms to choose from in its modern fleet of passenger ships. Boats go to Lombok twice a month as well; check with the PELNI office (Jl. Diponegoro near Jl. Hasanudin or at Pelabuhan Benoa, PO Box 386; Monday–Friday 7am–3pm) for days and costs.

Private Transport
Car Rental

Driving in Bali is a dangerous proposition. Other drivers are not defensive, the roads are narrow and poorly maintained, and stray dogs and chickens dart into the road all too frequently. If you collide with anything, you are responsible for all costs.

If you feel comfortable driving among unexpected processions – of both the people and animal variety – on potholed and narrow roads in a land where defensive driving means nothing, then by all means put yourself behind the driver's seat. Otherwise, hire a driver, relax and enjoy.

Self-drive cars are available in Sanur, Kuta and Ubud. You must have a valid Indonesian or International Driving License. Petrol is not included in the price. It's advisable to buy the extra insurance. Book a car through your hotel or from any of the companies listed below. They will deliver the car and pick it up. Test drive the car first before paying in advance.

RENTAL COMPANIES

Avis, Jl. Uluwatu 8A, Jimbaran, Tel: 701-770.
Bali Car Rental, Jl. Bypass Ngurah Rai, Sanur, Tel: 288-550, 288-359.
Bali Baru Wisata, Jl. Legian, Kuta, Tel: 223-998; Jl. Sumba 26, Denpasar, Tel: 231-784.
CV Agung Rent Car, Jl. Pratama Terora, Nusa Dua, Tel: 771-954.
Norman's Rent a Car, Holiday's Art Shop, Jl. Danau Tamblingan, Sanur, Tel: 288-328.
Nusa Dua Rent a Car, Jl. Pantai Mengiat 23, (100 meters from Hotel Bualu), Nusa Dua, Tel: 771-905.
Taman Sari Rent a Car, Jl. Danau Buyan, Sanur, Tel: 288-187.
Toyota Rent Car & Leasing, provides Ngurah Rai Airport, Tel: 753-744, Jl. Raya Tuban 99X, Tel: 751-356, 751-282; Jl. Bypass Ngurah Rai, Jimbaran, Tel: 701-747.

In Kuta, Candi Dasa and Ubud, you will see numerous "Rent Car" signs, which are fine to use.

Motorcycles

Each year, several tourists are killed in motorbike accidents, and many more end up spending their holiday in the hospital. If you do decide to rent a bike, drive slowly and very defensively.

This is a convenient and inexpensive way to get around the island, but roads are crowded and the traffic is heavy, so chances of having an accident are uncomfortably high. Helmets are required by law and the ones provided by rental agencies offer little protection. If you know you'll be using a motorcycle while in Bali, bring your own helmet from home.

The cost of hiring a motorbike in Bali is negotiable, and varies according to the condition of the machine, length of rental and time of year. There are 90cc, 100cc and 125cc models available for rent. You buy the petrol. It's a good idea to buy insurance so that you are not responsible for damages in case of an accident. Be sure to test drive it and see that everything is in good working order. You should have an International Driving Permit valid for motorcycles, or else spend a morning at the Denpasar Police Office to obtain a temporary permit, valid for six months on Bali only. This entails passing a driving test and paying an admin-

istrative fee of $30. Bring along passport and three passport-size photos, plus your driving license from your home country. Normally the person who rents you the bike will accompany you to the police station. Getting an International Driving Permit in your own country will save you this hassle.

Bicycles

It used to be that the only bicycles available were one-speed clunkers more dangerous to the rider than useful. Nowadays, mountain bikes (18-speed) are everywhere. Make sure the wheels are in good alignment, the brakes in good working order, and that you have a light.

On Foot

This is probably the most pleasant way to see Bali. As it is a small island, it is quite possible to traverse the entire island by foot. Most people do day hikes in and around Danau Batur, Danau Bratan in Bedugul, the national park in West Bali and around Ubud. The *Travel Treasure*, a map and guidebook available in Ubud, outlines a number of interesting walks throughout the island. Bali Bird Walks, from Insight Pocket Guides, is another winner (naturally).

Hitchhiking

Hitchhiking just isn't done and people probably wouldn't understand what you were doing. But this doesn't mean that you can't ask someone to take you somewhere. There are *ojek* or motorcycle taxis that will take you wherever you want to go for a fee; trying to get free rides from someone is not culturally appropriate. But you'll often find people offering to take you places; this is Balinese hospitality. (A warning to women: Be careful of "fast boys on fast bikes" as they want much more than just to give you a ride.)

On Departure

Leaving Bali by the airport, you must first make sure that your reservation is reconfirmed – do this three days in advance of leaving. Airlines, particularly Garuda, always overbook. To make your confirmations, go to the airline office in person, as a phone confirmation is not a "real" confirmation. Make sure you get the computer print-out that says you have a reserved seat. Not all international airlines require reconfirmation, such as Cathay Pacific. Seats cannot be assigned beforehand; arrive at the airport two hours prior to departure. An airport tax must be paid, Rp. 25,000 for international flights.

Where to Stay
Accommodations

There are a myriad of accommodations to choose from in Bali, from five-star luxury hotels to concrete slabs for just a few dollars a night. Recently, the basic comforts we take for granted (tiled bathrooms, hot-water showers, towels) have made their way even to the most remote regions. If staying in budget places, bring towel, soap, toilet paper and mosquito coils, as these are not provided. Most budget and intermediate range *losmen* (a small inn, usually family-run) and hotels provide breakfast; most luxury places do not.

Reservations are recommended for the larger hotels during July–August and around Christmas–New Year.

For the following listings: price categories for standard rooms (or suites in the larger hotels) are: (B)udget = under $29; (E)conomy = $30–$59; (I)ntermediate = $60–$99; (D)eluxe = $100–$149; (L)uxury = above $150.

Symbols (-B) and (L+) are used when rates are significantly below Budget or above Luxury, respectively.

Deluxe and luxury properties will include hot water, air conditioning, usually IDD telephone and other facilities, along with up to 21 percent government tax and service charge. Budget and economy properties often include a simple breakfast with rates.

All telephone codes are (0361) unless otherwise indicated.

Denpasar

There's no real reason to stay in Denpasar unless you have business that can't wait until after a commute in from Kuta or Sanur. If you really must stay here, the old Natour Bali Hotel or the Pemecutan Palace Hotel are the nicest places. The Bali Hotel was built in the early 1930s and was once the colonial oasis in Bali – the *rijstaffel* is still good and the swimming pool courtyard charming. The Pemecutan Palace is actually located in the Badung palace and one has the feeling, at least, of hobnobbing with Balinese royalty here in the extensive courtyards.

There are scores of other hotels in the $3–$20 category, most of them catering to domestic Indonesian tourists. Many are located on Jl. Diponegoro. There are also cheap but clean inns on Jl. Suli and Jl. Trijata, by the Lila Buana Stadium.

Adi Yasa, Jl. Nakula 23, Denpasar, Tel: 222-679. 14 rooms; price includes breakfast. *Losmen*-style rooms arranged around a central garden; restaurant. (B)
Natour Balil, Jl. Veteran 2, Denpasar, Tel: 225-681/5, Fax: 235-347. 71 rooms. Centrally located in Denpasar, just a block from the main intersection and town square. Good restaurant and bar. A/c and hot water. Swimming pool, tour service. (I)
Pemecutan Palace, Jl. Thamrin 2, Denpasar, Tel: 423-491. 40 rooms. This hotel takes one side of the extensive Badung palace, where day-to-day palace life continues all around. Half of the rooms have a/c. Restaurant; laundry services; no hot water. (B–E)
Wisma Taruna, Jl. Gadung 31, Tel: 226-913. 16 rooms. A youth hostel run by a friendly family. To get there, walk east on Jl. Hayam Wuruk from the center of town, then turn left at the Arya Hotel and go about 100 meters. It's on the right side. (B)

Sanur

Sanur is for gracious living, peace and quiet. More "international" but somehow far less cosmopolitan than frantic Kuta. Foreigners have been staying in Sanur since the 1920s, and they know how to take care of guests here. Strictly first-class, with a range of places for budget travelers. The main choice is between the convenience and luxury of the large 5-star establishments (Grand Bali Beach, Bali Hyatt and Sanur Beach) or the quietude and personality of a private bungalow by the sea. Reservations are advisable during the peak tourist seasons. During the low seasons (between January 15–July 15 and September I–December 15) a 10–20 percent discount from the published rates is available at many hotels just for the asking.

Abian Irama Inn, Jl. Ngurah Rai By-pass, Sanur, Tel: 288-415, 288-673, 288-792. 47 rooms. Ten minutes from the beach. Pleasant and reasonable rooms, some with a/c and hot water, all with laundry service and free airport transportation. Pool. (B)
Alit's Beach Bungalows, Jl. Raya Sanur, P.O. Box 302, Denpasar, Tel: 288-567, Fax: 288-766. 98 rooms. At the north end and two minutes from the beach. Cottages in a garden that borders a small road, and a beachfront packed with brightly-painted sailing craft. A/c and hot water. Pool. (E)
Baruna Beach Inn, Jl. Sindhu, Sanur, Tel: 288-546, Fax: 288-629. 7 rooms. Oldest hotel on the beach. Traditional thatched rooms furnished with Balinese antiques open onto a wide courtyard bordering the sea. Small and personal. A/c and hot water. (E–I)
BSB (Bali Sanur Bungalows) Besakih, Jl. Danau Tamblingan 45, Sanur, Tel: 288-424, Fax: 286-059. 50 rooms. Each hotel is set in a meandering garden that winds its way gracefully to the sea. A pool and two restaurants. All bungalows with a/c, western baths and hot water. (I)
BSB Peneeda View, Jl. Danau Tamblingan, Sanur, Tel: 288-425, Fax: 288-224. 46 rooms. A bungalow-style hotel right on Sanur beach. A pool and two restaurants. All bungalows with a/c, western baths and hot water. (I)
BSB Respati, Jl. Danau Tamblingan 33, Tel: 288-0461, Fax: 288-047. 27 rooms. A narrow string of duplex bungalows with white-tiled floors, twin beds, a/c, bathtub and shower. Comfortable but basic. Narrow beach, restaurant and small swimming pool. (E)
BSB Sanur Village Club, Jl. Hang Tuah 19, Sanur, P.O. Box 306, Denpasar, Tel: 288-421/2, Fax: 288-426. 41 rooms. All rooms surround a central garden with a pool, seven minutes from the beach. A/c and hot water. (E)
Bali Hyatt, Jl. Danau Tamblingan, Sanur, Tel: 288-271/2, 288-361, Fax:

287-693. 390 newly renovated rooms with television and suites overlooking the sea. A remarkably breezy, spacious feeling with public areas, clay tennis courts and fabulous gardens. Several restaurants, swimming pool, boutiques, convention facilities. (L)

Belcont, Jl. Hang Tuah, Tel: 288-250. 16 rooms. Seven minutes from the beach. All rooms have a/c and hot water. (B)

Diwangkara Hotel, Jl. Hang Tuah, Sanur, P.O. Box 120, Denpasar, Tel: 288-429, Fax: 288-675. 40 rooms. Private double bungalows in a secluded compound just behind the Le Mayeur museum, at the north end of the beach strip. All with a/c and have hot water. Swimming pool, one minute from beach. (E–I)

Grand Bali Beach, Jl. Hang Tuah, Sanur, Tel: 288-511/7, Fax: 287-917. 600 rooms. Ten stories, private beach, three swimming pools, four restaurants, bowling alleys, tennis courts, golf course, water sports, convention facilities, airline offices, banks. (L)

La Taverna Bali, Jl. Danau Tamblingan, Sanur, Tel: 288-387, 288-497, Fax: 287-126. 24 rooms. Delightful thatched bungalows with Italian stucco walls and elegantly-styled rooms set in a meandering Balinese garden. Private beach, pool and pizzeria. (D–L)

Laghawa Beach Inn, Jl. Danau Tamblingan 51, Tel: 288-494, Fax: 289-353. 22 rooms. Simple cottages with a/c or fan-cooled rooms in a garden; hot water. Five minutes from the beach. Excellent restaurant on premises. (B–I)

Puri Kelapa Garden Cottages, Jl. Segara Ayu No 1, Sanur, P.O. Box 236, Denpasar, Tel: 286-135, Fax: 287-417. 48 cottages. Each cottage is a/c with hot water shower and bathtub. Two-minute walk to the beach. (I)

Rani, Jl. Danau Buyan 33, Sanur, Tel: 288-578, 288-674. 24 rooms. Opposite the Post Office, 10 minutes from the beach. These *losmen*-style rooms are clean and quiet. There are no rooms with a/c, but all have cold-water showers and western toilets. (B)

Ramayana, Jl. Danau Tamblingan 130, Sanur, P.O. Box 366, Denpasar, Tel: 288-424, Fax: 288-675. 22 rooms. Clean a/c rooms with hot water, 5 minutes from the beach. This hotel takes pride in catering to the individual traveler's needs. (B)

Swastika, Jl. Danau Tamblingan 128, Tel: 288-693, 287-526, Tlx: 235-457. 60 rooms. Rooms have hot running water, most have a/c. Pool and restaurant. Breakfast included. (E)

Santrian Beach, Jl. Danau Tamblingan, Sanur, P.O. Box 55, Denpasar, Tel: 288-181/4, Fax: 288-185. 90 rooms. Private seaside bungalows in a spacious garden, some of which open into a garden and others with a view of the ocean. All rooms a/c with a private terrace. One pool, two restaurants, (I)

Sanur Beach, Jl. Mertasari, P.O. Box 279, Sanur, Tel: 288-011, Fax: 287-566. 425 rooms. This 4-story international hotel with attached bungalows is one of the older beachfront hotels in Sanur. Restaurants, swimming pool, ocean sports facility, tennis courts, mini-golf and a video viewing room with video cassette rental available. (D–L)

Sanur Indah, Jl. Danau Buyan, Sanur, Tel: 288-568. 15 rooms. Several *losmen*-style rooms with a fan, 10 minutes from the beach. Laundry. (B)

Sativa Sanur Cottages, Jl. Danau Tamblingan, Sanur, P.O. Box 163, Denpasar, Tel/Fax: 287-881. 50 rooms. Well-managed hotel. Very cozy and the restaurant food is excellent. (I)

Segara Village, Jl. Segara Ayu, Sanur, P.O. Box 91, Denpasar, Tel: 288-407/8, 288-231, Fax: 287-242, 288-022. 120 rooms. A variety of charming, private bungalows, some patterned after traditional rice granaries, arranged in tiny gardened "villages" bordering the sea. Two swimming pools, water sports facilities, classes in traditional Balinese dance, music, painting, woodcarving, batik, a children's recreation room, tennis courts and lots of personal attention from the staff. (I)

Sindhu Beach, Jl. Pantai Sindhu, Sanur, P.O. Box 181, Denpasar, Tel: 288-351/2, Fax: 289-268. 104 rooms. Bungalow hotel right on the beach, with a swimming pool. All with a/c and hot water. (I)

Taman Agung Beach Inn, Jl. Danau Tamblingan, Tel: 288-549. 24 rooms. Very pleasant, *losmen*-style rooms with a/c or fan, all have hot water and face a well-kept garden. Minutes from the beach. Laundry, restaurant. (B–E)

Tandjung Sari, Jl. Danau Tamblingan, Sanur, Tel: 288-441, Fax: 287-930. 26 rooms. Name means "Cape of Flowers". Serene and stylish, with private bungalows by the sea and lovely gardens. Excellent service and food. Swimming pool. (L)

Travelodge, Jl. Mertasari, Sanur; P.O. Box 2476, Denpasar, Tel: 288-833, 287-301/2, Fax: 287-303. 194 rooms. Down past the Sanur Beach Hotel at the very southern end of the strip. Rooms with tub, in-house video, IDD, restaurants, swimming pool and wet bar, tennis court, sauna and massage. Quiet and secluded. (D–L)

Villa Bebek, Jl. Mertasari, Sanur, P.O. Box 47, Denpasar, Tel/Fax: 287-668. 7 rooms. These are exquisite cottages and villas around an equally exquisite garden and swimming pool. Each villa has two rooms (upstairs and down) and fully-equipped kitchen and private garage. (D)

Kuta

Kuta in the 1990s is a malignant seaside Carnaby Street of the 1960s. Chaotic, noisy, lots of hype, but a great playground. Originally what drew visitors to Kuta was the wide beach and the surf. It still has the best seafront on the island, though now it is cluttered with hundreds of homestays, restaurants, bars, boutiques, travel agencies, artshops, car and bike rentals, banks and scores of tourists, both domestic and foreign. Though there are now many first-class hotels, the 5 km (3 mile) strip still caters best to the economy traveler who likes to be in the thick of things.

The Legian-Seminyak end of the beach is the best place to stay for any period of time – much quieter and more relaxed. Stay in Sanur or Jimbaran if you want solitude.

There are so many bungalows, hotels and homestays (called *losmen*, essentially a bed-and-breakfast) that no list could ever be complete, nor is a list really needed. Drop in and shop around. The difference between Kuta and Sanur is that one has far more choices in the lower price range here. The best way to find a budget room is just to walk around in any area that you fancy.

From the airport, the areas headed northward are: Tuban, Kuta, Legian, Seminyak, Kayu Aya, Petitinget, Canggu.

Tuban & Kuta

Barong Cottages, Jl. Legian, Gang Batu Bolong, Kuta, Tel/Fax: 751-804.

39 rooms. Two-story hotel with swimming pool, near the beach. (B)

Bali Dynasty, Jl. Kartika Plaza, Tuban, Tel: 752-403, Fax: 752-402. 267 rooms. Part of Shangri-la's international resort chain of hotels. Disco, conference facilities, beachfront restaurant. (D)

Bali Padma, Jl. Padma 1, Legian, P.O. Box 1107, Tuban, Tel: 752-111, Fax: 7521-40. 400 rooms. Big beachfront hotel with attractive wooden cottage-style rooms. Pool and lounge. (D)

Bintang Bali Resort, Jl. Kartika Plaza, Tuban Tel: 753-801 Fax: 753-292, Tlx: 235-833. 400 rooms. Pool and jacuzzi near beach, gym, tennis court, restaurants, and conference facilities available. (D)

Kartika Plaza Beach, Jl. Kartika Plaza, Tuban, P.O. Box 1012, Tel: 751-507/ 9, Fax: 752-475. 308 rooms. Beachside rooms and bungalows in a large garden. Table tennis, tennis court and swimming pool. (I)

Kuta Beach Club, Jl. Bakung Sari, Kuta, Tel: 751-261/2, Fax: 752-896. 100 rooms. In the middle of Kuta, quiet bungalows and rooms surround a patio garden. All rooms with a/c and hot water. Mini tennis, badminton, swimming pool and restaurant. (E)

Kuta Beach Hotel, Jl. Pantai Kuta, Kuta, Tel: 751-361/2, Tlx: 235-166. 50 rooms. A bungalow-style hotel 150 meters from the beach. Refrigerator, TV, private balcony or garden veranda. Restaurant, bar, disco and swimming pool. (I)

Maharani Hotel, Gang Poppies II, Tel: 751-863. Right next to the beach, this is a very friendly mid-sized hotel. Some rooms have hot water and a/c. (I)

Melasti Beach Bungalows, Jl. Kartika Plaza, Tuban, Tel: 751-860, Fax: 751-563. Swimming pool, close to the beach. (I)

Patra Jasa Beach Resort, Jl. Kuta Beach, P.O. Box 121, Tuban, Tel: 751-161, Fax: 752-030. 206 rooms. Located five minutes from the airport. This hotel was first built as a convention center by the state oil monopoly, Pertamina, and then opened to the general public in 1975. Restaurants, conference facilities, tennis courts, badminton, boating, water skiing, wind surfing, and a pool. Refrigerator, telephone, and in-house movies. (D)

Poppies Cottages, Gang Poppies I, Kuta (near Jl. Pantai Kuta and Jl. Legian), Tel: 751-059, Fax: 752-364. 20 rooms. Well-designed cottages in a beautiful garden, with hot water and refrigerator. Only 300 meters from the beach. Often filled to capacity, reservations is essential. Pool, restaurant. (I)

Poppies Cottages II, Poppies Lane II, Kuta (north of Poppies between beach and Jl. Legian), Tel: 751-059, Fax: 752-364. Smaller than Poppies – 4 rooms with fans only – but still quite popular; necessary to make reservations in advance. (B)

Ramayana Seaside Cottages, Jl. Kartika Plaza, Kuta, Tel: 751-864, Fax: 751-866. 45 rooms. Located 100 meters from the beach. All rooms with a/c, hot showers. Swimming pool, restaurant, laundry. (E)

Sahid Bali, Jl. Pantai Kuta, Kuta, P.O. Box 1102, Denpasar, Tel: 753-855, Fax: 752-019. 171 rooms. Just across from the beach, part of a large domestic chain. (I)

Santika Beach Hotel, Jl. Kartika, P.O. Box 1008, Tuban, Tel: 751-267/8, Fax: 751- 260. 157 rooms. An exquisite hotel with three swimming pools, coffee shop, restaurant, bar, tennis courts, and in-house video. All rooms are a/c and have refrigerators and taped-in music. (D)

Yulia Beach Inn, Jl. Pantai Kuta 43, Tel: 751-893, Fax: 751-055. 48 rooms. Variety of rooms from which to choose. (E)

Legian, Semiyak, Petitenget, Canggu

The villages of Legian and Seminyak lie at the north end of the Kuta Beach strip. As the beach continues northward, it becomes Petitenget and Canggu. These are the places to stay for the best of both worlds. Conveniently located 15–20 minutes from the center of Kuta, yet safely removed from the nerve-wracking intensity and hype, the villages are perfect for extended vacations. There are several first-class hotels, a great number of intermediate-range bungalows, and a plethora of inexpensive losmen. As is true in Kuta, you will find what suits you best by shopping around.

Bali Intan Cottages, Jl. Melasti 1, Legian, Tel: 751-770, Fax: 751-891. 150 rooms. This is the closest first-class hotel to Kuta. Tennis court, coffee shop, snack bar, and seafood restaurant. Wall-to-wall carpeting, color TV, and private balcony. (I–D)

Bali Mandira Cottages, Jl. Padma, Legian, Tel: 751-381, Fax: 752-377. 117 rooms. Built in 1982, this friendly and immaculate hotel provides tennis and squash courts, tours for skin-diving and snorkeling and an open view of the ocean. (I–D)

Bali Oberoi, Jl. Kayu Ayu, Petitenget, Tel: 751-061, 730-361, Fax: 730-791. 75 rooms. Luxury sea and garden-view rooms and villas with satellite television, sound systems, some with private pools. The hotel's coral-rock lanai and villas are adaptations of classic Balinese *puri*, or palace, designs. Secluded beach, shuttle to and from airport, pool. This is THE place to stay – pamper yourself. Massage and sauna in health center. (L+)

Blue Ocean, Jl. Legian Kaja, on "Double Six" Lane, Legian, Tel: 730-289. 29 rooms. Right on the beach; very popular with locals and surfers. A/c and hot water, swimming pool, restaurant, tour service. (B)

Dhyana Pura Beach, Jl. Dhyana Pura, Seminyak, Tel: 730-442, Fax: 730-463. 46 rooms. Close to the beach, this more isolated hotel has pool, restaurant, a/c rooms with hot water and bathtubs. Continental breakfast. (I)

Jayakarta Bali, Jl. Pura Bagus Teruna, Legian, P.O. Box 24, Denpasar, Tel: 751-433, Fax: 752-074. 280 rooms. A pleasant atmosphere which caters to the young, complete with two swimming pools, large garden, twice-a-week barbecue with performances of Balinese dance. (L)

The Legian, Jl. Kayu Aya, Petitenget, Tel: 730-622, Fax: 730-623. 71 suites on the beach, satellite television, sound system, pool and bar, restaurant, library, meeting room, shuttle to Kuta, airport transfers. (L+)

Legian Beach Hotel, Jl. Melasti, Legian, Tel: 751-711, Fax: 752-651. 190 rooms. Large complex wrapped in a relaxed atmosphere near the beach, the hotel offers free airport transport, hot water and tour service. (I–D)

Legian Garden Cottages, Jl. Double Six, Seminyak, Tel: 730-876, Fax: 730-405. 25 rooms. Not for those who want peace and quiet, as it's right next to a fashionable disco and gets noisy on party nights. Three minutes from the beach with a/c rooms, restaurant and a garden setting. (E)

Pelasa Cottage, Jl. Tunjung Mekar, Legian, Tel: 753-423/4, Fax: 753-424. 16 rooms. Very clean and well-maintained. Some rooms with a/c, hot water and kitchen. (B)

Pesona Bali, Jl. Kaya Aya, Petitenget, Tel: 753-914, Fax: 753-915. 69 rooms. Near the beach and far from the crowds. (I–D)

Rama Garden Cottages, Jl. Padma, Legian, P.O. Box 334, Tel: 751-971/2, Fax: 755-909. 34 rooms. Modern in style and comfort, offers refrigerators and a/c in every room, tiled bathrooms with hot water. Pool and restaurant. Breakfast and tax included. (E)

Jimbaran

The latest area to emerge as a hidden, luxury destination. The caliber of its hotels attract some of the jet-set for a hideaway holiday. Hotels are situated around a clean, white-sand bay facing toward Ngurah Rai airport. Native, beachside seafood grill restaurants are popular dining alternatives. Tranquil, with a charming fishing village. Continuing south on the dry Bukit peninsula, a new enclave of hotels is being constructed.

Bali Cliff, Ugasan, at the extreme south of Bukit peninsual. Tel: 771-992, Fax: 771-993. 200 rooms atop a 100 m cliff overlooking the sea. Cliff drops down to beach and seafood restaurant. (L+)

Bali Intercontinental, Jl. Uluwatu, Jimbaran, P.O. Box 35, Nusa Dua, Tel: 701-888, Fax: 701-777. 451 rooms. Set in 35 acres of Balinese landscaped gardens and lagoons, the resort has a beautiful beach and is the ideal viewing spot for Bali's sunsets. Squash courts, tennis courts, 3 swimming pools, water sports facilities, health club, restaurants and pubs. (L+)

Four Seasons Resort, Jimbaran, Denpasar, Tel: 701-010, Fax: 701-020. Built on a terraced hillside amidst landscaped gardens, the resort has a spectacular view of the bay and Gunung Agung. All individual villas, most with plunge pools. Four restaurants; conference facilities; full-service spa, swimming pool, tennis pro and courts, water sports. (L+)

Pan Sea Bali, Jl. Uluwatu Jimbaran, Tel: 701-605, Fax: 701-320. 41 villas with private baths and a/c. Great view of the ocean and bay. Pool, two restau-

rants, bar. Completely renovated in 1995. (L+)

Ritz-Carlton, Jl. Karang Mas Sejahtera, Jimbaran, Tel: 702-122, Fax: 702-123. 323 rooms in four-story resort, club rooms and villas, all perched on bluff overlooking white-sand beaches and the ocean. A/c, TV, pool, 18-hole golf putting course, tennis, kids program, gym, sauna, nursery, three restaurants. (L+)

Nusa Dua

As the newcomer on the scene, Nusa Dua is at a bit of a disadvantage, as it is rather isolated from the rest of Bali. On the other hand, the hotels here have made up for this by providing a "total" hotel environment – everything you could possibly ask for is available on the premises. Restaurants and souvenir shops line the road outside the complex, and the Galleria Nusa Dua shopping complex has expanded to feature 15 restaurants, 80 specialty shops, duty-free shopping, department stores and a supermarket. More upscale than Sanur and more inclusive than Jimbaran, this is a peaceful place but with little distinctive personality. Tanjung Benoa point, the northward continuation of Nusa Dua Beach, is lined with hotels catering to groups and watersports operations.

Amanusa, Nusa Dua, Tel: 772-333, Fax: 771-267. 35 suites. Part of the Amanresorts chain in Indonesia, this resort overlooks Bali Golf and Country Club, the ocean and Bali's coastline. There is a spacious swimming pool and an Italian restaurant, tennis courts and golf facilities. (L+)

Club Mediterranee, Nusa Dua, P.O. Box 7, Nusa dua, Tel: 771-521/3, Fax: 771-853. 350 rooms. Like its other international outlets, there's lots of sports and entertainment. (D)

Bali Hilton, P.O. Box 46, Nusa Dua, Tel: 771-102, Fax: 771-616. 540 rooms. Health center, tennis and squash courts, and water sports facilities. (D–L)

Bualu Village, Nusa Dua, P.O. Box 6, Denpasar, Tel: 771-310, Fax: 771-313. 50 rooms. Lush tropical gardens, a swimming pool about 100 meters from the beach. Transportation within Nusa Dua, tennis courts and sports available with or without instructors free of charge. (I–D)

Clarion Suites, Jl. Dalem Tarukan 7, Taman Mumbul, P.O. Box 133, Nusa Dua, Tel: 773-808, Fax: 773-737. 326 suites with living room, kitchenette. Tennis, gym, pool. (D)

Grand Hyatt Bali, P.O. Box 53, Nusa Dua, Tel: 771-234, Fax: 772-038. 750 rooms. Designed by architect of the world-famous Hyatt in Waikoloa, Hawaii, one of the most spectacular resort hotels in Southeast Asia. Four Balinese-style villages with five swimming pools. (L+)

Melia Bali, P.O. Box 1048, Tuban, Kuta, Tel: 771-510, 771-410, Fax: 771-360/2. 504 rooms. Newly renovated rooms and facilities. Club villas. Water sports facilities, five restaurants, swimming pool, gym and tennis courts. (L)

Nusa Dua Beach, P.O. Box 1028, Denpasar, Tel: 771-210, 771-220, Fax: 771-229. 380 rooms. A hotel on a scale of grandeur of Bali's rajas, owned by the Sultan of Brunei. The choice for heads of state visiting Bali. Huge pool, three restaurants, squash courts, tennis courts, international spa, and large beach front. (L+)

Sheraton Nusa Indah, P.O. Box 36, Nusa Dua, Tel: 771-906, Fax: 771-908. 380 rooms. Garden or ocean-view rooms, spectacular pool. Tuscany, seafood and bistro restaurants. Attached to Bali International Convention Center. (L+)

Putri Bali, Nusa Dua, P.O. Box 1, Denpasar, Tel: 771-020, Fax: 771-139. 384 rooms. All rooms with a/c, balcony, TV with two in-house video programs, four restaurants, two bars, pool, tennis courts, golf, water sports and recreation room. (D–L)

Sheraton Laguna, P.O. Box 2044 Kuta, Nusa Dua, Tel: 771-327/8, Fax: 771-326. 276 rooms with butler service. Beautiful setting with cascading waterfalls and blue swimming lagoons. (L+)

Tanjung Benoa

Bali Tropic Palace, Jl. Pratama 34, P.O. Box 41, Tanjung Benoa, Tel: 772-130, Fax: 772-131. 104 rooms, private terraces overlooking the sea. (D)

Grand Mirage, Jl. Pratama 74, Tanjung Benoa, Nusa Dua, Tel: 771-888, Fax: 772-148. 312 comfortable rooms with all the amminities, three restaurants, three bars, two tennis courts, swimming pool and meeting room. French spa is attached to hotel. (L)

Club Bali Mirage, Jl. Pratama 72, Tajung Benoa, Nusa Dua, Tel: 772-147, Fax: 772-156. All inclusive club with 100 rooms. Rate includes all meals, beverages, entertainment and non-motorized watersports. Balinese atmosphere. (D)

Novotel Benoa, Jl. Pratama, P.O. Box 39 Nusa Dua, Tanjung Benoa, Tel: 772-239, Fax: 772-237. 188 a/c rooms all in coconut wood. Two restaurants, room service, boutique and drugstore, children's program, shuttle bus to Nusa Dua, satellite TV. (D)

Central Bali

UBUD & ENVIRONS

The Ubud area has more rooms than one can count, as practically every month a new place is built. This used to be a budget traveler's dream, and even though cheap places abound, more and more *losmen* are upgrading by putting in swimming pools, tiled bathrooms and hot water.

Ubud encompasses a vast area, from Mas in the south, Andong, Sayan and Payangan in the north, Penestanan in the west and Peliatan in the east. Practically anywhere outside of Ubud town proper will give you more quiet, although the availability of food and transport could be a problem.

Ubud proper can be divided into **Andong** (north, out of town, views of rice fields, road noise); **Tebesaya** (walking distance to town, quiet, intimate family inns); **Padang Tegal** (walking distance to town, some places in rice fields, quiet); **Padang Tegal Kaja** (in center of town but off main road); **Monkey Forest Road** (close to everything, many with views or in rice fields, road noise if not set back); **Ubud Kaja** (center of town, noisy but convenient); **Campuhan** (five minute walk west of town, restful); **Penestanan** (up a long flight of stairs, rural feeling, very quiet, stunning panoramas of rice fields); **Sangginan** (further up the hill from Campuhan, tranquil, remote); **Sayan**, **Kedewatan** and **Payangan** (10–15 minute ride from Ubud, on a ridge which overlooks the Ayung River); **Pengoseken** (10–15 minute south of Ubud, quiet, many with views of rice fields, cheaper); **Peliatan** (village just south of Ubud, center of music, dance and woodcarving, food can be difficult here but a 20 minute walk from Ubud).

Sayan/Kedewatan/Payangan

Amandari Hotel on Sayan Heights, 3 km west of Ubud, Tel: 975-333, Fax: 975-335. 29 pavilions. Designed by Peter Muller of Oberoi Bali fame, this hotel overlooking the Ayung River is on top of the world, both in beauty and in price. Totally isolated from the village, it oozes solitude and relaxation as well as opulence. The main swimming pool (filtered with salt, not chlorine) is modeled after a Balinese rice paddy and is worth a trip to see. The rooms are huge, a/c with large bathrooms, verandas, refrigerators and sound systems. One type is two-story and has its own pool. The five-star restaurant has excellent food. (L+)

The Chedi, Desa Melinggih Kelod, Payangan, Gianyar, Tel: 975-963, Fax: 975-968. 60 rooms and villa suites about 15 minutes north of Ubud in a spectacular setting with mountain, rice terrace and river-valley views. Pool, two restaurants, complete spa with traditional treatments (L)

Kupu Kupu Barong, north in Kedewatan, Tel: 975-078, Fax: 975-079. Named for the butterflies that make this their home, this is another hotel with an even better view. Has 19 bungalows. All have sitting rooms and spectacular views. A/c, refrigerators in rooms, room service, tennis courts, whirlpool and traditional Balinese massage is available. Cuisine has been appraised in several magazines. (L+)

Sayan Terraces, 4 km west of Ubud, Sayan, Tel: 975-384, Fax: 9754-384. 10 rooms. Set high above the Ayung River with breathtaking views. The rooms are standard *losmen* type with fine views. (B–E)

Villa Indah, Kedewatan, P.O. Box 1, Ubud, 4 km from Ubud, Tel/Fax: 975-490. 8 suites in three villas with kitchen and private staff. Meals prepared to order and served on wraparound living terrace. Peaceful view over Sayan River valley. (I–D)

Sangginggan & Campuhan

Ananda Cottages, Campuhan, P.O. Box 205, Denpasar, Tel: 975-376, Fax: 975-375. 45 bungalows. In the rice fields of Campuhan is this lovely hotel. Here you can rent a "house" with 3 bedrooms, 2 baths and a huge sitting room or duplex rooms. All with hot water, fan. Pool, restaurant. (I)

Ibah, Campuhan, Tel: 974-446. Owned by the Prince of Ubud. Great views of the Wos River valley and Gunung Lebah temple. Large baths, in-room saes, mini-bar, television and sound system. Roman bath-style pool and spa area. (L)

Tjampuhan, Campuhan, P.O. Box I98, Ubud, Tel: 975-368/9, Fax: 975-137. 55 bungalows. Used to be the only "luxury" hotel around and is the former home of German artist Walter Spies, who strongly influenced Balinese painting. With a spectacular view, a large spring-fed swimming pool (open to the public) and restaurant, this is a quaint place to stay, although there are now many places which offer better service and rooms. The charm factor here scores high; 10-minute walk to the center of Ubud. Tennis and badminton courts, two pools. (E–I)

Ulun Ubud, Jl. Sanggingan, along the main road 1½ km west of Ubud, P.O. Box 333, Denpasar, Tel: 975-024, 975-762, Fax: 975-524. 26 rooms. Coming down the hill into Sanggingan village is this gem of a hotel carved into the hillside. Run by Ida Bagus Putu Suarta, brother of the famous woodcarver, the late Ida Bagus Tilem. Hotel grounds are filled with art. The swimming pool is down many, many steps and affords a stunning view of the paddy fields and ravine below. Restaurant is okay. Far from the center of Ubud, need transportation (available at hotel) to go out. (I)

Penestanan

Melati Cottages, P.O. Box 129, Ubud, Tel: 974-650. Set back in the paddy fields on hilltop, this isolated hotel is a real charmer. 12 huge rooms with two double beds, ceiling fan and large porch, attached bath, hot water. Clean, breezy and tasteful. Very quiet and idyllic. Pool, restaurant, have to be nimble to get here (down a narrow pathway, but the serenity is worth it). (B)

Ubud Proper

Abangan Bungalows, Jl. Raya Ubud, Tel: 975-977, Fax: 075-082. 17 bungalows, some with ceiling fans and fabulous views of rice fields. Just west of town on the north side of the street, these bungalows offer peace and quiet as well as convenience. All have hot water bathtubs, twin beds, screens and fans. Small pool, cafe. (B)

Menara, Jl. Raya Ubud, across from Puri Lukisan Museum, Tel: 975-142. Built by Cokorda Mas years ago, it has hosted illuminaries from all over the world. Cok Mas was one of the first Indonesians to study music overseas; his reference and lending library are impressive. Eight rooms, two of them overlooking rice fields, are in back of the restaurant. Cold water showers, very basic rooms. (B)

Murni's House, east of her famous *warung*, is up the stairs at Andangan and overlooks the rice fields, Tel: 975-165, Fax: 975-282. 4 rooms. This idyllic setting is perfect for those who want to rest. Famous Murni's breakfasts are served here. Rooms range from a single room with bath and veranda to large house with two bedrooms, two baths (can sleep six). All rooms are screened, have hot water and fans. Babysitter available. Free transfers to and from airport for stay of one week or more. Credit cards accepted. (E–I)

Puri Saraswati, Jl. Raya Ubud, Ibu Agung Arimas Sarawati Bungalows, Ubud Kelod, Tel: 975-164. 17 bungalows in a garden. Smack in the middle of town, next to the Lotus Cafe. Pool, breakfast nook (perfect for small-medium sized groups). (B–E)

Puri Saren, Jl. Raya Ubud, across from the market, Tel: 975-957, Fax: 975-137. 12 rooms. The home of the former king of Ubud, you will feel regal staying in one of the pavilions, which sport antique Chinese beds and fabulously carved wood panels. (E)

Ubud Kaja (North Ubud)

Lecuk Inn, Jl. Kajeng 15, Tel: 976-445. The rooms here are out back of the family compound. Rooms are very simple, concrete floors, basic bathrooms with shower and western toilet. Two rooms have bathtubs (cold water) and four have shower. Quiet and breezy in a garden setting. (B)

Rumah Roda, Jl. Kajeng, Tel: 975-487. 8 rooms. Another "family-style" place which emphasizes service to its guests. Some rooms in family compound itself, others out back. Standard concrete floor rooms with bathrooms. (B)

Siti Bungalows, Jl. Kajeng No 3, P.O. Box 227, Denpasar, Tel: 975-699, Fax: 956-43. 7 bungalows in the home of painter Hans Snel. Garden cottages in

a quiet setting, 5-minutes' walk into town. One of the few solar-heated hotels in the area. (I)

Jalan Wanara Wana (Monkey Forest Road)

Canderi's Homestay, Jl. Wanara Wana, Tel: 975-054. 5 rooms. Canderi's was one of the very first homestays in the early 70s and the best place to eat. Today her rooms are upgraded and shifted to the back of her compound, and the restaurant still serves simple, but delicious fare. Tiled rooms with screens, cold water showers. (B)

Fibra Inn, near the south end of Jl. Wanara Wana, Tel: 975-415, Fax: 975-165. 14 rooms. Rooms are set back from the road; downstairs rooms have lovely garden bathrooms, upstairs rooms a nice view of rice fields. Small swimming pool and cafe. Good place for groups. (I)

Oka Wati's Bungalows, off Jl. Wanara Wana, set in the rice fields, Tel: 963-86, Fax: 975-063. 19 rooms. Famous for her warung in the 70s, she moved it here, started a restaurant and then a hotel. Small pool. Some rooms with hot water showers. (E)

Pertiwi, Jl. Wanara Wana, Tel: 975-236, Fax: 975-559. 38 rooms in two-story bungalows with a lovely breeze and views of the paddy fields. Nice, simple rooms with tiled bathrooms and hot water, a/c. Pool. (E–I)

Ubud Inn, Jl. Wanara Wana, Tel: 975-071, Fax: 975-188. 34 bungalows. Has a fantastic pool set by a cafe in the middle of opulent greenery. The rooms have hot water and are screened and the ones upstairs have a nice veranda overlooking the rice fields. (B–E)

Ubud Village, Jl. Wanara Wana, Tel: 975-751, 974-071, Fax: 975-069. 28 rooms. Bungalow-style rooms (which need to be sound-proofed) with separate garden entrance. Full Western-style garden bathroom, ceiling fan, nice pool, restaurant, large pavilion suitable for group events. (E–I)

Padang Tegal

Matahari Cottages, Jl. Jembawan (behind the Post Office), Tel: 975-459. In a quiet and breezy setting, these very clean, tiled rooms have showers and western toilets. Some have hot water. Three single rooms which are quite small (but cheap!), plus one two-story

family house. Simple meals available all day. (B)

Nirwana Homestay, Padang Tegal Kaja, Tel: 975-415. 6 rooms. Run by Nyoman Suradnya (batik artist) and his wife Rai. The rooms range from simple *losmen* style to large, more isolated rooms with ceiling fan and hot water (can sleep 3). All rooms are screened. Batik studio and gallery on premises. Nyoman speaks fluent English (American, Aussie and British) and teaches batik courses. (B)

Nuriani Guest House, Tel: 975-346. At the south end of Padang Tegal Road and nestled far back off the road with a sweeping view of the rice fields. 8 rooms. The feeling here is what Ubud was like 10 years ago. The rooms are tastefully arranged around a central courtyard; parking is plentiful. Screened, clean rooms. (B)

Pengosekan

Agung Raka Inn, Pengosekan, Tel: 975-757, Fax: 975-546. 10 two-storey bungalows in the middle of rice fields. Marbled bathrooms with hot water and tub. Huge downstairs porch, small bedroom and veranda upstairs (stairs are extremely steep and not suitable for children). Large swimming pool. (I)

Bali Breeze Bungalows, Jl. Pengosekan, Tel: 975-410, Fax: 975-546. 15 rooms, all rooms have mosquito nets on beds. Among the first cottages to go up in the rice fields in this village. Good value; great view. (B)

Dewi Sri Bungalows, Jl. Hanoman, Padangtegal, Tel: 975-300, Fax: 975-777. 18 rooms. A small hotel at the junction of Padang Tegal and Pengosekan, set in the middle of rice fields. You can stay in a simple but nice room with hot water shower; in a poolside one-story bungalow; in a two-story cottage with a huge porch, outdoor bathroom and cramped upstairs bedroom; or opt for the larger bungalows with a decent-sized bedroom. Swimming pool, coffee shop. (B–E)

Guci House, Pengosekan. Quiet and in the midst of rice fields, there are three rooms and one bungalow for rent, tastefully decorated with the Nyoman Wijaya's (the owner) paintings and with an outdoor bathroom (cold water shower). (B)

Puri Indah, Jl. Pengosekan, Tel: 975-742, Fax: 975-332. 10 rooms. Bills itself as exclusive bungalows. Set in the rice fields with a view of Gunung Agung, these large rooms with matching verandas are tastefully furnished. Large pool. All rooms have hot water, bathtubs, mini-bar, fans. Free transport into Ubud for meals and performances. Part of the Agung Rai Museum of Art complex with restaurants adjacent. Houses many artists. (I–L)

Tiebesaya, Peliatan
Aji Lodge, Jl. Lorong Sukma 11 (behind Pura Dalem Puri). 4 rooms in a family compound, owner works for the Dept. of Education and Culture in Ubud and is a painter himself. Two rooms with shower, two with splash bath, all tiled and clean. (B)
Homestay Tebesari, Jl. Tebesaya No 29. Six rooms in a garden setting. Tiled, clean, shower, outdoor bathroom. Owner is a school teacher and loves to go on walks. (B)
Oka Kartini's, Jl. Raya Ubud by Jl. Tebesaya, Tel: 975-193, Fax: 975-759. 16 rooms, set in the midst of gorgeous gardens. Quiet and a short walk into town, you can have a drink at the bar in the front and chat with her innumberable sons. Fans and showers, some with hot water. (I)

South Peliatan
Ketut Madra, Banjar Kalah, Tel: 975-745. 10 bungalows. Set right by a river and with a stunning view of rice fields, Madra's has been popular with groups for years, with Gamelan Sekar Jaya from California making this their base since 1985. Madra himself is a very fine painter of the *wayang* style. The cottages are made out of *bedeg* (split bamboo) with squat and western-style toilets; most of these are in sore need of repairs and a thorough cleaning, but the price can't be beaten, though the newer rooms are cleaner. (B)
Mandala Bungalows, main road in Peliatan, Tel/Fax: 975-191. 8 bungalows. Owned by the Peliatan-Sukawati royal family. All rooms have hot water. Legong performances held here. (B)

Andong & Petulu
Andong Inn, Jl. Andong #26A, Tel: 950-76. Set off from the road, there are four basic tiled rooms with cold-water shower and six bungalow types with hot water. Large public pool in the front, restaurant. Behind Dr. Siada's house. (B)

Griya Loka Sari, Jl. Tegalalang, Petulu, Tel: 975-476, Fax: 975-120. These bungalows offer a relief from the standard rooms one finds all over Ubud and are quite reasonable. Extremely clean, each unit has its own simple kitchen, garden bathroom (with very creative decorating ideas) and ample bedrooms. Even though there's traffic noise in the daytime, a waterfall will lull you to sleep at night (and all day for that matter). Two bungalows with a downstairs and upstairs bedroom and a veranda; two one-story bungalows. (B)
Banyan Tree Kamandalu, Jl. Tegalalang, Banjar Nagi, P.O. Box 77, Ubud, Tel: 975-825, Fax: 975-851. 52 villas on the edge of the Petanu River valley, surrounded by rice fields. Deluxe and sensuous retreats. Full-range spa, Asian restaurant. pool, tennis, nature walks, conference facilities, swim up bar, private villa dining, shuttle to Ubud. (L+)
Petulu Village Inn, Jl. Tegalalang, Petulu, Tel: 975-209. Set far off the busy road, a complex of 4 rooms (2 up, 2 down) with cold-water shower and western toilet. Rooms are cool and breeze comes off neighboring rice fields. Even farther off the road are so-called family rooms, with a double bed, breakfast nook and veranda – overpriced, though these rooms are secluded and have a river view. (B)

Mas Village
Taman Harum is in Mas, two villages down the road. Duplexes with a sitting room and upstairs bedroom are tastefully furnished. Hot-water baths. Swimming pool. Restaurant is not great but there's nowhere else to eat in Mas. Breakfast included. (I)

BANGLI
There are two budget homestays in this town and both are part of puris or palaces. One of them, the **Homestay Darmaputra** is a Youth Hostel and the rooms are dirt cheap but full of dirt as well. **Artha Sastra Inn** on the other hand is quite clean and full of antiques and exquisite carvings.

KINTAMANI AREA
Telephone code (0366)
Most of the accommodations at Gunung Batur are basic, with cold (very cold, actually) mountain-spring water

and magnificent views. All room prices are subject to negotiation (most cost under $20) and generally reflect the market demand. Penelokan has the views, Kintamani is quieter and Toya Bungkah down at the lake gets great sunrises and sunsets.

On the Rim
Gunawan, outside Penelokan, Tel: 501-52. 2 bungalows, private bath, clean with crater view. (B)
Lakeview Restaurant & Homestay, Penelokan, Tel/Fax: 514-64. 17 tiny, overpriced rooms without private bath. Popular stop-off spot and restaurant with a view. (B)
Miranda, Kintamani, Tel: 510-96. 6 rooms in small, older place. Owner is a trekking guide for Gunung Batur. (-B)

In the Caldera
Hotel Puri Berning, Tel: 512-34, 512-35, Fax: (0361) 730-285. New modern block of hotel rooms under the volcano, international standard. (B–E)
Nyoman Mawa I (previously Under the Volcano I), Toya Bungkah, Tel: 511-66. 12 clean, nice rooms. Excellent dining room and service. (B)
Nyoman Mawa II (previously Under the Volcano II), Songan, Tel: 511-66. 8 rooms, some with hot water. Breakfast included. (B)
Surya Homestay, Kedisan, Tel: 511-39. 22 bungalows on hillside, spacious and clean, some with some without hot water. Breakfast included. (B)
Segara, Left before Kedisan from Penelokan. 42 rooms with private baths, restaurant. Rooms with hot water, over-priced. VIP rooms have television. Best to bargain. Rates include breakfast, laundry, tax & service. (B–E)

The East

KLUNGKUNG
Telephone Code (0363)
The only decent place to stay here is the **Ramayana Hotel** on Jl. Diponegoro, on the eastern edge of town, Tel: 210-44. The new rooms have baths and western toilets; old rooms are sparse but clean with shared bath and squat toilets. (B)

NUSA PENIDA & NUSA LEMBONGAN
The arid island of Nusa Penida has only one place to stay and that's a government-run *losmen* in Sampalan.

However, Nusa Lembongan (a surfing and snorkeling paradise) has a number of *losmen*. All rooms are usually under $10.

PADANG BAI

Telephone code (0363)

Padang Bai has a lovely white-sand beach, a few hotels and lots of boats, as this is one of the major ports on the island (the jumping off point for Lombok, Nusa Penida and cruises). Rooms cost less than $10.

Hotel Madya is near the wharf and has simple rooms. (-B)

Kerti Beach Inn's bungalows have two rooms each with the ocean in sight. (-B)

Rai Beach Inn, Tel: 413-85/6 has individual as well as a number of separate two-story bungalows with a huge downstairs veranda. 21 rooms. (B)

Topi Inn has 5 simple rooms in three-storey thatched bamboo structure and dormitory rooms over a restaurant. Beds with mosquito nets, squat toilets. (-B)

BALINA BEACH/MANGGIS

This is a spacious, gorgeous white-sand beach just 5 km from Candi Dasa. Currently, there are only a smattering of hotels and outrigger canoes here, going the gamut from luxury to basic. One of the major scuba diving centers of Bali.

Amankila, Manggis, Tel: 413-33, Fax: 415-56. 33 luxurious suites, seven with their own pool. Unsurpassed splendor but steep location. The main swimming pool has a fabulous view of Bali's east coast and of the Indian Ocean. The restaurant serves Asian and continental cuisine. (L+)

Rama Ocean View Bungalows, P.O. Box 334, Denpasar, Tel: 419-75, Fax: 4174. 74 rooms. A few hundred meters before Candi Dasa itself, these bungalows are set on the beach and have hot water, a/c and satellite TV. Fitness center, game room with video and TV. (I)

Sunrise, Jl. Raya Candidasa, Tel: 415-39, Fax: 415-38. 18 rooms. Very quiet, right on the beach. A/c or fan. (B) (breakfast included)

CANDI DASA

Until the last 10 years, this 2-km strip of exquisite beachfront was untouched paradise. A temple, Pura Pengumuman, was the only man-made fixture for miles around before an *ashram* was built in 1983. It was then that the tourists who were fed up with the growing commercialism of South Bali began to wander east and north for a more restful vacation.

A string of hotels, restaurants and shops have since cropped up, making Candi Dasa a veritable "tourist spot", but one with a low profile. There are several low-key discos in town, but most of the nightlife is confined to quiet walks on the beach at low tide; at high tide, there is no beach.

Being only a 2½-hour drive from Denpasar, it is the ideal place for a rest. The beach is encompassed by a coral reef, which was torn up by the locals, to make lime for new hotels.

Though the lack of indigenous village life lends a sort of open-ended, unrooted ambience to this community, it also keeps the clutter of arts and crafts down to a minimum. In short, the entire town exists for the sake of the tourist alone, and you will be treated here with the utmost of graceful, if not slow, service. Electricity is still on the low voltage side here, unless the accommodations have a generator. So if you want to do lots of reading at night, buy candles.

The Ashram. Built in 1983 by Ibu Gedong as a pipedream in Gandhian self-sufficiency, the ashram rents out rooms complete with three excellent semi-vegetarian meals a day. Ibu Gedong herself is a strong-willed, fascinating woman and a professor of English at Udayana University. If you want to volunteer as a worker here, then you pay a nominal charge for food and lodging. Regular guests' rates includes all meals. (B)

Bambu Garden Bungalows, non-oceanside. Has 7 bungalows with a panoramic view of Lombok to Padang Bai and fully-tiled sleeping and bathing areas. (B)

Candi Dasa Beach Cottage, Singkidu, Candidasa, Amlapura, Tel: 412-34, Fax: 411-11. 64 cottages and hotel rooms in tropical gardens, a/c, private bath and shower, satellite television, pool, tennis, fitness center. (I)

Candi Dasa Sunrise I, oceanside, West side of town, Tel: 415-39, Fax: 415-37. 20 bungalows. Near the town center, the bamboo bungalows are set in a garden; cozy and classy. All rooms with fan, some with Western baths. A gamelan orchestra performs once a week. (B)

Candi Dasa Sunrise II, Tel: 415-39, Fax: 415-37. 69 rooms. A/c and with hot water, this two-story building is a drab, concrete block. Rooms are immaculate but dark and sterile. Swimming pool, restaurant and bar, laundry and tour service. (I–D)

Homestay Segara Wangi, oceanside, West end. 7 rooms with single beds. Some of the friendliest people in town here. (B)

Ida's Homestay on the east end of "town", Tel: 410-96. Still one of the nicest places around. Not motivated to cram as many rooms onto the land as possible, the six bungalows here are set in a huge coconut plantation next to the ocean. Two-story houses with garden bathrooms. No hot water. (B)

Pandawa Bungalows, oceanside, on East end of lake. 10 bungalows, each with shower, breakfast, and coffee or tea all day. (B)

The Water Garden, P.O. Box 39, Amlapura, Tel: 415-40, Fax: 411-64. Run by the folks at TJs, this elegant hotel has 12 enclosed a/c rooms built of teak in the midst of pools and gardens. Across the street from the beach, private. Swimming pool. (I)

AMLAPURA & ENVIRONS

There's really no reason to stay right in Amlapura; there are a few funky *losmen* here. Just east of town in Abian Soan is a cute little place in the middle of the paddyfields called **Homestay Lila** (-B). A perfect place to get away from it all and just be. There's no electricity, but each bungalow has its own bath. And you can't beat the price. **Balai Kiran**, (E) has four rooms within the grounds of Amlapura's Puri Agung palace. Breakfast and dinner are provided. **Losmen Lahar Mas**, (-B) Jl. Gatot Subroto 1, Tel: 213-45, has 20 rooms in a typical losmen, clean and friendly.

The North

SINGARAJA

Telephone code (0362)
There's no real reason to stay in Singaraja, as the beach resorts are so close by.

Hotel Cendrawasih, Jl. Jen. A. Yani. (B)
Hotel Sedana Yoga, Jl. Imam Bonjol. (B)
Losmen Dama Setu, Jl. A Yani 46, Tel: 232-000. (-B)
Losmen Duta Karya, Jl. A. Yani 59, Tel: 214-67, (fan-cooled or a/c rooms – and it gets quite hot up here). (B)

AIR SANIH

These freshwater springs sport a number of bungalows by the pools, themselves just by the ocean.

Apilan Beach Front Hotel, Bukti village, Buleleng. Bookings: (P.O. Box 188, Singaraja, Tel: 811-13, Fax: 211-08. c/o Telcom Singaraja. Beach house with attached dining. Private cottages with verandah and double beds. (B)
Sunset Graha Beach Hilltop Garden Bungalow, Jl. Raya Kubutambahan Singaraja, Fax: 211-08. 6 rooms on steep hill overlooking beach and springs, private bath, shower, fan, mosquito net, restaurant adjacent. (B)

LOVINA BEACH

A northern beachfront alternative to Kuta and Sanur, this is a serene and frequently-visited vacation spot 10 km west of Bali's original capital and port, Singaraja. Black-sand beaches and quiet waters protected by extensive coral reefs distinguish this idyllic beach. Snorkeling is superb here and the reef is close enough that even beginner swimmers feel comfortable.

Best news is that the local government has passed a moratorium on building, thus preventing any new hotel development along the non-ocean side of the main road, and limiting building on the oceanside. Rice paddies that currently separate the accommodations into three major sections are required by law to stay put, ensuring an open and uncluttered beachfront for the future.

Do not be swayed by the condition of the signs you see on the road, for the quality and upkeep of an establishment often has little to do with its advertising skills. Most places do not include breakfast.

Higher-priced accommodations are on the oceanside of the main road, with private bath with shower/tub, Western toilet, a/c, hot water and swimming pools. All of these are characterized by good management and cleanliness. Reasonably-priced lodgings are abundant, with shower and private bathroom. Nearly all include a simple breakfast.

Aditya Bungalow, Jl. Seririt, west end, P.O. Box 35, Lovina, Tel: 410-59, Fax: 413-42. 75 rooms, all with hot water. Restaurant and bar on premises, laundry services and water sports. (B–E)
Banyualit Beach Inn, center of town, P.O. Box 116, Kalibukbuk, Tel: 417-89, Fax: 415-63. 20 rooms, some with a/c, some fan-cooled. Isolated, quiet, and exquisitely managed. Advance reservations recommended. Excellent restaurant, money changer, laundry, tour services, water sports. (B)
Homestay Agung, east end, P.O. Box 124, Anturan. 10 rooms. Very friendly staff. Bamboo is used to built this hotel. Shared baths. (-B)
Jati Reef Bungalows, east end of beach, P.O. Box 52, Tukad Mungga, Tel: 410-52. 16 rooms. Thoughtful touches such as outdoor showers, safety deposit lockers, laundry service, towel, soap, and daily sheet changes. Four bungalows with four fan-cooled units in each, tiled floors, large garden bathrooms, thatched roofs, ideal location behind rice paddies, close to beach. (B)
Nirwana Seaside Cottages, center of strip, Kalibukbuk, Tel: 412-88, Fax: 410-90. 37 rooms. Close to a popular section of the beach, yet also far from the road. Has its own restaurant and bar. Bicycle rental, snorkel equipment, tours to Kintamani available. All rooms have fans. (B)
Puri Tasik Madu, Tel: 413-76. 12 rooms. One of the original *losmen* in the area. Friendly staff, rooms were recently renovated. (-B)

Western Beaches

Telephone code (0362)
Up along this coast north of Kuta and Legian lies a stretch of black sand beach known only to surfers. With a dangerous reef and heavy undertow, these beaches are not ideal for swimming or beginner surfers and should be avoided by the inexperienced.

TANAH LOT

You can actually stay here, if you can stand all the hype surrounding this beautiful temple.

Dewi Sinta Cottage, Tel/Fax: 812-933, has 11 cottages, 4 suites with hot water and fans. They offer an Indonesian buffet, breakfast included. (B)
Mutiara Tanah Lot, Tel: 812-939, Fax: 222-672, has a/c or fan rooms. (E)

PEMUTERAN & MENJANGAN

About 125 km (75 miles) north of Sanur lies the sizable Menjangan Island. Part of the West Bali National Park, this is a haven for all-season diving and snorkeling. Many stay at Pemuteran on the north shore and take a 30-minute boat ride to the island. Accommodation and professional dive facilities are available in Pemuteran.

Matahari Beach Resort, Pemuteran, Singaraja, Bali, Tel: (0362) 923-12, Fax: 923-13. 32 Balinese style bungalows with international hotel facilities; a/c, garden shower, watersports and dive center, 200 m from beach. (D–L)
Pondok Sari, Pemuteran, Grokgak, Singaraja, Tel: (0362) 023-37. 20 bungalow rooms with a/c or fan, restaurant. (B)
Taman Sari Hotel, Pemuteran, Grokgak, Singaraja, Tel: (0362) 926-23, Fax: (0361) 289-285. 21 a/c and fan rooms, restaurant. (E–I)

Western Interior

KRAMBITAN

Krambitan is a small, rustic village near the western coast of Tabanan. It is most famous for its "Puri Night" when, by commission, the village escorts you by torchlight to the palace (*puri*), where you are entertained with either a *joged* flirtation dance or the *Calon Arang* dance-drama (featuring Rangda and the Barong), all the while feasting on a myriad of Balinese foods. The Calon Arang performed here, even though done for tourists, often involves real trance, as the Rangda mask here is quite powerful.

You can also stay at two of the *puri* here: **Puri Agung Wisata**, Tel/Fax: 812-667, has simple elegant rooms (18 rooms total), no hot water. (B)

Down the road at **Puri Anyar Krambitan**, Tel: 812-668, there are seven rooms. Here there are three *saren* (bungalows) for rent, part of the five *saren* which the royal family used to live. Each *saren* has two rooms with a shared bathroom. The proprietor, I Gusti Ngurah Sangka, speaks several languages fluently and is an expert on Balinese literature. Contact him at Tromolpos I, Krambitan, Tabanan. (E)

BEDUGUL

Telephone code (0368)
This resort is famous for its air.

Bali Handara Kosaido Country Club, Pancasari, by Gunung Bratan, Tel: 226-46, Fax: 230-48. 37 rooms. Located on an 18-hole golf course, all rooms with hot water, TV, private bathrooms, refrigerator; tennis court, gym, restaurant, laundry. (I–D)
Bedugul, on main road south of Bedugul, Tel: 211-97, Fax: 211-98. 16 bungalows by the lake with hot water. Wide range of watersports available; restaurant by lake. (E)
Bukit Mungsu Indah, on main road, Baturiti, Tel: 214-453. 13 rooms. There are fireplaces in all rooms. Some bungalows face Bedugul's Botanical Garden. Breakfast included. (E)
Hadi Raharjo, is on the way into town. 18 rooms. This is a basic *losmen* with private showers and a small restaurant, breakfast included. (-B)
Pacung Mountain Resort, Jl. Raya Baturiti, Desa Pacung, 9 km south of Bedugul, P.O. Box 3297. Tel: (0361) 262-460/2, Fax: 210-43. 26 rooms with hot water, impressive views, heated pool, two restaurants. Choice Hotel chain affiliate. (I–D)
Strawbali Hill, south of Bedugul at Bedugul Hotel turnoff, Tel: 214-42. 10 rooms managed by famous Poppie's Cottages of Kuta. Clean and simple, blankets provided. (E)

NEGARA

Telephone code (0365)
In this western town, there are a number of low-budget losmen costing below $5. On the main road, you'll find Hotel Ana. Losmen and Rumah Makan Taman Sari, Jl. Nakula 18.

Eating Out

What to Eat

Centuries of contact with other great civilizations have left their mark on the wonderfully varied cuisine of Indonesia, particularly in Bali. Indian and Arab traders brought not only merchandise, Hinduism and Islam, but also a variety of new spices such as ginger, cardamon and turmeric. Later the Chinese and (to a lesser extent) the Dutch added their own distinctive touch to the cooking pot.

Spices abound in Balinese cooking, and are often partnered by coconut milk (the juice is made by squeezing the grated flesh of the coconut), which adds a rich flavor and creamy texture to dishes containing intriguing tropical vegetables, poultry, meat and fish. Happily for the unaccustomed foreign palate, Balinese cooks (in restaurants, that is) are light-handed with both spices and chilies. They are fond of using sugar as well as fragrant roots and leaves, and the final result is food which tastes subtle and sophisticated.

The basis of a Balinese meal is rice. Each person helps himself to a serving of steaming white rice and then to a little of the three or four dishes of vegetables or meat (known as *lauk*), which are placed in the center of the table for all to share. Balinese do not swamp their plates with food on the first round, but help themselves to a little more of their fancy as the meal progresses.

A side dish or *sambal*, made with red-hot chilies ground with dried shrimp paste and other seasonings such as lime juice, should be approached with caution. (If you scorch mouth or throat with chilies, don't rush for the nearest water, as it aggravates the problems, and cold beer or other fizzy drinks are worse. The quickest relief comes from plain boiled rice, bread, cucumber or a banana. Common side dishes are *tempe*, a protein-rich savory cake of fermented soybeans, and small crisp cookies

(*rempeyek*) made of peanuts. Both are delicious.

The Dutch word *rijsttafel* (rice table) is sometimes associated with Indonesian food. The name was originally given to gargantuan banquets or rice and countless dishes of vegetables and meats accompanied by savory offerings such as *krupuk* (fried prawn or fish crackers), *acar* (cucumber pickles), fried banana, peanuts, chilies and anything else capable of adding fragrance and flavor to the spread. Full-scale extravagances are seldom witnessed (let alone eaten) these days, although a few hotels make a modest attempt at imitation, and all of the individual dishes of the old rijsttafel can still be found and enjoyed.

National favorites include *gado-gado*, a lightly-cooked vegetable salad which includes beansprouts, greenbeans, cabbage and potatoes covered with a rich peanut sauce. *Sate*, sometimes regarded as Indonesia's national dish, is a tempting assortment of meat, chicken or seafood grilled on skewers over a charcoal fire, served with a spicy sauce. A tasty, chicken soup known as *soto ayam* is found everywhere.

Chinese influenced noodle dishes such as *mie goreng* (fried wheat-flour noodles) and *bakmi* (rice flour noodles, either fried or in soup) are also common. *Cap cai* (previously *tjap tjai*) is very popular and better than its Western name "chop suey" would suggest.

You will, of course, find *nasi goreng* (fried rice) everywhere; topped with a fried egg, it makes a good and cheap meal for breakfast or anytime. *Nasi campur* is the name given to the daily staple: rice with side dishes.

The speciality of Bali is *lawar*, usually made of minced pork, coconut and spices. There are other kinds of lawar: chicken, egg, green bean, jackfruit – the list goes on. If it's red, you know you've got pork lawar made with fresh raw blood: stay clear of it if you want to avoid running to the bathroom.

Sate lilit is another Balinese specialty: the meat and spices are rolled onto a stick and grilled (as opposed to barbecued chunks of skewered meat). For vegetarians, *jukut urab* is a taste sensation. Cooked vegetables, usually sweet potato leaves or beans are minced and mixed with shallots, chilies, garlic and coconut.

Something few foreigners get to try (mainly because they don't know about it) is *tupat*. Steamed rice in coconut-leaf packages, these are cut up into small pieces with tofu, cucumber, spinach and sprouts and then mixed with a fiery peanut sauce. (You can specify the number of chilies used, however, as each dish is made to order.) Just look for hanging packets of woven coconut leaves at a friendly *warung*.

For breakfast or dessert, don't miss *bubur injin* or black rice pudding. Black rice, which actually is black, is cooked and then coconut milk and palm sugar are poured over the top. Delectable!

Fruits & Snacks

The tropical fruits of Bali are excellent: pineapples, bananas (ranging from tiny finger-sized *pisang mas* up to the footlong *pisang raja*; green bananas, *pisang kayu*, are ripe and very sweet), papayas and mangoes are joined by even more unusual seasonal fruits. Some of the most outstanding are *rambutan* (hairy red skins enclosing sweet white meat, akin to a lichee), *mangosteen* (staining, purplish black skins with a very sweet juicy white fruit inside – don't eat the seeds or skin), *jeruk Bali* (pomelo) and *markisa* (passion fruit).

Of course, the best fruit of all is *salak*, called the snakeskin fruit. This brown scaly-skinned fruit encloses a crunchy white fruit with a pear-like flavor – Bali is famous throughout Indonesia for its *salak*. The huge spiky *durian* has (to most people) a revolting smell, but its butter-rich fruit is adored by local people and a few adventurous visitors. One fruit visitors often overlook is the *nangka* or jackfruit. Akin to the breadfruit, this large fruit has stringy yellow pulp inside – its smell is reminiscent of bubble gum but its taste is distinctive and sweet. Unripe and cooked, it is a great vegetable.

Notes for vegetarians: With all the fresh vegetables and fruits and soybean products here, one would think it would be easy for vegetarians to find decent food. However, the Balinese are a meat-loving peoples and pork is a mainstay in their diet. Most soups are made with chicken stock (called *kaldo*) and often fish and chicken are not considered "meat" (*daging* in Indonesian). So you must always ask if there is any meat or fish in a dish or whether it's been cooked in meat – best to check with the cook as often the staff are ignorant of ingredients. The only pure meatless dish is *gado-gado* (steamed veggies with peanut sauce), although sometimes the peanut sauce is made with *terasi* or shrimp paste. Fried noodles and fried rice often are made with chicken, as are fried greens (*sayur hijau*), but these can be easily made without meat by request. *Tempe* is often fried with peanuts and *tofu* can be bought plain and fried.

Thirst Quenchers

Most familiar Western drinks are available in Bali, though some take on an exciting new dimension.

Tea is usually very fragrant, and similar to Chinese tea in flavor. Served hot or cold, *manis* (with sugar, and LOTS of it) or *pahit* (without), it is delicate and refreshing.

Coffee is a delight to real coffee lovers, being served almost Turkish-style with grounds floating around (known as *kopi tubruk*). Balinese coffee is made like instant coffee and will keep you up all night. If you ask for it with milk, it's condensed milk and so will be sweet. For all drinks, you must specify no sugar – if not, you'll end up with flavored sugar.

Locally manufactured **beer** (Anker, Bintang and Bali Hai) is similar to European lager beer and is excellent. It's moderately priced and everywhere, but it won't be cold in outlying villages.

Fresh fruit juices are popular. *Air jeruk*, as orange juice is called, is actually oranges or limes mixed with water. Getting it hot is delightful, especially if you're feeling under the weather. There are also juices made from bananas, pineapples and other fruits, which are blender drinks made with ice. Westerners accustomed to regarding avocado as a vegetable will probably be amazed at the *apokat* drink, but it's wonderful. In the Ubud and Kuta area are *lassi*, a yogurt drink nothing like the original in India. You can get it plain or with fruit.

Es kopyor is a favorite concoction of rose syrup, ice, scoops of jelly-like flesh from the inside of the *kopyor* coconut. You can ask for it without the rose syrup (no sugar). *Es campur*, a mixture of shaved ice with fruits and "jelly beans" made from tapioca (called *cendol*); *es tape*, made from fermented rice or sweet potato; and *es cendol*, akin to *es campur* but made with coconut milk, are all delicious.

The best thirst quencher of them all, **water**, is widely available. Almost everyone these days is savvy enough to boil their water; all piping-hot drinks are perfectly safe. In most of the larger cafes and restaurants, ice drinks are safe as well. Bottled spring water, under the names of Aqua, Spring, Fresh, etc., is safe, but be sure the seal is still intact.

Alcohol: For those who like the harder stuff, try Balinese *brem*, a rose-colored sweet rice wine, or *arak*, distilled palm liquor. A favorite drink in the bars is the potent combination of brem, arak and orange or lime juice. *Tuak* is fermented palm wine and on the sweet side. Imported alcohol has become scarce and expensive due to heavy taxation.

Where to Eat

Note: For some reason, Indonesians love to cook with MSG (called Ajinomoto or Vetsin in Bali). So if you're not fond of MSG, be sure to tell your waiter/waitress that you don't want any Ajinomoto, *tanpa ajinomoto*.

Denpasar

Near the market are a number of eateries, most of them Chinese. The Hawaii in the Kumbasari Shopping Center, 2nd floor, Tel: 435-135, 437-139, is popular.

Rumah Makan Polaris, Jl. Sulawesi 40, Tel: 222-640, just south of the market is a tiny hole in the wall but has good chicken and vegetarian dishes.

Depot 88, Jl. Sumatra 88, has Chinese and Indonesian food at good prices in clean restaurant.

The Balinese always head down to Warung Wardani in Tapakgangsul. You can walk there by turning north at the Bank Indonesia 1946 and going a couple of blocks. Just north of the bank is a popular Chinese place, Siefu.

The Natour Bali Hotel, Jl. Veteran 3, Tel: 225-681, does a nice *rijstaffel*. A favorite of expatriates is Rumah Makan Betty, Jl. Sumatra 56, Tel: 224-502, which has a not-so-spicy menu of Javanese and Chinese dishes. Try the *tahu goreng kentang* (tofu and potato curry), *bubur ayam* (rice porridge with chicken) and their *nasi campur*.

If you can't get to Lombok, but want to try the famous Taliwang chicken, head down to Ayam Bakar Taliwang on Jl. Teuku Umar, near the Simpang Enam (six crossroads).

Sanur

For elegant as well as informal western dining, Sanur's Bali Hyatt, Grand Bali Beach and Sanur Beach hotels offer a wide choice of poolside lunches, buffets, barbecues, coffee shops and supper clubs with or without evening dance performances and/or live musical entertainment. The menus are predominantly Western, Indonesian, Chinese and Japanese. The prices are not cheap. Most Sanur restaurants provide transportation to their establishments from your hotel.

The Tanjung Sari Hotel restaurant has a formidable reputation for Indonesian rijsttafel and a sublime atmosphere. A bamboo *tingklink* orchestra provides the ideal accompaniment to dinner in a cozy, antique-filled dining area by the beach.

At Kuri Putih, in the Bali Sanur Irama Bungalows, chef Nyoman Sana of Ubud has brought his kitchen to Sanur. Try the barbecued specials from the grill. Choose from a wide range of salads and juice drinks. Reasonably priced, with a complimentary welcome drink of real Bali *brem*.

The Kul Kul Restaurant, Tel: 288-038, near the Hyatt has an elegant bar and serves good Western, Indonesian and Chinese cuisine in its handsome garden pavilion. Book for the dinner-dance night (Batuan's famous "Frog Dance" troupe).

The Telaga Naga, Tel: 288-271 opposite the Bali Hyatt, is a spectacularly stylish Sichuan restaurant under the stars overlooking a lotus pond. The food is good and the prices are non-hotel, though the restaurant is owned and operated by the Bali Hyatt.

The nearby Swastika Gardens, Tel: 288-573, for those who are tired of paying hotel prices. The food is quite good and the menu varied enough to satisfy most tastes – try the Balinese specialty, smoked duck (*bebek tutu*) and their grilled fish. The Swastika I Restaurant, Tel: 288-373, up the road has some of the best grilled fish and grilled chicken around at good prices.

The best Italian food on Bali is available at Trattoria Da Marco, Tel: 287-642, where Reno and Diddit da Marco have guarded their reputation and clientele for over 15 years. Try the grilled fish, spaghetti carbonara, bean salad and delicious steaks.

La Taverna, Tel: 288-497, is part of a Hong Kong-based chain of Italian restaurants in Asia. The Sanur branch is a charming bar and open dining area on the beach, with a menu that features imported cheese, French pepper steak, seafood and pizza from a real brick pizza oven.

In Banjar Semawang, right on the ocean, is Terrazza Martini, Tel: 288-371, a tiny Italian restaurant that is always full – with Italians. The food is good and the prices are quite reasonable. A free drink and appetizers.

For a meal by the seaside, try the inexpensive Sanur Beach Market, on Jl. Segara at the beach, Tel: 288-574, a little outdoor restaurant run as a cooperative by Sanur's mayor. Great for lunch (*sate, nasi goreng* and fresh grilled fish) or dinner (grilled lobster) with delicious Balinese desserts, all at reasonable prices. Once a week they have a dance performance and a special set dinner, though there is no cover charge and you may order from the regular menu.

For fresh seafood at decent prices, try the restaurant at the Leghawa Hotel right on Jl. Tanjung Sari. The Sanur Food Market on Jl. Bypass Ngurah Rai 70, has a variety of food stalls offering everything under the sun at reasonable prices.

If it's decent and cheap Indonesian food you're after, then head down to the Rumah Makan "Mini" on the bypass near Jl. Segara. Here you can get *nasi cap cay* and sate for less than $2. And the last *warung* (Mak Beng's) on the left on Jl. Raya Sanur by the beach (just past the entrance to the Grand Bali Beach) has good grilled fish. The Jawa Barat in Semawang is quite popular with locals.

You also can get a reasonably-priced buffet dinner at the Restaurant Bhinneka on the corner of Jl. Bypass and Jl. Segara.

Kuta & Legian

Kuta Beach and Legian Beach offer cuisines from all over the world at very reasonable prices. Most of the resident foreigners come to Kuta-Legian when dining out.

Made's Warung on Jl. Pantai, Kuta, Tel: 751-923, hasn't missed a beat in its metamorphosis from one of only two foodstalls on the main street of a sleepy fishing village, to a hip "Cafe Voltaire" in this St Tropez of the East. It has great food (spare ribs, Thai salads, escargot, turtle steaks, home-made ice cream and yogurt, chocolate-mint cake, capuccino, freshly-squeezed juices, breakfast specials), great music and always a host of the young international Balinese demi-monde. Made also serves a fabulous rijstaffel on Saturday night. This is THE place to see and be seen. It's new branch is in the quieter "suburbs" of Seminyak.

Poppies Restaurant (Tel: 751-059) on Gang Poppies I, a narrow lane parallel to Jl. Pantai Kuta, is another Kuta fixture. Avocado seafood salads, sashimi, chicken liver pate, tacos, grilled lobster, steaks, kabobs and tall mixed drinks pack this garden idyll to capacity during the peak tourist seasons. Get there early.

Nearby TJ's Mexican Restaurant serves the best enchiladas, tacos, tostadas, nachos and Margaritas this side of the Pacific. Try the eggplant or tahu/bean dip with chips, great with a cold beer. A second outlet, Cafe Seminyak, serves a similar fare on Jl. Seminyak. Cajun buffet night is Thursday and Tequila night is Friday.

For Indian food, go to Goa 2001 on Jl. Legian in Legian. Perhaps better known for its pre-disco hours bar than its food, it has wonderful Tandoori dishes. Opens after 7pm. Another place that serves Indian as well as Lebanese food is Warung Kopi, Jl. Legian Tengah 427, Tel: 753-602. Inexpensive, they serve falafels, curries and have delectable desserts. The former George and the Dragon, now Griya Delta behind the Panin Bank on Jl. Legian serves sumptuous tandoori dishes. Pica Pica, Jl. Dhyana Pura 7, Seminyak, Tel: 730-485, serves the best, if not only genuine tapas and pallea. Ask the Spanish owner Carlos for his recommendations.

Marilyn's Warung at Jl. Pura Bagus Taruna is a new place which is open only for dinner and has excellent grilled fish and a cozy atmosphere.

The best Italian food and atmosphere combined are found at La Lucciola Restaurant Bar and Beach Club, Jl. Kayu Aya, Petitenget, Tel: 261-047. The big, two level thatched structure looks out over Kayu Aya beach, offering beachfront chairs and service during the day. Great for sunset cocktails and packed for dinner. Reservations essential.

Warung DJ's and Warung Murah on Jl. Legian serve a great nasi campur (combination rice) for the best price. One of the most popular spots is the Pasar Senggol or Night Market behind the main Post Office in Kuta. Try the fresh fish and steamed crab!

Ubud

Ubud's eateries are almost as varied as Kuta's with everything from egg lawar to yogurt shakes, to feta salads and brown bread, to some of the best nasi campur on the island.

Probably the most famous restaurant here is Cafe Wayan, run by Ibu Wayan and her ever-smiling family, about a kilometer south on the Monkey Forest Road. Her Wayan Special Salad is delicious with a bowl of soup and garlic toast to go along with it. The seafood here is scrumptious, as is the pizza. Sit at the table way in the back where rice fields still exist. Prices here are at the high end (for Ubud that's about $5 a meal, including drinks).

At the other end of the scale (and the north end of the road) is Ibu Rai's, the place where you can get home-cooked Indonesian cuisine at cheap prices. The grilled fish is one of their specialities.

The old stand-bys of Murni's and Lotus Cafe are being replaced as the places to be, as more and more eateries co-run by Westerners are opening up. Murni's location over the Campuhan river can't be beaten – there are now three levels of seating, and on Sundays and in the evenings, the grill is open for scrumptious barbecues of fish, prawns and chicken.

The Lotus Cafe, Jl. Ubud Raya, Tel: 975-660, is located in a charming open-air courtyard. The menu includes fantastic homemade pastas, yummy cheesecake and brownies, and a delightful es cendol. You can dine al fresco right next to a huge lotus pond in front of the palace temple.

Ary's Warung, across the street and a bit east, Tel: 975-053, has some of the best gado-gado on the island. Check out their Balinese feast specials. The food is of a high standard, though on the reasonable side. Taking in the neighboring banjar, a new two-level bar and dining terrace offers great breezes in a nice atmosphere. Nearby, Casa Luna, Tel: 96283, serves Balinese and vegetarian food, and has a kid's menu. Jungle Chicken is a favorite as is the smoked duck feast, ordered a day in advance. Casa Luna holds Balinese cooking classes 10 am to 1 pm Monday and Wednesday, with a minimum of 8 students.

One of the newest establishments is Bebek Bengil or The Dirty Duck, Tel: 975-489, right at the Y junction between Padang Tegal and Pengoseken. An open-air cafe in the rice fields, with a spectacular view of Gunung Agung and a refreshing breeze, this is where the "scene" is happening. The portions are on the small side (and expensive for Ubud – about $3–$6 a portion). Often there's live music.

Mumbul Garden Terrace, Tel: 975-346, on the main road near Puri Lukisan Art Museum, is a small, intimate cafe with an extensive menu. The cook at Mumbul can whip up a Balinese banquet or a salak pie at extraordinarily low prices for such a chic place. The girls in the kitchen have published a cookbook with their favorite recipes in it. Its sister restaurant, Bumbu, around the corner on Jl. Sueta, serves Balinese, Indian and vegetarian food. Griya Barbecue has mouth-watering grilled tuna, chicken, and beef along with a regular menu. The room overlooking the gorge out back has a breathtaking view. Nomad's, at the other end of the main street serves pizza and grilled fish, and their tsetsuke skewers are out of this world.

Down the road in Peliatan village is Mudita Inn, a tiny hole-in-the-wall, that has the best fried noodles (mie goreng) and french fries this side of Lombok, and some of the best Balinese-style banana pancakes around. (You can change money and buy postcards while you're waiting for your lunch next door.) The most popular place to eat in Peliatan for the locals is Ibu Made's Warung (across the street from Banjar Tengah), where chicken dishes take on a new meaning. Hot and spicy, an incredible meal here costs around one dollar.

If you need to impress someone, then take them to the restaurant at the Amandari Hotel, Tel: 975-333, for reservations, in Sayan, north of Ubud. Prices are high but the view of the Ayung River and the surrounding rice fields is superb. An even more spectacular view of the Ayung can be seen from the upstairs room at the Kupu Kupu Barong in Kedewatan, east of Sayan, Tel: 975-078. A grand place for cocktails. More moderately priced, but with a million-dollar view, is The Restaurant at The Chedi in Payangan, Tel: 975-963. Here you can get Indonesia, Asian and Continental cuisine, served by Bali's only female executive chef.

For those wanting a Balinese feast in a Balinese home, contact Ketut Suartana at the Suci Inn. For less than $10, Ketut takes you up to his parent's home for a scrumptious meal.

The East

Candi Dasa

It seems that every eatery here serves the same thing: grilled fish, french fries and vegetables, along with all the other standard Indonesian dishes. The most popular place for grilled fish (and mighty inexpensive) is Candra's. TJ's Cafe, Tel: 0366-41540, opened a branch here, but it doesn't specialize in Mexican food. Excellent salads and desserts served in an elegant atmosphere, with prices to match.

Pandan Restaurant, Tel: 0366-41541, right on the beach, serves a Balinese buffet, including fruit and a cocktail. Pondok Bamboo has excellent grilled fish and whopper iced juices. Ibu Rasmini's Warung is by far the favorite of regulars. Just past the lagoon on the other side of the street, she serves a mean nasi campur (mixed vegetables, tempe, chicken and rice). Kubu Bali, Tel. 0366-41532, specializes in seafood and has an open kitchen.

The North

In Singaraja, good eateries are few and far between. One of the most popular is the Chinese Gandhi Restaurant, Tel: 0362-21163, which offers an extensive menu at moderate prices.

In the Lovina area, fresh seafood is the meal of the day. Most restaurants offer a variety of Indonesian dishes, but the food here is like the life: simple and satisfying. One of the most popular tourist hang-outs is Badai Restaurant, right over a river on the main road. Here you can find inexpensive yet delicious fish dishes. Vegetarian dishes are also available. The Banyualit Hotel has the freshest fish and vegetables in town. The Dhyana Bar and Restaurant on the ocean side of the road is a well-managed place that offers home-cooked food. The mixed seafood grill and yogurt lassies are house specialities. Meals for the budget traveler can be found at Khi Khi Restaurant. Other places with good food are Homestay Agung, Superman's, and Johni's.

Attractions

Things to Do

Most people come to Bali to experience the rich cultural heritage; some come for the beaches and the waves, others for pure relaxation. The major urban centers are Denpasar, Kuta and Sanur. Discotheques abound in Kuta and a few good ones are in Sanur as well. The major movie theaters are in Denpasar, although there are current videos shown in Kuta at bars and restaurants. For culture lovers, rituals abound all over the island. You can consult a Balinese calendar or pick up a calendar of events from the Tourism Office in Denpasar.

Many travel agencies also have information on rituals open to the public. Be wary of tour companies selling "tickets" to cremations and other rites. Dress and behave with decorum, you are welcome at cremations.

Other life-cycle rites (weddings, tooth-filings, etc) are by invitation only and you should not attend if you do not know the host personally.

Amusements

Taman Burung-Bali Bird Park. With more than 300 species winging over the mountains and rice fields, Bali could be described as the 'Island of birds'. The Bird Park is the first international-quality animal preserve on the island. The 2-hectare park at Singapadu contains more than 800 specimens of 125 bird species – a third of which are endangered - from Indonesia and around the world. Paved paths wander through gardens, leading to large aviaries in a natural setting. The landscape is populated with a tremendous selection of tropical plants and cacti from around the world. The facilities are well-signed for a self-guided tour.

The park's breeding program preserves rare and endangered species. Eggs and hatchlings, housed in a nursery, can be viewed through on observation window. Taman Burung is open 9am–7pm, Tel/Fax: 2990-352, Jl. Serma Cok Ngurah Gambir, Singapadu.

Waterbom Water Park. Centrally-located in Tuban, south of Kuta, Waterbom Park has a fully-certified staff of lifeguards, lockers and towels for rent. Main gate admission gives access to all park facilities, including water slides, numerous pools, lazy rivers, sun loungers, game areas, etc. Children under age 12 must be accompanied by an adult. Dining and bar facilities available. Open 9am–6pm daily, Tel: 755-676/78, Fax: 753-517, Jl. Kartika Plaza, Tuban. Adults $10, children $5.

Hiking and Outdoor Activities

Bali Bird Walks, Beggar's Bush, by the bridge, Campuhan, Ubud, Tel: 975-009. See a sampling of the more than 100 species of birds in Bali. Easy walk along trails, across rice fields and rivers, through coconut groves with experienced Balinese guides. Price, $33, includes drinking water, binoculars, lunch, tea and coffee and a bird list.

Sobek Adventure Specialists, Jl. Tirta Ening 9, Bypass Ngurah Rai, Sanur, Tel: 287-059. Sea kyaking, birdwatching, volcano trekking, mountain and off-road bicycling.

Cruises

A cruise can be a lovely way to see a different part of Bali. There are numerous yachts for hire and most offer a day cruise and a sunset cruise. Listed are some of the more popular ones:

Spice Island Cruises. Offers 3- and 4-night cruises to Komodo Island on the M/V Bali Sea Dancer, a 100-meter (330 ft) cruise ship with 73 cabins for 140 passengers. With Friday and Monday departures, stops include Sumbawa, Komodo and Lombok (on 4-night cruise). Casual cruise with food food and comfortable cabins, friendly crew. Optional snorkeling and diving during shore excursions, optional tours, (Komodo island tour included). On-board facilities include small gym, doctor, salon, gift shop/boutique, laundry, pool, two bars, evening entertainment, sun deck, library/game room. Inclusive rates (meals, cabin, Komodo tour, hotel transfers) from $450/person. Children under age 2 not permitted. Spice Island Cruises, Jl. Padang Galak 25, Sanur, Denpasar, Tel: 286-283, Fax: 286-264.

Golden Hawk. Sail to Lembongan Island on an 1880s-era tall ship. The cost of $88 per person includes lunch, snacks and refreshments, snorkeling equipment and hotel transfers. Departs from Benoa, 9am. Tel: 289-508.

WakaLouka. Day-cruise to Lembongan Island on a catamaran. Including continental breakfast, lunch with beer and wine, sunset cocktails, soft drinks all day, afternoon tea and coffee, all island facilities at WakaNusa resort, water sports, hotel transfers. $86. Tel: 484-085.

Bali Hai Cruises. Day-cruises to Lembongan Island and and sunset harbor/dinner cruises aboard catamarans. Day-cruises include hotel transfers, morning and afternoon tea, lunch, watersports, snorkel equipment, beach club or sea pontoon activities for $68 to $80, island tours and diving optional; dinner cruise with transfers, cocktail, buffet dinner, entertainment, $38. Tel: 720-331, 771-463, Fax: 720-334.

Tour Packages

The tour companies listed below are reputable and can arrange island-wide tours; a guide is furnished (languages widely spoken are English, French, Japanese, German and Dutch; some companies have Italian-, Spanish- and Chinese-speaking guides).

There are many standard tour packages from which to choose, or you can design your own and hire a driver and a guide for the day (from $60–$125 per day; air-conditioned vehicles are more costly). For either type of tour, contact one of the agents below or inquire at the hotel travel desk. The most experienced agents for English-speaking travelers are BIL and Pacto.

Exotic wildlife safaris start at $60 and go up to $400, which includes airfare to see the Komodo dragons, to the Buluran Wild Game Reserve in East Java, and the Sukomade tour, continuing the above to Turtle Bay renowned for surfing, diving and the impenetrable jungle of the Meru Betiri National Park. Tours are also available to Bali Barat National Park, where lives the few remaining wild Rothschild Bali starling, an extremely rare blue-faced white starling found nowhere else in the world. These tours can be made through Bali Ekawista Tours (BEST).

For cheap airline tickets, try Astrindo, Jl. Raya Kuta 109, Kuta, Tel: 753-138; KCB, Jl. Raya Kuta 79, Tel: 751-517; and Vayatour, 223-757.

WakaLouka provides half-day land trips to the "secret soul of Bali" aboard four-wheel-drive vehicles. Travel grassy tracks through terraced rice fields, up mountain roads to where spices, tea and coffee grow, see birds and scenery, mineral hot springs, stone quarries. Lunch in the WakaLouka Rainforest Camp. Rate includes transfers, soft drinks, lunch with beer and wine. $80+. Return transfers by 25-minute helicopter, $195 (minimum 8 passengers). Tel: 484-085, Fax: 484-767.

TOUR GUIDES

Almost all of the travel agencies listed above have qualified guides. Freelance guides abound and some of them are not really qualified (either in language or in expertise).

Culture

Museums

Bali has many museums with fine collections of traditional and modern art. The **Bali Museum** (Tel: 235-059, 222-680) in Denpasar offers a vivid picture of Balinese life and art from prehistoric times up to the 20th century, with emphasis on the antique. **Museum Le Mayeur** (8am–2pm Tuesday–Sunday), just north of the Grand Bali Beach Hotel in Sanur, has the collection of the late Belgian painter, Le Mayeur. **Museum Puri Lukisan** (Tel: 975-636) in Ubud displays works dating from the late 1920s, when Balinese painters first began to break away from the formality of traditional painting styles, up until the present. Many were gathered by Dutch painter Rudolph Bonnet, with the assistance of Ubud's prince. It contains excellent contemporary paintings and carvings, most created during the past 20 years by artists living in or around Ubud. A gallery has been added where selected works of arts are on sale. Open daily, 8am–4pm.

The **Lempad Museum** on the main street in Ubud houses the paintings of the famous I Nyoman Lempad, who died in 1978 at 116. Noted for his pen-and-ink drawings (both erotic and otherwise), his style is quite unlike traditional Balinese painting and in a class of its own.

Nyoman Suradnya in Padang Tegal, Ubud (at the Nirwana Losmen) is a fine batik painter and has a gallery and studio at his home. Classes in batik are available. Call 975-415.

Visit also the many private galleries in the homes of artists. One of the most lavish is the gallery/home of an American, Antonio Blanco, (Tel: 975-502, 975-551) up on the left after the bridge in Campuhan (Ubud). This old building is a well-preserved example of Balinese architecture. Inside you can meet the artist's family, and view his private collection of erotic paintings and collages. Open daily 8am–5pm.

Hans Snel is another well-known foreign artist living in Ubud, a Dutchman painting in the Gauguin/Spies/Bonnet tradition of native-modern art. His gallery has recently been expanded to include a guest house, bar and restaurant. After viewing his work, sit and have a cozy drink.

The **Neka Museum** (Tel: 975-074, 975-034), several kilometers to the west of Ubud, contains the finest collection of paintings on Bali, better than the Puri Lukisan. Neka is a Balinese art dealer known to all the great painters of Bali over the years, and this is his private collection. Paintings are sold in a gallery on Ubud's main street. Open daily 9am–5pm.

Down the road in Peliatan is the **Agung Rai Museum of Art** (ARMA) (Tel: 976-659, 964-95, Fax: 974-229, www.nusantara.com/arma/) houses an impressive collection of traditional and modern Balinese paintings, as well as works of foreigners who have lived in Bali. The permanent collection, which has moved to Jl. Bima in Pengoseken, should not be missed. The gallery is open daily 8am-6pm.

The **Archaeological Museum** by the main road in Pejeng, (Tel: 942-354, 943-357) less than 1 km north of Bedulu on the Tampaksiring Road, contains a collection of Bronze Age remains found in this area, including huge stone sarcophagi and tiny Hindu lamps. Open 8am–3pm weekdays.

In Mas, you can see the layout of a typical (but wealthy) Balinese compound at **Adil Gallery** and Siadja & Son. The staff will gladly explain what each structure is used for and how things are built according to the traditional system of architecture.

The late Ida Bagus Tilem was the most famous woodcarver of Mas. His house is on the main road just south of Ubud. His son, himself a talented carver, now manages a gallery exhibiting his father's work. Many contemporary carvings are also sold in adjoining showrooms. Open daily 8am–5pm.

The **Museum Manusia Yadna** in Mengwi, just across the moat from the Puri Taman Ayun Temple, was founded with the admirable idea of preserving, in a single collection, examples of the arts of Balinese temple offerings. Unfortunately, the museum has not been well kept and receives few visitors, but if fascinated by Balinese ritual life, this collection is a must. Exhibited are all sorts of offerings used for various rites of passage and temple ceremonies. Open every day (but often left unattended).

Just before Tabanan town, on the right side of the road, is the **Subak Museum** in the village of Sanggulan. Opened in the early 1980s, this museum houses an eclectic and small collection depicting the *subak* (water irrigation for paddy fields) system and a typical Balinese household, including all the implements used in a traditional wood-burning kitchen.

The **Gedong Kirtya** in Singaraja (Tel: (0362) 25141, 7am–3pm Monday–Thursday, until noon Friday, closed weekends) is a unique library of old *lontar* (palm-leaf) manuscripts and scholarly Dutch books. It was founded by the colonial government in the 1930s. Open daily 7am–3pm.

Performing Arts

The best way to see Balinese dance-dramas, *wayang kulit* (shadow puppet) and gamelan orchestras is to attend a village temple festival. There is one going on somewhere on the island almost every day. Ask at the hotel, or consult the *Bali Post* or Yayasan Bina Wisata in Ubud, Tel: 96285.

For visitors whose time in Bali is more precious, public performances are given at numerous central locations. These are mainly for the benefit of tourists, but that doesn't mean they are inferior to genuine temple performances. Some of Bali's best dancers and musicians participate in tourist performances, a good source of additional income. The times and locations change constantly, but the following are fairly well-established venues and schedules. The shows last no longer than 90 minutes and begin on time. (Camera flashes are normal in these performances, and can be distracting.) Tickets average Rp. 7,000.

Sunday: Kecak Fire & Trance, Padang Tegal, Ubud, 7pm or Bone Village, 6.30pm; Wayang Kulit, Oka Kartini Ubud 8pm; Mahabharata Ballet, Ubud Palace, 7.30pm; Women's Gamelan, Peliatan, 7.30pm.
Monday: Legong, Ubud Palace, 7.30pm; Kecak Fire & Trance, Bone Village, 6.30pm or Singapadu, 7pm; Ciwa Ratri with classical Gamelan Gebuyg, Pura Dalem Puri Ubud, 7.30pm.
Tuesday: Mahabharata dance, Teges village, 7.30pm; Ramayana Ballet, Ubud Palace, 8pm; Spirit of Bali, Jaba Pura Desa Kutuh, Ubud, 7.30pm.
Wednesday: Wayang Kulit, Oka Kartini Ubud, 8pm; Kecak Fire & Trance, Bone Village, 6.30pm, Padang Tegal Ubud 7pm; Legong & Barong, Ubud Palace 7.30pm, Banjar Tengah, Peliatan, 7pm.
Thursday: Gabor Dance, Ubud Palace, 7.30pm; Kecak, Puri Agung peliatan, 7.30pm; Calonarang Dance, Mawang Village, 7pm.
Friday: Barong, Ubud Palace, 6.30pm; Kecak Fire & Trance, Bone Village, 6.30pm, Pura Dalem Ubud, 7.30pm; Legong Dance, Peliatan Village, 7.30pm.
Saturday: Legong Dance, Ubud Palace, 7.30pm; Calonarang dance, Mawang Village, 7pm; Kecak Fire & Trance, Padang Tegal Ubud, 7pm.

Many of the large hotels have regular evening dinner shows. Call for information. It is possible to charter performances. In Krambitan, at the Puri Anyar and Puri Gede, they perform a Calon Arang story accompanied by the unique *tektekan gamelan* or *joged* (flirtation dance). With a minimum of 10 people, guests will be met with a torch-lit procession, and you can feast on local Balinese food and be entertained by the dancers and musicians of this small village, in the west of Bali.

Other gamelan troupes can also be hired. The dance academies SMKI and STSI, in Batubulan and Jl. Nusa Indah in Denpasar respectively, frequently have student recitals; some of the best young dancers on the island can be found there.

Nightlife

The real night scene is in Kuta and Legian Beach. Here the streets come alive after 10pm and pub-crawls happen nightly. Not a Balinese scene at all, drinking in Kuta caters mainly to Australians. Discos are becoming more fashionable for young Indonesians, but drinking is still not a way of life here.

Kuta is full of Indonesian gigolos just waiting to go in for the kill; these are very slick operators who offer love and romance and expect to be taken care of. Prostitution by another name, with the genders reversed. Lots of foreign women fall for it.

Sanur is more sedate, and older Indonesian businessmen often frequent the discos here, more for a place to relax than for the dancing.

Gambling is not legal in Indonesia; there are no casinos or other types of gambling establishments here.

Discos

Again, Kuta is the disco scene, although there are some good ones in Sanur as well. Discos in Kuta change clientele and popularity, so something top this year may not be in favor the next. In Sanur, the scene is a bit more mellow. Hotel discos in Tuban and Nusa Dua are popular with locals, but sedate and expensive.

Festival

Balinese Calendar

Trying to figure out the Balinese calendar requires mathematical genius, as three systems are in use simultaneously.

The indigenous *pawukon* calendar consists of a series of weeks, numbering from 1–10 days, which converge together after 210 days. The Balinese refer to this as the *wuku* system, wuku meaning a week (but not necessarily of 7 days). The most important wuku are the three-day week (Pasah, Beteng and Kajeng), the five-day week (Umanis, Paing, Pon, Wage and Kliwon) and the seven-day week. The three-day week is based on the revolving market – large market days are held in the village every three days. There are a number of holy days which occur when certain days fall together: Anggara Kasih which is when a Tuesday and Kliwon fall together; Kajeng of the three-day week and Kliwon of the five-day week occur every 15 days, and this is a time considered to be conducive to the darker powers, a kind of Friday the 13th, if you will. Wednesdays are often days of special religious ritual and Saturdays are days of honor.

Another ancient system is the **lunar calendar**. Many of the temple festivals in the mountain villages occur on *tilem* (the new moon) or *purnama* (the full moon), and occur once a year instead of every 210 days. This system is called the Hindu *saka* calendar and is divided into 12 months, or *sasih*, of 29–30 days. Every two or three years, an additional month is added to bring the lunar calendar in accord with the solar calendar. This calendar is named after the Indian Saka dynasty, which began in AD 78 – 1920 in the saka calendar is 1998 in the solar calendar.

The third calendar system is the

Gregorian, which is used for national holidays. Balinese calendars hang in every home, as no one is able to memorize all the configurations. In the case of a large ceremony, a Brahman priest must be consulted to ascertain an auspicious day. These calendars are available in all the bookstores and are quite interesting to look at and make intriguing gifts.

Major Balinese Holy Days
Nyepi

The New Year by the *saka* calendar falls on the day after the new moon of the ninth month, usually in March. It is celebrated by a day of stillness, Nyepi, when no fires may be lit, no transport taken, and no work done. On the day before Nyepi, the last day of the year (*pengerupuk*) and marking the end of the rainy season, a great purification offering is made by all the villages to cleanse the country of dark forces. Laid on the ground at every crossroad are huge offerings of wines and flesh from wild and domestic animals (*caru*). These are to feed the ground spirits, while from a raised platform, high priests recite powerful formulas to exorcise them. That night, everyone is out in the streets sounding gongs, cymbals and other noise makers to chase the spirits away. In Denpasar, a huge parade (*ogoh-ogoh*) of papier-mache monsters (some riding papier-mache motorcycles) is held; at the end of the parade, some of them are burned. Even though its roots are exorcistic, this is now a competition between hamlets to see who can make the best ogoh-ogoh.

Galungan

Every 210th day by the *wuku* calendar, the Balinese hold a great feast commemorating the victory of the people over the legendary demon-king Mayadanawa. According to myth, this king strictly forbade his subjects' worship of their ancestors and deities. Assisted by the god Indra and his divine allies, the people revolted and, in a great battle, defeated the demon-king. Thus, they were free again to worship according to their own beliefs. On Galungan, it is believed that the supreme god, Sanghyang Widi Wasa, followed by other deities and ancestral spirits, descends from heavens to temples on earth to feast. For 10 days, they receive many offerings and processions, dances and songs. All the *barong* are marched from the temples and paraded from village to village, often stopping at the roadside and dancing on the spot. The 10th day, Kuningan, is the last day of their sojourn on earth and the spirits ascend.

Temple Festivals (Odalan)

Each temple holds a festival on the anniversary of its consecration, either every 210th day or every lunar year. To the villagers, it means an all-day, all-night celebration. (Some odalan, such as the one at Besakih, can go on for 35 days.) From early morning, the *pemangku* priest is on duty to receive and bless the offerings brought by the women. By afternoon, a cockfight is in full swing, vendors have set up their refreshments, a medicine man is laying out his paraphernalia for demonstrating cure-alls, processions of people in festival dress are arriving... and so it continues. In the evening, gods and mortals alike are entertained with dance-dramas and gamelan music, *wayang kulit* and sung poetry.

Days of Honor

Besides national holidays and festivals, the Balinese set certain days (*tumpek*) aside to honor individual deities who are guardians of special disciplines. Once a year by the wuku calendar, a day is devoted to Saraswati, goddess of wisdom. Offerings are made to *lontar* manuscripts and no one is allowed to read or write on that day. Another day is dedicated to Batara Sangkara, the lord of all crops. Offerings are presented to coconut trees "dressed up" in wrappings of fine cloth; climbing them is prohibited on that day.

On the day devoted to the divinity of prosperity and financial success, no business is done. The day honoring weapons forbids the use of any sharp objects. There is also a day of the "golden blessing", when offerings are made to all objects of gold, silver and precious stones, and to the lord of gold, Mahadewa, guardian of the West. Little of nature or of the tools that serve the people is left unattended. One day is reserved for all offerings to domestic animals, another for all utensils and equipment used in rice farming (during which time no rice may be husked or sold), and still another for all musical instruments, dance costumes, puppets and even motor vehicles. In Bali, there are no off-seasons. Every day brings celebrations; no matter when you arrive, you are bound to encounter a celebration on the island.

Many important temple festivals fall at much the same time as Galungan and Kuningan. Festivals also occur during the fourth month (September/October) and the tenth month (April).

Shopping

Thousands of artisans, craftspeople, seamstresses, woodcarvers, and painters are kept busy supplying the tourist demand. Swarms of vendors crowd the beaches and streets of Denpasar, offering friendship bracelets, necklaces and watches. Many shopkeepers have developed a hard-sell sales pitch reminiscent of Hong Kong or New York. Sometimes it is a bit overwhelming, but rare is the visitor who comes away without at least one bag of souvenirs. The variety is literally endless. Most handicrafts and paintings can be found in the Gianyar district; textiles in Gianyar, Klungkung (Sideman), Karangasem (Tenganan), Kuta and Denpasar. Kuta has the best shopping, but you have to deal with the crassness of the shopkeepers.

Antiques

The "antique" business in Bali is booming. Carve a split piece of wood, paint it and bury it in the ground for a month and, *voila!* – an antique. Be very careful when buying antiques. There's no guarantee as to age. Intricately-carved doors, doorways, huge ornate wedding beds, wavy ceremonial kris, textiles, old Dutch lamps, masks, Chinese ceramics and sculptures from many parts of Indonesia, as well as China and Japan, are available to the discriminating buyer, however.

The antique shops, adjacent to the Kerta Gosa in Klungkung, house collections of rare Chinese porcelains, old Kamasan wayang-style paintings, antique jewelry and Balinese weavings. Prices are reasonable. Singaraja has some of the best antique shops in Bali. They are all on the main streets of this port town.

Cassette Tapes

Pirated (and cheap) cassette tapes are a thing of the past now, thanks to new trade agreements and government regulations. But there is still a great variety of rock, pop, classical and folk music available, for around $5 a tape. Probably the best selection is at Mahogany on Jl. Seminyak, Seminyak. Ubud Music across from the Lotus Cafe also has a good selection. For traditional Balinese and Indonesian music, you can't beat Toko Melati on Jl. Kartini, a block north of the main Denpasar market. The owner is knowledgeable about the latest and will play the tapes before you buy them.

Ceramics

The village of Pejaten in Tabanan has whimsical and serious tiles, as well as stoneware plates, bowls and the like. Good quality stoneware can be found in Kapal (at the bend in the road just past Pura Sadah). Jenggala in Batujimbar, Sanur, is another source for tea sets, dinnerware, vases, etc. Also in Sanur is Sari Bumi on Jl. Danau Tamblingan; in Ubud the outlet is just past the post office, on the south side of the street. All of these outlets sell lead-free pottery.

Clothes

Bali now has one of the biggest garment industries in Southeast Asia. There are perhaps 500 designers and exporters working out of Kuta and Legian (including many young Italians and Japanese). The clothes are ideal for casual summer wear in warm climates. The best way to find a store that specializes in designs to your liking is to walk along Jl. Legian, or down

Jl. Bakung Sari in Kuta. Overruns are available at Mama and Leon, Jl. Danau Tamblingan 99A, Sanur, on the west side of the street near Pacto; Bali Garments behind Segara Village in Sanur; and Sari Busana, Jl. Raya Menguntur 21, Tel: 298-569, just south of the Y-junction in Tohpati.

For more upscale sportswear, try Kartini, Tao and Kingkong in Legian. Uluwatu (on Jl. Bakung Sari), Kekal (Jl. Legian and Jl. Pantai Kuta) and Bali High on Jl. Semawang in Sanur offer lacy women's wear. Surfwear can be found all over, but the most popular shops are The Curl and Ulu's Shop on Jl. Melasti and Bali Barrel on Jl. Legian. For gorgeous ikat designer clothes, go to Nogo's on Jl. Batujimbar in Sanur and Jl. Legian in Kuta.

Gold & Silver

Inventive Balinese jewelers smelt, cast, forge and spin delicate flowers, bowls and images of demons studded with semi-precious stones. The centers for metalworking are Celuk, Kamasan in Klungkung, and Bratan in Buleleng, where all such ornaments are on sale at reasonable but negotiable prices. These craftsmen will also produce pieces and settings to order – bring them a drawing or a sample to copy. If you don't like it, they'll smelt it down and start over.

For traditional Balinese jewelry (and that means gold), visit the shops at Jl. Hasanudin (Melati is a reputable one - most of the gold is 22–24K) and Jl. Sulawesi. You'll see women sitting out in front of the shops buying and selling gold as well. If you want to take your chances with them, you can usually take the jewelry into one of the shops and have them test it to see how dense the gold is.

One of the best goldsmiths around is Nyoman Sadia, at Jl. Sersan Wayan Pugig No 5, in Sukawati. His prices are high but his work is exquisite. If coming from Denpasar, you'll see his placard on the right side of the road, past the police station. A new upscale shop in Ubud, Treasures, Jl. Ubud Raya next to Ary's Warung, features pricey jewels in gold settings by local designers-in-residence, Penny Burton, Carolyn Taylor and Jean-Francois Fichot. In Ubud, go to Putra's for silver. Fixed prices here but it's a blessing as they aren't inflated (nor quoted in dollars

like in Celuk). He has two shops on Monkey Forest Road, one across from Griya Restaurant on the main road; his wholesale outlet is in Puri Agung, in Peliatan. Kuta is a great place to shop for jewelry as the designs are quite modern and contemporary. Try Jonathan, Mirah, Mario's and Jusuf's on Jl. Legian.

Handicrafts

Bamboo implements, *wayang kulit* figures and ornaments made of coconut shell and teakwood are sold at most souvenir shops. Bone carvings can be bought at good prices at Tampaksiring, while plaited hats and baskets are the specialty of the women of Bedulu and Bona. Pasar Seni Sukawati and the row of stands opposite Goa Gajah (Elephant Cave) are the best places to buy baskets; to see them made (and sold, of course), go to Pengoseken near Ubud. Wooden earrings (the animals and geometric-design styles) can be found at Tampaksiring and the kiosks at Gunung Kawi, as well as in shops in all the major tourist resort areas. Sandalwood fans can be ordered with your name on it at Toko Susila on Jl. Hasanudin 29 near Jl. Sumatra in Denpasar. Orders can be filled within a day. Make sure to specify real sandalwood, as most fans are coffeewood soaked in sandalwood perfume. Ebony nameplates can be ordered in Sanur in front of the Swastika II Restaurant.

The **Handicrafts Center** (Sanggraha Karya Hasta) in Tohpati, Denpasar, has a collection of the handicrafts from Bali and the other islands of Indonesia, such as baskets and weavings. This center is not really a museum, but a government-sponsored cooperative selling Indonesian and Balinese handicrafts. Open 8.30am–5pm, until 4.30pm on Saturday, closed Sunday.

Musical Instruments

If it's gongs, xylophones, or drums you're after, head on out to the gong foundry in Blahbatuh and look up Pande Gableran and sons. They churn out instruments for gamelan clubs all over the world and always have some stock on hand. For bamboo flutes in the Ubud area, look up Cok Agung in Banjar Teruna. Any kind of bamboo instruments (*bumbung, tingklink*) can be made by the master Pak Rembang, in

Banjar Tengah, Sesetan, Denpasar (on the way to Kuta past Sangglah).

Paintings

The classical wayang style has its origins in Kamasan, Klungkung. Cheap renditions can be bought in the parking lot across from Kerta Gosa in Klungkung. For traditional paintings, go to Batuan, Pengoseken (fish and birds) and Peliatan, Ubud and Penestanan (Young Artist style). The best thing to do is to visit major galleries, see which artist you like and then seek them out at their home. Smaller galleries often have gems at a much lower price.

Stonecarvings

For traditional sandstone carvings, stop in at the workshops in Batubulan. Wayan Cemul, an Ubud stone carver with an international following, has a house full of his weird and wonderful creations.

Textiles

The spiraling designs and geometric patterns of Javanese batik are seen everywhere on the island, as part of the daily dress of the Balinese. Buffaloes, birds, masks and puppet figures are some of the motives entwined in characteristic compositions. Most of what is being sold on the streets by vendors is not batik, but printed materials the Balinese use for tablecloths.

Be careful what you buy for "temple clothing", as a lot of it is inappropriate (not wrong, just funny to the Balinese sensibility). A good starting point for batik is Batik Populer, a small shop west of the river on Jl. Gajah Mada in Denpasar. Here you can find everything from simple *cap* (stamped) batik to the glorious *tulis* ("written", the batik artist uses a canting to make the designs) batiks.

For the Balinese hand-loomed *ikat* cloth, there are a number of "factories" one can visit; each part of the island specializes in certain motifs.

The most accessible and well-known factories are those in the town of Gianyar. Cap Togog and Cap Cili are two showrooms which also have tours of the process. Cap Anoman in Beng (just north of Gianyar) doesn't provide a tour, but you're welcome to wander through the factory. Their showroom in Blahbatuh is fancy and overpriced. Other centers of ikat are Sideman and

Gelgel in Klungkung, and Singaraja in the north.

Songket is another traditional Balinese cloth which has gold and silver threads in the weft. It is worn for rituals by both men and women. The villages of Blayu, Sideman, and Singaraja are well-known for their songket. Other types of weaving, such as *selendang* (temple sashes) are done in Batuan, Ubud, and Mengwi. The famous *geringsing* (double ikat) is made only in Tenganan, where ikat cloth from all over the Indonesian archipelago is for sale. Textiles such as the Sumbanese *hinggi* and Batak *ulos* may also be bought in many shops in Kuta and Denpasar. **Arts of Asia**, Jl. Raya Tuban, Tel: 752-860, and **Suryajaya**, Jl. Gajah Mada 128, Tel: 422-254, have the highest quality and most variety, respectively.

Woodcarvings

You are sure to find good woodcarvings in the shops along the main road of Mas (particularly well-known is Ida Bagus Tilem's Gallery and Museum – pricey but the work is gorgeous) and in the village of Kemenuh. For masks, try Ida Bagus Anom in Mas, I Wayan Tangguh in Singapadu and I Wayan Regog in Lantanghidung near Batuan. Kemenuh, on the way to Gianyar, also has fine exponents of ebony and other types of wood carvings. Pujung (past Tegalalang north of Ubud) is the banana-tree capital of the world (the wooden variety, that is). Jati is known as the home of "primitive" carving.

For exquisite work carved onto delicate roots, no one can surpass Muja in Singapadu. All sorts of indigenous woods are used, ranging from the butter-colored jackfruit wood to inexpensive bespeckled coconut. Woods imported from other islands - buff hibiscus, rich brown Javanese teak and black Sulawesian ebony – are also hewn into delicate forms by the Balinese craftsmen.

Packing & Shipping

If you've gone overboard on shopping and can't fit it all into your two suitcases, don't despair. There are a number of ways to get things home. First, find yourself a reliable shipper. For a small fee, they'll do your packing. If you have something quite delicate or

fragile, you might want to oversee the packing yourself.

Air cargo is charged by the kilo (minimum 10 kg/22 lbs) and can turn out to be pretty expensive. Sea mail is another option, taking 2-3 months to get to its destination. Packages less than a meter in length and under 10 kg (22 lbs) can be sent through the postal service. Insurance is highly recommended; read the fine print. If you have a lot of stuff, then send it by sea cargo - you can send a minimum of a cubic meter to Europe and the US for around $350, including packing. Insurance is 2.75 percent of the claimed value. Sea and air cargo go to the closest port and international airport, post goes to your door; therefore you have to think about how you'll get your goods home from the port/airport. Shippers will even pick things up from the shop or come to your hotel. What remains is to be aware of what problems, restrictions or expenses you might encounter in your home country.

Shippers

Alpha Sigma, Jl. Raya Imam Bonjol 605X, Kuta, Tel: 752-872.
Angkasa Jaya, Jl. Raya Kuta 105A, Kuta, Tel: 751-390.
Bali Delta Express, Jl. Kartini 58, Denpasar, Tel: 223-340.
Bintang Bali Cargo, Jl. Nangka, Gang Murni l8, Banjar Tegeh Sari, Denpasar, Tel: 421-802.
Pacific Express, Jl. Arjuna 21, Denpasar, Tel: 235-181.

There are branches of many other agents throughout Kuta, Legian, Ubud and other areas.

Body Treats

How about a rub down with exotic herbs followed by a steam bath? Or an hour-long facial to get rid of all the grit from the exhaust and the dust? Or a "creme bath" for your hair: an hour-long conditioning treatment including massage and steam?

Almost every "salon" now offers these services. Creme baths and facials run around $5; the whole-body treatment around $10. If a purist, make sure you ask for the "traditional" herbal treatments, otherwise you'll get cheap chemicals put on your head. The most popular salon in Denpasar is

Sari Ayu, just across from the flower stalls and before Tiara Dewata. In Kuta, try Jamu Traditional Salon at Kul Kul Resort, Jl. Pantai Kuta, Tel: 752-520. In Ubud, try Nur's Salon, Jl. Hanoman 28, Padang Tegal, Tel: 975-352, or Milano Salon II, Jl. Wanara Wana, behind Le Chat, Tel: 96488.

Indonesians have been using herbs for centuries to cure ills and beautify themselves. *Jamu*, as it is called, is now available in pill form (the traditional form is a bitter powder mixed with lime juice and honey). Everything from tonics to post-partum purifiers to cough medicine is made by several jamu companies in Java (Nyonya Meneer, Mustika Ratu, Martha Tilaar and Cap Jago). The pills and the powders are available at the major Chinese apothecaries on Jl. Gajah Mada and at Nur's Salon in Ubud. Just look for the jamu signs.

For massages, there are now a number of *panti pijit* (legitimate massage parlors) all over Denpasar. For around $5, you can get a relaxing rubdown. In Kuta, one can still get a perfunctory massage on the beach for cheap. In Ubud, I Wayan Weda, Jl. Hanoman 1, Padang Tegal, Tel: 974-001, gives accupressure, relaxation and reflexology massages for under $10 a session. Blind masseuse I Wayan Surtana, in Kedewatan, does deep-tissue work, reflexology and sport massage for under $10.

International spas are opening up left and right. Single treatments start at about $30. In Ubud, The Spa at the Chedi, Tel: 975-963, in Payangan has a variety of treatments in private villas – massage, facials, body scrubs – and specializes in couples. The Banyan Tree Kamandalu Spa, Tel: 975-825, in Petulu, has a full range of spa and salon services. In Jimbaran, the Four Seasons Resort, Tel: 701-010, has a great spa, as does the Nusa Dua Beach Hotel, Tel: 7721-210, in Nusa Dua. All of these resort spas offer hotel facilities, including pool use, tennis where available, and add 21 percent tax and service to your bill.

For lower key massage and body scrubs, plus full salon at reasonable prices, visit Bodyworks, Jl. Raya Seminyak 63, Tel: 730-454.

Sports

Participant Sports

The most recent boom in sports in Bali has been of the liquid variety: the government is encouraging the development of marine sports. There are a wide variety of watersports available.

Bungy Jumping

Bungy jumping took Bali by storm in 1995 when several towers opened. The attraction to the sport here is that it is much cheaper and just as safe as elsewhere. Usually included are a T-shirt and beer with the jump.

A.J. Hackett, Jl. Double Six, Legian, Tel: 731-144.
Bali Bungy Co, Jl. Pura Puseh, Kuta, Tel/Fax: 752-658. $49.

Golf

Grand Bali Beach, Sanur, Tel; 288-511. A small 9-hole course that can be used for 18 holes. $50 for 18 holes. Guests of the hotel can use it for half price. Equipment and caddies are available. A miniature golf course is also available at $2 for 18 holes.
Bali Handara Country Club, Desa Pancasari, Bedugul, Tel: 228-866. The serious golfer will want to visit this 18-hole championship course, designed by Peter Thompson. It is the only course in the world set inside a volcano. It is also gazetted among the world's top-50 most beautiful courses. If you stay at the adjoining hotel, there is a 50-percent discount on the green fees of $75-90.
Bali Golf and Country Club, Nusa Dua, Tel: 771-791. Within walking distance of Nusa Dua's main hotels. Exquisite course with 9 holes by the sea and 9 holes on the edge of the Bukit. Green fees, $125 plus tax.

River Rafting

White-water rafting adventures are offered down several rivers near Ubud. All-day excursion with lunch provided and a free cocktail up on the ridge afterwards. Cost is $65 per person, 4 persons minimum. Includes transport to and from hotel, insurance and professional guides.

Sobek Bina Utama, Tel: 287-059, Fax: 289-448.
Bali Safari Rafting, Tel: 221-315, 221-316, Fax: 232-268.

Sailing

For those who just want a ride in a *jukung*, an outrigger canoe with sails, Sanur, Candidasa and Lovina all have locals who will take you out for around $3/person. For more professional sailing, head on down to Benoa Harbor. The **Bali International Yacht Club** at Benoa Harbor, Tel: 723-415, is planning to build a modern 50-berth marina in Benoa. Those who require permission to bring their own boats into Indonesian waters can contact them for assistance in obtaining all the necessary documents. Other yacht operators: **Camar Yacht Charter**, Tel: 720-591, 7710956, Fax: 720-592; or **Beluga**, Tel: 771-997, Fax: 771-987.

Surfing

Kuta is the central location to rent/buy boards and find out surfing conditions. Lili's Surf Shop, on the north side of Jl. Legian in Kuta near Midnight Oil, is probably the best source of information. Bali Bagus on Jl. Legian rents and sells surfboards.

Best places for surfing are Kuta, Legian and Seminyak for beginners. Intermediate surfers should go to Bingin, south of the airport reef in Kuta. Also Canggu, 20 minutes northwest of Legian. Much further west are Lalang Linggah village (Soka Beach) and Medewi. For real expert surfers, Kuta Reef is accessible only by boat, in front of the Sunset Club; Uluwatu and Padang Padang. Great surfing at Nusa Lembongan as well.

Swimming

For a fee ranging from $2–$5 per day, the pools at some of the larger hotels in Denpasar, Sanur, Kuta and Nusa Dua are open to non-guests. In Ubud, the pools open to the public are at Ubud Inn (great kiddy pool), Hotel Campuhan, Ubud Village Inn, Oka Wati's, Villa Rasa Sayang, Dewi Sri and Fibra Inn. Most charge around $2 per day.

One of the best kept secrets (not any more, actually) in Ubud is the cave pool on the way to Pejeng. At the T-junction of Peliatan and Ubud, go east on the asphalt road. After around 200 meters is a fabulous view of a gorge and river; there is a slippery path that goes down to the river. You can swim in crystal-clear water here, and if adventurous, dive under a cave and come up in a private, natural pool. All the locals know about it.

Water Sports

Over the last 10 years, surfing, snorkeling, scuba diving, spearfishing, windsurfing and deep-sea fishing have all become very popular in Bali. Nusa Lembongan, the small island directly opposite Sanur, has developed into a haven for surfers and divers alike. Group charters and safari tours are available, together with equipment and instruction if needed. A complete scuba outfit and a ride out to the reef at Sanur is available. Ask about taking out insurance.

Baruna Water Sports, Jl. Bypass Ngurah Rai 300B, Tuban, Tel: 753-820. They offer tours to all the main scuba diving attractions on the island. Also, parasailing, jetskiing, waterscooter, windsurfing, canoe and paddleboard, glass-bottom boat, waterskiing, trolling, coral/deep sea fishing.

Bali Marine Sports, Jl. Bypass Ngurah Rai, Belanjong, Sanur, Tel: 287-872, 289-309, offers a number of different boating expeditions, including snorkeling and diving.

Beluga, Benoa Harbor, Nusa Dua, Tel: 771-997. Swimming pool, diving and watersports, parasailing, dolphin tour, submarine, restaurant.

Dive Sites

Sanur and Nusa Dua: Convenient access, dives at 2–12 meters (6–39 ft) deep are rewarded by beautiful underwater panoramas. Gigantic table and trophy-shaped coral and sponge grow for miles on barrier reef, but limited variety. Coral better at Nusa Dua. Variety of colorful fish.

Padangbai and the Gili Tepekong Islands: Located about 60 km (40 mi) northeast of Sanur. Ideal for dives at 3–20 meters (9–66 ft) depths. Full growth of coral and fish. The Gili islands offer a variety of fish life and larger species. Water is cool and wetsuit essential. Currents are strong and unpredictable.

Lembongan Island: About 20 km (12 mi) east of Sanur and two hours by motor boat, this is actually one of the three sister islands of Bali. White sandy bottom and crystal-clear, cool water offer assorted fish and marine vegetation. Underwater grottos are the wonders of this area.

Tulamben: Located about 100 km (60 mi) northeast of Sanur. On location, 30 m offshore are remnants of the US merchantman *Liberty* sunk during World War II. The wreck is fully grown with anemone, gorgonia, sponge, and coral, and fish are tame.

Singaraja: Located about 80 km (50 mi) due north of Sanur, where the calm waters of the Bali Sea create pool-like conditions ideal for snorkeling. The best spots are around Lovina Beach, suitable for beginners, and Gondol Beach having slight currents from 5–15 meter (16–50 ft) depths.

Menjangan National Park: The tiny adjoining island 120 km (70 mi) northwest of Sanur is accessible in 30 minutes by boat. All-season, undemanding diving where magnificent underwater vistas (up to 50 m visibility) will surprise even the most seasoned diver. It is rich with all kinds of sponges, sea plants, coral and fish. This area is considered the diver's paradise in Bali. Also an old wreck at 40 m (130 ft) and superb coral in 5–7 m (16–23 ft.)

Pemuteran: The access point for Menjangan Island, easy access in a few minutes by boat. Slight current, good variety of fish and abundant soft corals at 3–8 m (10–26 ft) make this a good dive and snorkel area. **Tabuhan Islands**: Coral reefs, tropical fish and shark sites are the main diving draws. **Amed**: Located near Tulamben. Slope and drop off 3–40 meter (10–130 ft) depth, has coral, plantation, sinall, large fish and drop-off. Mild current, best variety of hard coral in Bali, dense fish population on deep walls. Coral near the beach.

Nusa Penida: This is the adventure dive. Two hours by boat from Padangbai. Drift dive, flat slope and drop-off between 3–40 meters (10–130 ft). White sandy bottom, crystal-clear and cool water present assorted fish, crayfish and coral reef. Water typically cool from upswell. Currents can be strong.

DIVE OPERATORS

Bali Marine Sports, Jl. Bypass Ngurah Rai, Belanjong, Sanur, Tel: 287-872, 289-309.

Balina Diving in Balina (near Candidasa) offers snorkeling, and diving. Call Bali Nusa Granada in Sanur at 288-451.

Dive 'n Dives, Jl. Bypass Ngurah Rai 23, Sanur, Tel: 288-052.

Reef Seen Aquatics Dive Center, Desa Pemuteran, Gerokgak, Singaraja, Bali, Tel/Fax: (0362) 92339, e-mail: reefseen@denpasar.wasantara.net.id. Specializing in dives around Menjangan Island; Australian PADI instructor who has pioneered the area. Equipment rentals, dives and certification, cruises, sailing, dive trips.

Serendipity Divers, Bali Hai Cruises, in Benoa Harbor, Tel: 730-206.

Stingray Diving at Puri Bali Homestay (Tel: 225-844) in Candi Dasa.

Planning The Trip

Lombok's **telephone code 0370** precedes all phone numbers listed below, unless otherwise noted.

Touring Lombok

Lombok is an excellent escape from the tourist scene of Bali. Those with only a few days on Bali should probably leave Lombok for the next trip. But if you have a few weeks on Bali and would like to see more of Indonesia but without traveling great distances, consider Lombok. For any traveler, a three-day excursion is a good sampler of Lombok's attractions – all of its sights are located within an hour or two of the old capital, Cakranegara. Diving at Gili Air or climbing to the summit of Mount Rinjani require at least three days.

Getting There

Choose between a quick 20-minute flight from Bali's Ngurah Rai to Lombok's **Selaparang Airport**, a leisurely cruise on the modern ferry that shuttles between Padang Bai, on Bali's eastern coast, and the port of Lembar, on Lombok's west coast, or a speedy hydrofoil from Bali's Benoa Harbor to Lembar. By air, Bouraq, Sempati, Merpati, Garuda and Silk Air serve Lombok from Denpasar, Surabaya and Singapore.

The 4-hour sea passage by ferry, with the majestic volcanic peaks of Bali and Lombok in the distance, is well worth the inconvenience of traveling to and from the ports. The ferry departs every two hours, around the clock, from Padang Bai (Bali) to Lembar (Lombok). From Sanur or Kuta, it takes more than 2 hours to get to Padang Bai by private car, 3 hours or more by public transport, so get an early start. Better yet, go to East Bali the day before and spend the night in a beach bungalow at Candi Dasa, just 20 minutes from Padang Bai.

Ferry tickets are about $3 each way first-class, and $2 for economy. Cars are charged $25 for passage. There is a snack bar on board serving *nasi rawon*, soft drinks, beer, coffee and tea. Or buy food packets from vendors at the port before departing.

Mabua Intan Express (Tel: 772-521 in Bali, 37224 in Lombok) hydrofoil catamaran departs Benoa Harbor daily at 8am and 2.30pm, and departs Lombok's Lembar harbor at 11.30am and 5.30pm. Three classes of fares: $12.50, $17.50 and $25.

Useful Addresses

Travel Agents & Tour Operators

Tours of Lombok can be arranged, but consider one of the English-speaking taxi drivers at the airport and negotiate a fee for a day-trip around the island (up to $30).

For an expedition up to the top of Gunung Rinjani, including food, tents, sleeping bags and a guide (all for $75), contact Mr Batubara at Wisma Triguna, on Jl. Koporasi, Ampenan.

Bidy Tour, Jl. Ragigenep 17, Ampenan. Tel: 32127, Fax: 31821.
Citra Lombok Indah, Jayakarta Lombok Hotel, Jl. Raya Senggigi, km 4, Meninting, Gunung Sari, Batu Layar 83351. Tel: 93838, Fax: 93287.
Dewi Sri Murni Tours & Travel, Jl. Raya Senggigi. Tel: 93013.
Express Rinjani Utama, Jl. Adi Sucipto 10, Mataram, Tel: 35968.
Harum Permai Tours & Travel, Jl. Langko 15. Tel: 25679.
Kapitan Tour, Jl. Raya Senggigi km 8, Senggigi. Tel: 93052, 93054 Fax: 93055.
Mataram Vista Wisata, Jl. Pejanggik (complex APMH Cilinaya). Tel: 22314.
Perama Travel Club, Jl. Pejanggik 66, Tel: 35936, 35928; Senggigi, Tel: 93007, 93008, Fax: 93009.
Saka Tours & Travel, Jl. Langko 48. Tel/Fax: 23114.
Senggigi Sunshine Tours & Travel, Jl. Raya Senggigi. Tel: 93232.
Sunda Duta, Pasar Seni Senggigi, Tel, 93390, Fax: 22344, 35753, email: lombok@mataram.wasantara.net.id; Homepage: http://www.vol.it/lombok.
Wannen Tours, Jl. Erlangga 4, Mataram. Tel/Fax: 31177.

Airlines

Bouraq Airways, Jl. Pejanggik 45, Ampenan, Tel: 27333, 33370.
Garuda Airways, at Hotel Lombok Raya, Jl. Panca Usaha 11, Mataram, Tel: 37950, Fax 37951.
Merpati Nusantara Airlines, Jl. Pejanggik 69, Mataram, Tel: 36745, 32226, 31037, 23762, 33844, 32127, 22314, 33469.
Sempati, Jl. Pejanggik, Komplek APHM Cilinaya, Blok B, Mataram, Tel: 21615.
Silk Air, Jl. Senggigi Raya, Komplek Pasifik Supermarket, Tel: 93877, Fax: 93822.

Practical Tips

Emergencies

Medical Services

There are three hospitals in Mataram, one each in Praya and Selong. The **Mataram General Hospital**, Jl. Pejanggik 6, has a tourist clinic with an English-speaking doctor, Dr Felix. Tel: 21354.

Getting Around

Orientation

The port of Lembar, where the ferry and hydrofoil arrive from Bali, is about 20 km (12 mi) south of Mataram. Lombok's Selaparang Airport is right in Mataram and no more than 3 km (2 miles) from any hotel in the city area. A daily ferry departs for Alas on Sumbawa from the port of Labuhan Lombok, on Lombok's eastern shore. A trunk highway cuts right across the island, from Ampenan to Labuhan Lombok, a distance of only 76 km (48 mi). Air-conditioned shuttle bus/ferry packages to Sumbawa depart daily for about $13 to $20, depending on destination, or $7 to $10 for the return trip to Bali. **Wannen Tours**, Jl. Erlangga 4, Mataram, Tel. 31177, can book.

The Ampenan-Mataram-Cakranegara stretch is the island's main business, administrative and shopping district. Call at the **West Nusa Tenggara Regional Tourist Office** (DIPARDA), Jl. Langko 70, Ampenan, Tel: 31730, 31829, 37828 or Fax: 37838, for brochures and maps of the island. They haven't much information on cultural activities, unfortunately. The regional tourism ministry office, DIPARDA, also can be helpful: Jl. Singosari 2, Tel: 35308, Fax: 37233.

Women should be aware that exposed thighs and plunging necklines are severely frowned upon, particularly by Lombok's Muslim majority (this applies particularly to towns on the eastern and southern parts of the island, where the most staunch Muslims live). Cases of harassment have been reported – women thus attired are considered unworthy of respect – and women are advised not to travel alone outside of the urban areas.

If you keep yourself discreetly covered, you should have no problems.

On Arrival

Once in Lombok, transportation is easy, though it is time-consuming to rely upon public transport. Taxis and mini-buses (bemos) are readily available for charter. Bring a motorcycle from Bali on the ferry (rental cars cannot leave Bali). It is possible to rent motorcycles in Ampenan, Mataram and Senggigi for $7–$8 per day. Ask at your hotel, or at any motorcycle shop. (You should have an international or Indonesian license). Lombok's Selaparang Airport is right in Mataram, so the taxi fare to any hotel in urban Ampenan/Mataram/Cakrangegara will be no more than $3. Major hotels will pick up for free. Call them from the airport or contact their representative in the arrival hall. To Suranadi, expect to pay up to $7 with some bargaining, up to $12 to Tetebatu.

You may charter a taxi for a day-trip around the island for between $35 and $40, depending on the itinerary. Do this through the hotel or at the airport. Try to get a Lombok Balinese driver who speaks English. The taxis here are

all old cars not permitted to operate on Bali any more.

Lendang Express Taxi has the island's only metered cabs for about $0.50 at flagfall and $0.25 per kilometer. The main office is Jl. Adi Sucipto 10, Mataram, Tel: 35968 or 22688. Booking stations in Senggigi are at the Sheraton and Holiday Inn hotels.

Bemo and buses service all towns on the island. Buy your bemo ticket at the snack bar on the ferry for the ride into Mataram from the port of Lembar. The central bemo and **bus terminal** is at the crossroads at Sweta, just to the east of Cakranegara; there is a signboard here displaying the official fares to all points on the island.

You can charter a bemo for the day for between $25 and $30 and they will take you anywhere on the island. Bemos are slow and uncomfortable, so you are better off paying a bit more for a taxi (perhaps with an English-speaking driver). The best option for a comparable price is renting an air-conditioned car and driver by the day or hour. Choose from Suzuki Jimny jeep, $30 daily without driver, $45 with driver; Mitsubishi minibus $40 without, $55 with; and Toyota Kijang, $40 without, $55 with driver. Hourly rates with driver are $8.

Transportation

Lendang Express Taxi, Jl. Adi Sucipto 10, Mataram, Tel: 35968 or 22688. Booking stations in Senggigi are at Sheraton and Holiday Inn hotels.
Mabua Express, hydrofoil to Bali, Lembar Harbor, Tel: 81225, 81224.

Rental Cars

Lendang Express, Jl. Adi Sucipto 10, Mataram, Tel: 35968.
Rinjani Rent Car, Jl. Bung Karno 6, Tel: 32259.
Star Rent Car, Jl. Raya Senggigi, Tel: 93518.
Surya Rent Car, Jl Malase, Batu Layar, Senggigi, Tel: 93076; Jl. Raya Senggigi, Tanah Embet, Senggigi, Tel: 93172.
Vanessa Rent Car, Jl. Harimau 24, Mataram, Tel: 37293.

Where To Stay

Accommodation

The consistently best international-standard accommodation is centered along **Senggigi Beach**. A good mix of losmen and hotels, in all price ranges, suits every pocketbook.

Nestled high in the west Lombok hills, but only a 30-minute drive from the airport, is the old **Hotel Suranadi** (Tel: 33686) dating from colonial times. Adjacent to the Suranadi temple and surrounded by a nature reserve, the hotel boasts spectacular views and cool, serene evenings. Its cottages wrap around a large spring-fed swimming pool and several concrete tennis courts. The pool-side restaurant, serving Chinese food, is excellent if a bit expensive. A variety of rooms are available from $25 a night (for a single with external bath) on up to $50 for a private air-conditioned bungalow, plus 21 percent tax and service. There is also a losmen nearby with rooms for under $10.

The island's most exclusive and secluded resort for the rich and famous, **The Oberoi Bali**, nestles along Madana Bay, between Pemanang and Tanjung in northwest Lombok. Villas with private swimming pools can be had in the $500 range, and lanai rooms around $200, plus tax and service. Facilities and pampering matches the price.

Lombok's northwestern reefs are among the most spectacular in the world. Aquatic enthusiasts stay at the **Sasaka Beach Hotel** at Meniting, 5 km (3 mi) north of Ampenan, and travel daily from here to Pantai Sira or Pantai Pemenang beaches and Gili Air island (cross to the islands from Bangsal harbor by motorboat or local sailing prahu). Rooms at the Sasaka Beach are less than $30, inclusive of 21 percent tax and service (substantial discounts are available for longer stays).

There are several home-stays at Sira Beach and on the Gili islands at budget prices. Losmen on Gili

Trawangan island average only $5 a day with home-cooked meals. Gili Air's 29 accommodations range from $5 to $45, Mawar Bungalow being on the lower end and the air-conditioned Hotel Gili Air at the top. Take a mosquito net if you plan on losmen accommodation in the Gilis.

Hotel Lombok Raya in Mataram is the island's best hotel. Air-conditioned rooms and suites are between $50–$80 (plus tax and service). The **Selaparang Hotel** in Mataram is also very pleasant, near to the temples and markets in Cakra. Rooms cost under $21. Both hotels have restaurants, and they will pick you up at the airport on arrival.

Just across from the Selaparang, the **Hotel Mataram** in Cakra has air-conditioned rooms for as little as $15 (including tax, service and breakfast). The delightful mountain resort of **Tetebatu (Wisma Sudjono)** has added some bungalows to its restaurant complex – a much simpler alternative to the Hotel Suranadi and less than $10 a night for a double. **Air Buka**, reached via Kembang Kering in Central Lombok, is another very reasonably priced highland spring resort with bungalows. Besides these, there are many other losmen and home-stays found throughout the island.

Senggigi

DELUXE ($80 UP)

Dame Indah, PO Box 1128, Lendang Guar, Pemenang Barat, Tanjung, 83352, Tel: 93246, 93246, Fax: 93248, 93249. Air-conditioned rooms with mini-bar, sound system and fun, eclectic furnishings in hillside hotel overlooking Gili islands. Pool, Jacuzzi, restaurant, library.

Holiday Inn Resort, Mangsit, Tel: 93444, Fax: 93092. 159 international-standard air-conditioned rooms in two-story buildings, chalets and villas situated in coconut grove around pool. Mini-bar, satellite television, coffee/tea making facilities. Two restaurants, bar, pub, health club, tennis, clinic, beach shuttle to Senggigi.

Hotel Hilberon, PO Box 1062, Mataram, Desa Pemenang Barat, Senggigi, Tel: 93898, Fax: 93252. European-style bungalow villas with mini bar and television. Manicured gardens. Pool, restaurant, beach.

Hotel Lombok Intan Laguna, PO Box 1049, Mataram, Jl. Raya Senggigi, Tel: 223680, Fax: 752193. 123 air-conditioned rooms and bungalows with satellite television and mini-bar. Restaurant, bar, room service, pool, tennis, watersports, arcade, beach.

Hotel Senggigi Beach, PO Box 1001, Mataram, Jl. Raya Senggigi, Tel: 93210, Fax: 93200, 93339. 150 air-conditioned rooms and bungalows with satellite television and mini bar. Three restaurants, bar, room service, tennis, sports. Area's first hotel; mature grounds, set on point with two sweeping beaches.

Hotel Sheraton Senggigi Beach, PO Box 1154, Mataram, Jl. Raya Senggigi km 8, Tel: 93333, Fax: 93140. 156 international-standard, air-conditioned rooms and suites with satellite television, mini-bar, balconies. Resort wraps around inviting lagoon pools with water slide, two restaurants, disco, lounge, room service, business center, tennis, beach, airport departure lounge.

FIRST CLASS ($40–$75)

Graha Beach Senggigi, Jl. Raya Senggigi, Batu Layar, Gunung Sari. Tel: 93401, 93101, Fax: 93400. 29 air-conditioned, beachfront bungalows with expansion under way .

Hotel Jayakarta, PO Box 1112, Jl. Raya Senggigi, Tel: 93045, 93048, Fax: 93043. 76 air-conditioned, international standard rooms with mini-bar, sound system, television with in-house movies. Two restaurants, two bars and karaoke, pool, tennis, conference center, pool, jogging track, beach.

Hotel Nusa Bunga, PO Box 1118, Mataram, Jl. Raya Senggigi, Klui, Tel: 93035, Fax: 93036. 5 km north of Senggigi. 13 air-conditioned bungalow rooms along beach with pool. Garden restaurant and room service.

Pantai Pacific, PO Box 1035, Jl. Raya Senggigi, Kerandangan, Tel: 93006, 93068, 93069, Fax: 93027. 26 air-conditioned rooms and beachfront bungalows with restaurant, pool, room service, television, mini-bar.

Puri Saron, Desa Krandangan, Jl. Raya Senggigi, Tel: 93424, 93425, Fax: 93266. 20 air-conditioned, deluxe rooms in five beachfront bungalows with mini bar television, video, pool, restaurant and room service. Opened in late 1995, Lombok style setting with manicured gardens.

INTERMEDIATE ($15–$35)

Batu Bolong Cottages, Jl. Raya Senggigi km 12, Batu Bolong, Senggigi. Tel/Fax: 92198. 30 rooms.

Hotel Puri Bunga, PO Box 51 Mataram, Senggigi Beach, Tel: 93013, 93353, Fax: 93286. 50 air-conditioned rooms with mini bar, television. Restaurant, bar, pool, sauna fitness center. Overlooking Senggigi.

Hotel Puri Mas, PO Box 1123, Mataram, Jl. Senggigi Raya, Mangsit, Tel/Fax: 93023. 15 beachfront villas and bungalows in homey surroundings. Must book two months in advance, many repeat and long-stay guests. Vegetarian restaurant, pool, library, room service.

Mascot Berugan Elen Cottages, PO Box 1099, Mataram, Jl. Raya Senggigi, Tel: 93365, Fax: 93236. 20 ocean- and garden-view rooms.

Pondok Senggigi, Jl. Raya Senggigi. Tel: 93275, 93273, Fax: 93276. 48 rooms.

BUDGET (UNDER $15)

Kebun Rohani Cottages, Jl. Raya Senggigi, Tel: 93018. Cool tropical garden setting, inviting and trendy restaurant, rooms with fan only.

Pondok Damai, Jl. Raya Senggigi, Tel: 93019.

Mataram-Ampenan-Cakranegara

FIRST CLASS ($45–$75)

Hotel Granada, Jl. Bung Karno, Mataram. Tel: (62-364) 22275, Fax: 36015. 99 air-conditioned rooms. with video. Pool, tropical gardens with birds and monkeys.

Hotel Lombok Raya, Jl. Panca Usaha 11, Mataram, Tel: 32305, Fax: 36478. 48 large, clean rooms with air conditioning, mini-bar, television. Pool, restaurant, room service.

INTERMEDIATE ($15–$35)

Hotel Mataram, Jl. Pejanggik 105, Cakranegara, Tel: 33675, Fax: 34966. 32 air-conditioned rooms with television, mini-bar. Restaurant, bar, pool.

Hotel Pusaka, Jl. S. Hassanuddin 23, Cakranegara, Tel/Fax: 33119, 34 rooms, air conditioning or fan.

Hotel Ratih, Jl. Pejanggik 127, Cakranegara, Tel: 31096, Fax: 24865. 42 rooms with private bath, fan or shower.

Nitour, Jl. Yos Sudarso 4, Ampenan. Tel: (62-364) 23780. 25328, Fax: 36579. 20 air-conditioned rooms with television, carpet, balcony.

Sasaka Beach Hotel, Jl. Meniting, Ampenan, Tel: 222711. 24 rooms.

Selaparang Hotel, Jl. Pejanggik 40, Cakranegara, Tel: 222670, 223235. 19 rooms either air-conditioned or fan-cooled, with hot water and television. Airport pick-up available.

Wisma Melati, Jl. Langko 80, Ampenan, Tel: 25328. 20 rooms.

BUDGET (UNDER $15)

Hotel Kertayogo, Jl. Selaparang 82, Mataram. Rooms with private bath, fan and breakfast.

Hotel Pusaka, Jl. S. Hassanudin 23, Cakranegara, Tel: 223119. 48 rooms. Centrally located. Rooms with private bath and fan.

Hotel Tigamas, Kampung Melayu Tengah, just off Jl. Pabean, Ampenan.

Hotel Zahir, Jl. Koporasi 9, Ampenan, Tel: 34248. 14 rooms.

Losmen Pabean, Jl. Pabean 146, Komplek L. Yos Sudarso/M, Ampenan, Tel: 21758. 10 rooms. Near the waterfront on the main street, opposite several restaurants. Popular with budget travelers.

Puri Indah, Jl. Sriwijaya 132, Gebang, Mataram. Tel: 37633, 37609. 30 rooms.

Wisma Triguna, Jl. Koporasi, Ampenan. A losmen near the airport.

Other Areas

Air Buka Homestay, Air Buka. Reached via Kembang Kering; highland spring resort with bungalows. (Budget)

GEC Rinjani Country Club Resort, Golong, Desa Peresak, Narmada, Tel: 33839, 37316, Fax: 33488. 20 km east of Mataram. 40 rooms in blocks and villas surrounding 18-hole golf course. Club house, restaurant, Japanese baths, coffee shop, pool, tennis, conference room. (Deluxe)

Kuta Indah Hotel, Kuta, Tel: 53781, 53782, Fax: 54628. Air-conditioned rooms with satellite television. Airport transport, beach view. (Intermediate)

Matahari Inn, Kuta, Tel: 54832, Fax: 54909. Bungalows and restaurant. (Budget)

Sasaka Beach, Meniting, 5 km (3 mi) north of Ampenan. A favorite with aquatic enthusiasts wanting to explore Lombok's spectacular northwestern reefs. Many travel daily from here to Pantai Sira or Pantai Pemenang beaches and Pulau Gili Air (cross to the islands from Bangsal harbor by motorboat or local sailing prahu).

Suranadi Hotel, PO Box 1009, Mataram, Jl. Raya Suranadi 1, Narmada, Tel: 33686, 36411, Fax: 35630. 24 rooms with fans. Adjacent to Surnadi temple at 300 m above sea level in cooler climate. Restaurant, pool, tennis. (Intermediate)

The Oberoi Lombok, Madana Bay, Tel: (62-361) 730361, Fax: (62-361) 730791. 50 luxury, air-conditioned villas along Madana Bay, all with sunken baths, garden showers, satellite television, sound systems, ocean views. Most villas with private pool. Facilities include restaurants, bar, pool, health club, beach club. (Luxury)

Wisma Sudjono, Tete Batu, delightful mountain resort has some bungalows attached to its restaurant complex; a much simpler alternative to the Hotel Suranadi. (Budget)

In Senaru: Homestays at launching point for Gunung Rinjani trek include the Rinjani, Homestay, Guru Bakti and Pondok Senaru. All are priced between $5 and $10. (Budget)

Gili Air: Among recommended homestays is Gili Indah. Hotel Gili Air, Jl. Wahidin 39, Mataram, Gili Air, Tel/Fax: 33003. ($10–$30) Air-conditioning or fan, private showers, hot water, bar and restaurant. (Intermediate)

Gili Meno: Among recommended homestays are Indah Ceman, Blue Coral and Ceman. Gili Trawangan: Among recommended homestays are Paradisa, Trawangan and Karin Homestay.

Eating Out

What & Where To Eat

The Balinese roast suckling pig, *babi guling*, done by the Lombok Balinese beats anything on the mother island. Arrange a feast (through hotel or driver) and ask if it can be served in one of the spacious courtyards of a Lombok Balinese home. Ask for *tuak* (palm toddy) to go with the pig, and a folk dance performance (also easily arranged).

The old Chinese restaurants on Jalan Pabean in Ampenan (the Tjirebon and the Pabean) are central and good, favorite hang-outs of budget travelers. The Tjirebon has cold beer and steak with chips (don't eat the salad). The Arab restaurants of Mataram often serve both Yemeni and Lombok dishes. The Taliwang in the shopping center on Jalan Pejanggik specializes in *ayam pelicing* - the searing hot curried chicken that is Lombok's specialty. The Garden House Restaurant, nearby on Jl. Pusat Pertokoan, Tel: 22200, serves both Indonesian and Chinese food.

In Cakranegara, there are many restaurants along Jalan Selaparang. The Asia and the Harum serve Chinese food, as does the Friendship on Jl. Panca Usaha, Tel: 22706. The Minang has *nasi padang* and the Istimewa and the Hari Ini both serve ayam pelicing. Other Indonesian dishes can be had at Siti Nurmaya, Jl. Palapa 34, and Indonesia, Jl. Selaparang 62. For western dishes, your best bet is at the hotels.

Both the Hotel Suranadi (in Suranadi) and the Wisma Sudjono (in Tete Batu) enjoy good reputations for tasty, fresh fish from their icy ponds. If staying in town, go there for lunch (and for a swim, at the Suranadi). The main road from Batu Layar to Senggigi is lined with an increasing number of restaurants. Some offer transportation within the Senggigi area if you telephone ahead.

Kafe Alberto, 6 km from Senggigi toward Ampenan, Tel: 93758, serves real Italian pizza, grilled seafood and homemade pasta in tropical garden setting. Beachside Dynasty, just south of Senggigi Beach Hotel, Tel: 93313, 93039, offers Chinese food and a karaoke bar. Marina Pub, Tel: 93136, roadside Oriental and Western food, seafood and steak grill.

In the heart of Kuta, Putri Lombok, Tel. 93011, serves up steaks, Mexican food, barbecue, grilled food in upstairs restaurant. The downstairs pub features the cold draft around and a wide drinks list, billiards, darts and video. Pasifik Restaurant, at Pacific Supermarket, has a menu with Indonesian, Chinese, European, Italian. The Blue Ocean bar is upstairs. Kafe Espresso, Tel: 93148, has a Thai menu, sandwiches, soup and pasta.

A wide-range of cuisine is available from beachfront eateries at Senggigi Art Market (Pasar Seni). Alfredo and Putri Lombok both have outlets along with Cafe Coco Loco, serving western and Lombok dishes; Gede's Warung, with traditional Lombok and Indonesian fare; Warung Lino, a seafood grill; and Kafe Senggigi Indah, offering Italian, barbecue, and Indonesian.

North of Senggigi, the hillside Lombok Coconut has spectacular sunset views across Lombok Strait to Gunung Agung. Alang-Alang, adjacent to Puri Mas, serves seafood.

Shopping

Traditional textiles and pottery are the best buys on the island. Visit the villages where the threads for **traditional textiles** are dyed and woven by hand: Sukarare (for *tenun Lombok*), Pujung (for *kain lambung*), Purbasari (for *kain Purbasari*) and Balimurti (for the sacred *beberut* cloth). Labuhan Lombok also produces fine blankets.

The best weaving factories for **contemporary textiles** are found in Cakranegara. Many of Bali's resident Italian couturiers buy fabrics from Pak Abdullah of C.V. Rinjani Handwoven, next door to the Hotel Selaparang (on Jl. Selaparang). His stockroom often has leftovers from bolts of top designer fabrics. His silk sarongs and matching *selendang* scarves are highly regarded among the rag conscious of Bali and Jakarta. The Selamat Ryadi weaving factory in the Arab quarter on Jl. Ukir Kawi (one block north and one

block west of the Pura Mayura water palace) is another excellent source. The Balimurti factory nearby produces weavings in the Purbasari style.

Three villages – Banyumulek, Masbagik Timur and Penujak – produce **pottery**. Wander behind the roadside stalls in any of the three villages to see pots being thrown and fired. Sofia, at the Pottery Art Shop in Banyumulek, worked five years with the New Zealand project and can provide concise information on methods. The Lombok Pottery Center, Jl. Majapahit, Mataram, Tel/Fax: 33804, offers high-grade products for sale and offers information on the project. Lombok clay also is crafted into more contemporary ceramic tableware at Citra Lombok Ceramics, Jl. Brawijaya 26, Cakranegara, Tel/Fax: 34502.

Lombok's **rattan and grass baskets** are extremely fine and sturdy. Many are produced in the eastern Lombok villages of Kotaraja and Loyok. Baskets, pots and crafts are cheap and abundant at the main market by the bus and bemo terminal in Sweta, or in the Cakranegara Market to the west of the Pura Meru temple.

For **general souvenirs**, batiks, paintings and Lombok-produced pearls, visit Kencana near the airport, Jl. Adi Sucipto 12, Tel: 35727, or Sari Kusuma Workshop, Jl. Selaparang 45, Cakranegara, Tel: 23338, Fax: 93122. The Senggigi Art Market (Pasar Seni) has kiosk-style shops selling souvenirs, local clothing and artwork, along with eateries.

Sudirman's Antiques, a few hundred meters down a side lane from Jalan Pabean in Ampenan (enter across from the bemo station, and ask for directions). Enterprising merchants of **antiques** will often call on you in your hotel. They have old Chinese ceramics, antique carvings and ceremonial weavings. Bargain hard and nonchalantly, never appear eager or rushed. A second outlet is along Jl. Raya Senggigi.

Parmour Antiques also has two outlets, the original location at Jl. Niaga II/2, Tel: 33778, in Ampenan and the large gallery at Jl. Raya Senggigi, km 10, No 13, Tel: 93692, Fax: 35753, near Jayakarta Hotel. The gallery shop features fine antiques and furniture collected by owner Agus Heri Gomanthy, an excellence source of in-

formation on such arts. He also exports. There are a few factories in Lombok doing a booming trade in primitive bottletops, wooden spoons and carved canisters-in some cases these are excellent reproductions of traditional pieces. Most of what you see is new and made to look antique.

The 6-km (4-mi) main street running through the centre of Ampenan, Mataram and Cakranegara (Langko/ Pejanggik/ Selaparang street) is one long shopping mall. For sundries, basic necessities, groceries and drinks, especially for Gunung Rinjani treks, there are two **supermarkets** in the center of Senggigi: Senggigi Abadi and Pacific Supermarket.

Sports & Leisure

Diving

There are more than 15 mapped dive sites around the three Gili islands. Certified foreign and Indonesian dive instructors offer certification courses in Indonesian, English, German and other foreign languages. Introductory dive courses are available for $60 to $80; 2-day PADI open-water dive courses for certification are under $300; PADI advanced open-water certification is around $200; rescue and other advance courses vary.

Daily dive trips to the Gilis and beach dives start from about $25 for one-tank dives. Dive and snorkeling equipment rentals are available.

Albatross Dive Center & Pro Shop, Jl. Raya Senggigi km 8, Senggigi, Tel: 93399, Fax: 93388. PADI English- and Indonesian-speaking instructors. Also offers deep-sea fishing from $200, troll-fishing from $300, glass-bottom canoes.

Blue Coral Diving Adventures, Jl. Raya Senggigi km 8, Senggigi; Tel: 93441, 93033, Fax: 93251. On Trawangan island, Tel: 34496. PADI English- and German-speaking instructors. Dive equipment rental, sales and service. **Rinjani Divers**, Jl. Raya Sandik 25, Pakel Gunung Sari, Tel/Fax: 36040; Senggigi counter, Hotel Intan Laguna Lombok, Tel: 93090, ext. 8192. ISSA/CMAS International certification.

Golf

Rinjani Country Club Golf & Resort at Golong, Narmada, 20 km east of Mataram, Tel: 33839, Fax: 33488, is a Japanese joint-venture, 18-hole golf course and hotel. The simply-landscaped par-72 course, designed by Shunji Ohno, is in a quiet setting under the shadow of Gunung Rinjani. A Japanese golf pro is in residence. Facilities include club house and restaurant. Reasonable rates: weekdays $30 and weekends $40 for green fees, club rental $10, shoes $5 and caddy fee $10. Simple hotel rooms and villas around the course start at $60 nightly. Guests may use the pool free, others pay a nominal sum to splash. Tennis and restaurant also on the grounds. A miniature golf course is at Sandik, south of Senggigi, and a new golf resort is under development at Tanjung Sira, north of Senggigi.

Climbing Gunung Rinjani

Lombok's central highlands, circling the upper reaches of Gunung (Mount) Rinjani (Indonesia's second-highest peak at 3,726 meters/12,220 ft), are sparsely-populated due to the vagaries of climate and rough terrain. Up to about 2,000 meters (6,500 ft), the mountain is covered in dense jungle and forest, but above this level, scattered stands of pine and low scrub take over. The volcano's windswept rim is quite barren, and from here are spectacular morning views across Lombok to Bali and Sumbawa on either side. The only time to attempt the climb is during the dry season (June–October), and even then you must reach the top in the early morning hours, as swirling mist envelops the peak soon after 10am.

Inside the vast crater is a large lake, **Segara Anak** (Child of the Sea). The steep descent from the rim down into the crater is precarious, and only possible from a single point at the northern side. Definitely not for the timid. It is important to have warm clothing (temperatures can drop below freezing near the summit at night), a tent, boots or sturdy shoes, sleeping bag, water bottle, cooking utensils and enough food for up to four days. (Remember to bring extra food for the guide.) The widest range of camping equipment is available in Ampenan from Mr Batubara at the Wisma Triguna Hotel or Wisma Sorja on Jalan Koperasi. Cooking utensils may be borrowed or rented, along with guides and porters, at villages along the way.

Packages through travel agents in Senggigi or Mataram average $150 per person (volume discounts) including transportation, equipment, food, drinking water, guides and porters. The journey can be arranged more economically from Batukok, Senaru or Sendang Gila.

Guides are essential. There are two principal ways of approaching the crater's rim. Many people begin from the eastern hill town of **Sapit**, which can be reached by bemo from the main highway at Pringgabaya, about 3 hours from the central Sweta terminal. From Sapit, it is about a 5-hour hike along a well-worn trail up to the villages of Sembalun Bumbung and Sembalun Lawang. You can make arrangements through the village chief of **Sembalun Lawang** for a guide (and porters) to the summit and spend the night there.

The next day, hike up to a base camp just below the rim and spend the night, so as to make the final 1-hour ascent in the early morning when it is clear. Return via Sembalun Lawang and Sapit, or continue on to the north coast at Bayan.

A shorter and easier route begins from the northern village of **Bayan**, reached via the northwestern coastal road by bus (a 3-hour journey from Sweta). From Bayan, where the bus stops, you may be able to get a lift on a truck farther on to the end of the road at Batukok, where you should contact school teacher Pak Guru Bakti to make arrangements for guides and porters. If you arrive early enough in the day (before noon), you may be able to begin the ascent immediately.

Otherwise spend the night at Losmen Pak Bakti. From **Batukok**, it is about an 8-hour hike past the traditional Sasak village of Senaru to a base camp just below the crater's rim. Camp overnight here, and climb up to the summit early in the morning. From this point, you may want to turn back, or you can descend into the crater and spend the night comfortably by the crater lake (after soaking your sore muscles in the adjacent hot springs). There are three security posts along the way where you must register.

The return journey to Batukok from within the crater takes 12 hours and you will have to spend the night here unless you have your own transportation, as the last bus leaves Bayan for Sweta at 6pm.

Languages

Indonesia's motto, *Bhinneka Tunggal Ika* (unity in diversity) is seen in its most potent form in language. Although there are over 350 languages and dialects spoken in the archipelago, the one national tongue, Bahasa Indonesian, will take you from the northernmost tip of Sumatra through Java and across the string of islands to Irian Jaya.

Bahasa Indonesian is both an old and new language. It is based on Malay, which has been the lingua franca throughout much of Southeast Asia for centuries, but it has changed rapidly in the past few decades to meet the needs of a modern nation.

The construction of basic Indonesian sentences is relatively easy. A compact and cheap book, *How to Master the Indonesian Language* by Almatseier, is widely available in Indonesia and should prove invaluable in helping you say what you want to say. Indonesian is written in the roman alphabet and, unlike some Asian languages, is not tonal.

When speaking Bahasa Indonesian, you need to keep a few basic rules in mind. Adjectives always follow the noun: *rumah* (house) and *besar* (big) together are *rumah besar*, meaning big house. When constructing a sentence, the order is usually subject-verb-subject: *saya* (I) *minum* (drink) *air* (water) *dingin* (cold). The possessive is made by putting the personal pronoun after the noun: *rumah saya* is my house.

Indonesians always use their language to show respect when addressing others, especially when a younger person speaks to elders. The custom is to address an elder man as *bapak* or *pak* (father) and an elder woman as *ibu* (mother), and even in the case of slightly younger people, who are obviously VIPs, this form of address is suitable and correct. *Nyonya* is polite when speaking with a married woman, *nona* with an unmarried woman.

Greetings & Civilities

thank you/*terima kasih*
good morning/*selamat pagi*
good day/*selamat siang*
good afternoon, evening/*selamat sore*
good night/*selamat malam*
goodbye (to person going)/*selamat jalan*
goodbye (to person staying)/*selamat tinggal*
I'm sorry/*ma'af*
welcome/*selamat datang*
please come in/*silakan masuk*
please sit down/*silakan duduk*
what is your name?/*siapa nama saudara?*
my name is.../*nama saya...*
where do you come from?/*saudara datang dari mana? or dari mana?*
I come from.../*saya datang dari...*

Pronouns/Forms of Address

I/*saya*
you (singular)/*saudara, anda/kamu* (to children)
he, she/*dia*
we/*kami* (exclude the listener)
we/*kita* (including the listener)
you (plural)/*saudara-saudara, anda*
Mr/*Pak/Bapak*
Mrs/*Ibu*
Miss/*Nona*
young boy/girl/*adik*

Directions/Transport

left/*kiri*
right/*kanan*
straight/*terus*
near/*dekat*
far/*jauh*
from/*dari*
to/*ke*
inside/*didalam*
outside of/*dilaur*
here/*disini*

there/*disana*
in front of/*didepan, dimuka*
at the back/*dibelakang*
next to/*disebelah*
to ascend/*naik*
to descend/*turun*
to walk/*jalan*
to drive/*stir, bawa*
pedicab/*becak*
car/*mobil*
bus/*bis*
train/*kereta-api*
airplane/*kapal terbang*
ship/*kapal laut*
bicycle/*sepeda*
motorcycle/*sepeda motor*
where do you want to go?/*mau kemana?*
I want to go to.../*saya mau ke...*
stop here/*berhenti disini, stop disini*
I'll be back in five minutes/*saya akan kembali lima menit*
turn right/*belok kekanan*
slowly, slow down/*pelan-pelan/ perlahan-lahan*

Important Places

hotel /*hotel, penginapan, losmen*
shop/*toko*
train station/*stasian kereta-api*
airport/*lapangan terbang/bandara*
cinema/*bioskop*
bookshop/*toko buku*
petrol station/*pompa bensin*
bank/*bank*
post office/*kantor pos*
swimming pool/*tempat pemandian, kolam renang*
Immigration Dept/*Departemen Immigrasi*
tourist office/*kantor pariwisata*
embassy/*kedutaan*

Restaurants

restaurant/*restoran, rumah makan*
dining room/*kamar makan*
food/*makaan*
drink/*minuman*
breakfast/*makan pagi*
lunch/*makan siang*
dinner/*makan malam*
boiled water/*air putih, air manang*
iced water/*air es*
tea/*teh*
coffee/*kopi*
milk/*susu*
rice/*nasi*
noodles/*mie, bihun, bakmie*
fish/*ikan*
prawns/*udang*
vegetables/*sayur*

fruit/*buah*
egg/*telur*
sugar/*gula*
salt/*garam*
pepper/*merica, lada*
cup/*cangkir*
plate/*piring*
glass/*gelas*
spoon/*sendok*
knife/*pisau*
fork/*garpu*

Shopping

shop/*toko*
money/*uang*
change (of money)/*uang kembali*
to buy/*beli*
price/*harga*
expensive/*mahal*
cheap/*murah*
fixed price/*harga pas*
How much is it?/*Berapa?/Berapa harganya?*
Can you reduce the price?/*Bisa saudara kurangkan harganya?*
I'll take it/*Saya akan ambil ini*

Understanding Signs

Many Indonesian words have been borrowed from other languages, and quickly reveal their meanings: *sekolah, universitas, mobil, bis, akademi, sektor, proklamasi* and *polisi*. Other important signs leave you guessing. This short list may help you.

open/*buka, dibuka*
closed/*tutup, ditutup*
entrance/*masuk*
exit/*keluar*
don't touch/*jangan pegang*
no smoking/*jangan merokok*
push/*dorong*
pull/*tarik*
gate/*pintu*
ticket window/*loket*
ticket/*karcis*
information/*keterangan*
public/*umum*
hospital/*rumah sakit*
pharmacy/*apotik*
house/*wisma*
central/center/*pusat*
city/*kota*
district/*daerah*
zoo/*kebun binatang*
market/*pasar*
church/*gereja*
golf course/*lapangan golf*
customs/*beadan cukai*

281

Index

A
B
C
D
E
F
G
'
I
J
b
c
d
e
f
g
h
i
j
k
l

The Insight Approach

The book you are holding is part of the world's largest range of guidebooks. Its purpose is to help you have the most valuable travel experience possible, and we try to achieve this by providing not only information about countries, regions and cities but also genuine insight into their history, culture, institutions and people.

Since the first Insight Guide – to Bali – was published in 1970, the series has been dedicated to the proposition that, with insight into a country's people and culture, visitors can both enhance their own experience and be accepted more easily by their hosts. Now, in a world where ethnic hostilities and nationalist conflicts are all too common, such attempts to increase understanding between peoples are more important than ever.

Insight Guides:
Essentials for understanding
Because a nation's past holds the key to its present, each Insight Guide kicks off with lively history chapters. These are followed by magazine-style essays on culture and daily life. This essential background information gives readers the necessary context for using the main Places section, with its comprehensive run-down on things worth seeing and doing. Finally, a listings section contains all the information you'll need on travel, hotels, restaurants and opening times.

As far as possible, we rely on local writers and specialists to ensure that the information is authoritative. The pictures, for which Insight Guides have become so celebrated, are just as important. Our photojournalistic approach aims not only to illustrate a destination but also to communicate visually and directly to readers life as it is lived by the locals.

Compact Guides
The "great little guides"
As invaluable as such background information is, it isn't always fun to carry an Insight Guide through a crowded souk or up a church tower. Could we, readers asked, distil the key reference material into a slim volume for on-the-spot use?

Our response was to design Compact Guides as an entirely new series, with original text carefully cross-referenced to detailed maps and more than 200 photographs. In essence, they're miniature encyclopedias, concise and comprehensive, displaying reliable and up-to-date information in an accessible way.

Pocket Guides:
A local host in book form
However wide-ranging the information in a book, human beings still value the personal touch. Our editors are often asked the same questions. Where do *you* go to eat? What do *you* think is the best beach? What would you recommend if I have only three days? We invited our local correspondents to act as "substitute hosts" by revealing their preferred walks and trips, listing the restaurants they go to and structuring a visit into a series of timed itineraries.

The result is our Pocket Guides, complete with full-size fold-out maps. These 100-plus titles help readers plan a trip precisely, particularly if their time is short.

Exploring with Insight:
A valuable travel experience
In conjunction with co-publishers all over the world, we print in up to 10 languages, from German to Chinese, from Danish to Russian. But our aim remains simple: to enhance your travel experience by combining our expertise in guidebook publishing with the on-the-spot knowledge of our correspondents.